Donald Ogden Stewart, aged four years.

BY A STROKE OF LUCK! AN AUTO-BIOGRAPHY BY DONALD OGDEN STEWART

BY A STROKE OF LUCK! AN AUTO-BIOGRAPHY BY DONALD OGDEN STEWART

PADDINGTON
PRESS LTD

THE TWO CONTINENTS
PUBLISHING GROUP

For Ella

Library of Congress Cataloging in Publication Data

Stewart, Donald Ogden, 1894-
    By a stroke of luck.

    1. Stewart, Donald Ogden, 1894-   –Biography.
I. Title.
PS3537.T485Z52   818'.5'209[B]   75-11172
SBN 0-8467-0063-8

Printed in the U.S.A.
Designed by Richard Browner

The publishers would like to thank the following persons for use of photographs from their personal collections: Mrs. Philip Barry, Kevin Brownlow, Katharine Hepburn, John Kobal, Honoria Murphy.

IN THE U.S.A.
PADDINGTON PRESS LTD
TWO CONTINENTS PUBLISHING GROUP
30 East 42nd Street
New York City, New York 10017

IN THE UNITED KINGDOM
PADDINGTON PRESS LTD
231 The Vale
London W3 7QS

IN CANADA
PADDINGTON PRESS LTD
distributed by
RANDOM HOUSE OF CANADA
5390 Ambler Drive
Mississauga
Ontario L4W 1Y7

A Note from Katharine Hepburn

Donald Ogden Stewart is a man who is willing to pay the price of his own passionate beliefs. He went in one quick step from being the highest-paid writer in Hollywood (Spencer Tracy and I were only two of his beneficiaries) to a man without a job.

This remarkable man was one of the great wits of the late 20's, 30's, and 40's; the creator of laughter and delight in movies, plays, books, and high society. Yet he was direct and over- sensitive to his fellow man. His life tells the story of the American-style late 20's. He laughed his way to the top of the heap and looked down. Saw the bottom of the heap and thought, "this is not fair." He forsook his giddy companions for serious thinking and had to leave the country of his birth.

He never regretted it, never moaned, never excused himself. He simply believed passionately.

Donald Stewart considers himself lucky. This must have taken doing. He's my friend. I think I'm the lucky one.

Introduction

Although my profession since the age of twenty-six has been that of a writer, there were serious considerations in my mind, when I began this autobiography, of asking for the assistance of a ghost-writer. My chief reason for doing this was a concern about truth. I have tended throughout my whole life to avoid searching for the truth about my friends and acquaintances. The basic cause of this is that I have been cursed from childhood with an almost obsessive need to be liked by others. If, therefore, some man or woman became my friend, I accepted that blessing so gratefully that it never occurred to me to attempt any analysis of judgment of his character. If I had become, as I originally intended, a business man or a banker, I would necessarily have had to analyze and judge my employees and clients. If, as a writer, I had ever had any training as a journalist or a novelist, I would presumably have become versed in what Ernest Hemingway called "the way it was; what you really saw and felt – not what you were supposed to." I never fulfilled that obligation about my friends, including Ernest. I was, in life and in literature, a romantic amateur living in a happy dream-world. This is why, in my telling of that life, I thought that perhaps I should have balanced my romance with the challenging "truthfulness" of a trained analytical mind.

But this is not a story about my friends. It's about me. And in that respect I think I have told the truth about "how it was" – just as, in my plays, I have given "what I truly saw and felt," because the characters in my plays were in reality true bits and pieces of myself. When I could translate my dream world onto the stage, it became real. In that sense, this autobiography is my last play – with only one character. But he, I believe, is a real person, about whom I have truthfully described the belated transference of a childhood playtime world into an understanding of the real world and his obligation to it. And in that sense I feel that I have (to quote Hemingway once again) "put down what I saw and felt in the best and simplest way I could tell it."

1

I was born on the 30th of November, 1894, in Columbus, Ohio. This came as more or less of a shock to my parents, who were surprised that I had ever been conceived at all. Their financial situation was what might be termed "modest" and they had considered the family fairly satisfactorily complete with the birth, some ten years before, of a daughter Anne. Brother Bert (Gilbert Holland Stewart Junior) was her senior by four years; older brothers had succumbed to childhood diseases. Anyway, Gilbert senior and his wife Clara had thought that their contribution to the total Columbus population (1894 – around 150,000) of Anne and Bert was sufficient.

This is not to say that my arrival was considered a complete disaster. Gilbert, my father, was a lawyer with a fair practice. Born in Cambridge, Massachusetts into a low-income family, he had been too young to fight in the Civil War. He had entered Harvard and had then heeded the cry of "Go West, young man!" In Worthington Ohio, just outside Columbus, he had met and married the young red-haired Clara, daughter of the educator John Ogden.

This John Ogden was ultimately to play a considerable role in the true education of his unexpected grandson. Not directly, for I only saw him twice and remembered chiefly a pure white beard and an admonition about throwing stones at birds. But later in my life the "idea" of John Ogden was to have a profound influence.

John Ogden was devoted to education. He was teaching in Wisconsin when the Civil War broke out, joined the First Wisconsin Cavalry, became a lieutenant and was captured in one of the early battles. The rest of his own personal war was spent amid unheroic miseries in Libby (Andersonville) prison, which he later described in *Prison Life in the South*. After the war ended, he elected to remain in Tennessee in order to educate the recently freed slaves. This was an idea which did not particularly appeal to the former owners, and the fervent young idealist had some fairly tough going, including the comparatively mild experience of having charming young Southern belles spit in his face as he walked the streets of Nashville. In spite of this local disapproval, however, he helped to found Fisk University for Negroes, of which he became the first president. He is probably one of the few university presidents who slept with a pistol under their pillow every night.

So much for my mother's father. I never saw her mother, and the only time I remember Clara talking about her was when she described discovering her mother one day with tears running down her cheeks. "President Lincoln has been shot," was the explanation between sobs. "But Mother," asked the puzzled Clara, "why are you crying so? Did you know him?"

Clara told me this story on the day in 1901 that President McKinley was assassinated. We were then living in The Normandie, an apartment-hotel on Long Street to which we had moved about a year after my birth. At The Normandie mother and father, Bert, Anne and I lived in a six or seven room apartment on the fourth floor. We took our meals in a large dining room on the top (seventh) floor. That room shines brightly in the memories of my youth. Breakfast consisted of a choice of several kinds of fruit *and* (not "or") cereals. And fried steak. And "eggs as ordered" (I never did understand what that meant). And buckwheat cakes, griddle cakes, waffles. My first appreciation of the aesthetic side of life came with a realization of the beauty of the pewter syrup jug; its proportions seemed somehow just right (unless it was empty). Another artistic experience was when the management repainted the dining room ceiling with cherubs who smiled approvingly as I piled sugar on my oatmeal. It was in the dining room that balls and other functions were held; my sister Anne's "coming-out" party was celebrated up there. I was not allowed to attend it as I was only seven or eight, but I can remember lying in bed and hearing music.

Other sounds which came to me in bed were the exciting whistles from the trains in the Union Depot about a mile away, and the bells of the streetcars below the window as they went out Long Street on their way to Franklin Park, or turned into Mt. Vernon Avenue toward where the Negroes lived. There was great excitement whenever a brilliantly-lighted streetcar called "Electra" went past with a party of merrymakers who had rented it for a joy ride around the city. There was the music of singing from the Welsh church nearby, and the terrifying noises on the Fourth of July when older boys would put explosives on the car tracks, some of which were powerful enough to lift the front wheels right up in the air.

The Fourth was a wonderful day, even for a boy living in a hotel. It wasn't so wonderful for the other residents but they just gritted their teeth and waited for the evening when the "bangs" let up and the pretty sky-rockets started. The intense anticipation of the night before the Fourth made it, next to Christmas, the most exciting in the year. All my firecrackers, torpedoes, pinwheels, etc. were displayed on a table in my room so that I could see them as soon as my eyes opened. Then, right after a feverish breakfast, father and I would go down to the curb in front of the hotel. He would solemnly light a stick of dried camels' dung (known as "punk"), hand it to me, and my fun would begin. I can still remember the wonderful smell of gunpowder, although I was very timid about loud explosions – a timidity which later extended to all theatrical productions where guns were to be fired. In the afternoon, since it was a holiday, father and mother and I would take the North High Street trolley out to Olentangy Park. There were few automobiles, we couldn't afford a horse and carriage from Fred Atcheson's nearby Gay Street livery stable, and these streetcar rides were sheer joy. I would be allowed to stand up in front beside the motorman. Occasionally he would let me stamp on the bell and my cup would run over. And when we arrived at Olentangy Park there was everything a young heart and stomach could wish. Not only a merry-go-round and a zoo, but also popcorn fritters, lemonade, a "naphtha launch" for a ride on the Olentangy River, and the Fourth of July band concert. Then home to The Normandie where we would go up on the roof and watch the fireworks.

Streetcar rides were usually the way we spent our Sunday afternoons. Besides Olentangy there were two other parks – Franklin in the East End and Minerva to the North. Neither of these had merry-go-rounds or any "attractions" except trees and lakes and grass, but life was simple and the mere fact of going somewhere was excitement enough for me. I was even delighted when we went out to

Green Lawn Cemetery to put flowers on the graves of brothers Ben and Carl whom I had never seen. Occasional Sundays we would take the South High streetcar to the German district and "Steelton" (whose blast furnaces lighted the skies every night) or on the West side to the State Institute for the Feeble Minded where we would call on one Ione Black, who was a nurse there.

I never quite understood about Ione except that she was somehow a friend or relative of a mysterious Otho Hayes (they named people "Ione" and "Otho" in those days) whom I had overheard mother and father whispering about in connection with the "O.P." When I got older I discovered that those intitials referred to the Ohio Penitentiary and that Otho was serving time there because he was a victim of the financial ambitions of the notorious Cassie Chadwick of Cleveland, Ohio whose criminal manipulations brought several banks crashing down. There was a song at the time that went "Who Got Rich quick? Cassie Chadwick!" Anyway, poor Otho was cashier of one of the banks and (according to my father) took the rap for some of the higher-ups.

The "O.P." became one of the terror words of my childhood vocabulary – words you thought about while lying in bed. Another word I puzzled about was "Catholic." We passed the Catholic Cathedral on our walks to the Trinity Episcopal Church at Third and Broad, but somehow or other Catholics were "different." So (to a much lesser degree) were Methodists, Presbyterians, Congregationalists and Democrats. And as for Jews, I didn't know anything about them. When, later on, I found myself sitting next to Jeffrey Lazarus in school, I knew about him all right. His father ran the Lazurus Bros. store on High Street where you got a free baseball and bat whenever you bought a new suit.

But my first conscious memories begin with the three and one-half years I stayed in Sullivant School until I was eight and a half. It was here that grandfather John Ogden addressed our little class one morning – to my horrible embarrassment, when everyone looked at me as he and mother were introduced to us by the principal of the school. Another moment which sticks because of the embarrassment was when, in the second grade, I wrote "I love you" on my slate and passed it forward to a very pretty girl named Josephine Baldwin. This spontaneous if somewhat premature Casanova-like gesture did not, I think, have anything to do with sex; if it did, it certainly had a most negative effect, not only on the beautiful Josephine but particularly on me, because of the cruel teasing which I got from my schoolmates. I dimly remember them trying one day to force me to kiss a girl, and later three older Negro girls in my class chased me down Fifth Street, caught me hiding in a doorway and screamed with laughter as they kissed me. I was terrified – and I have been afraid of girls ever since. And, for a long time, I was afraid of sex.

About this time I had an experience with an older boy on the roof of The Normandie when he tried to get me and two or three other little boys to play with his penis. I was the only one who declined; it was, again, a terrifying experience, and I felt so bad that I told father about it next day. He and mother were very sensible and my guilt was eased.

Sullivant School was four blocks away, Trinity Church the same distance. On the walk to either, one passed Mr. Roehm's drugstore, whose windows displayed two large jars filled with blue and red liquid in the window and, on Sundays, the papers, with Buster Brown and Happy Hooligan temptingly on display (we didn't take that paper). Farther down Long Street was Tommy's West's saloon, out of which came exotic odors and an occasional (terrifying) drunk. Around Thanksgiving in front of the saloon there would be a captive live turkey which was being raffled. Along Fourth Street was the Masonic Hall. "People in Society didn't belong to the Masons except for business or political reasons" – I forget who put that into my head, but one of my best friends at The Normandie was a Mr. Moore who was a Mason as well as a conductor on the railroad and I loved him dearly. Besides, the Masons were responsible for wonderful funeral parades. At the corner of Fourth and Broad was a Lutheran church, but that was only for Germans, and across from that was father's Columbus Club. The only true church (Trinity) was on the next block, right across from the ten-acre State House yard which was full of squirrels and statues of Civil War heroes. Then came the center of town, the corner of Broad and High, and just beyond that, (overlooking the bridge which crossed the broad Scioto river) was the only tall building, the twelve-storied Wyandott, where father had his law office. High Street was notable for Hatton's Drugstore where I had my first ice cream soda (I thought the ice cream was soap and cried bitterly) and Dobbie's Drygoods store with its cashboxes whizzing by on overhead wires. I used to squirm impatiently on a stool while mother talked to Mr. Richter, who lived at The Normandie and was head of the linen department. I can still smell that linen, and also Mr. Richter who used perfume and was in the habit of playfully pinching my cheeks in The Normandie elevator. Across from Dobbie's was the Lazarus store of ball and bat memory. And, of course, the Catholic cathedral at Broad and Fifth, across from which was the large yard of Mrs. Collins who kept a cow. A block farther along was State Street and Sullivant School and Dr. Kinsell's office which I remember painfully. Father took me there one morning because my penis had become inflamed and I ran home alone, terror-stricken because I had seen the doctor make a scissor-like gesture while explaining my case to father. I suppose that it was an ordinary recommendation for circumcision, but to mother's arms I fled and the operation was never performed.

When I was eight I transferred from Sullivant to Douglas School. The Douglas school was way out on 17th Street near Broad Street in the fashionable East End and necessitated a walk of over a mile each way. Why I changed was never clear to me. It was, I imagine, my parents' idea that Douglas was a "better" school, in a "better" district. This may have been the beginning in me of a sense of class distinction which gradually came to be connected with "security." It is difficult to trace back the origins of one's prejudices, but one of my earliest is that obsession with the relationship between Society and Security.

The walk out to Douglas school opened up new territory, the East End. Starting out from The Normandie, one passed the Welsh church from which in the evening came the sound of the singing of strange hymns – strange at least to Episcopal ears. Near the church was the wonderful lumber yard, a perfect hiding place for cowboys, Indians, outlaws, cops, or robbers. Across from the lumber yard was a vacant lot, too full of tall weeds to be any good for baseball, but with a little imagination the weeds became jungles, and traps could be set for whatever wild animals were on their savage way to the "water hole." In the three or four years of my life as a trapper (with my base in room 43 of The Normandie) I caught one kitten and a great deal of hell from the kitten's owner. On Gay Street lived Beans Horn, who owned a pony and whose father owned a saloon. Then one came to Broad Street, lined on both sides with beautiful trees all the way out to Franklin Park and Alum Creek. Most anybody who was anybody lived on or near East Broad. An invitation to play in the large yard between the Platts' and the Mitchells' houses was my first contact with social status. The Platt boys, Bob and Ruddy, were not snobs; nor were Barry Wall and Harry Heil, who lived at the Mitchells' with their older cousin Grant Mitchell who was later to make a hit on the Broadway stage. But when I started at Douglas School I gradually shifted my sights from the alleys and vacant lots around The Normandie to the grassy yards of East Broad; it was not that I was ever forbidden to play across Long Street with the McKee boys (whose mother worked in The Normandie kitchen) or the Gilchrist girls (whose father was a policeman).

This was my world – a very small world but very complete. One did not go "abroad" in those days, and only rarely outside of Columbus. Father, when he was a judge on the Circuit Court, traveled to Dayton, Springfield and one or two similar small cities. He took me once to Dayton to visit the Soldiers Home where the veterans of the Civil War were being taken care of by the State. In those days the veterans – the Grand Army of the Republic – were very much in evidence. It was only thirty-five years after the end of the Civil War. Grandfather's cavalry shoulder straps were in mother's dried roseleaf-scented top drawer. These roseleaves were kept in a special jar and were later, rolled in toilet paper, to provide me with my first – and, for several years, last – cigar.

I think that this fifty-mile trip to Dayton was my only voyage until I was almost ten. The universe was exciting enough as it was.

We Stewarts were "in Society" in Columbus. Father was Judge Stewart, one of the few citizens who had attended an Eastern university and a member of the exclusive Columbus Club. Anne had "come out" into Society. I'm not sure at what age I became aware of any implications of superiority in all this. The Columbus Club was a place where once or twice a year I was allowed to have oysters. Mother gave whist parties (no bridge yet); occasionally she took me with her in a rented carriage to pay calls or leave calling cards. I also remember overhearing a bitter quarrel between her and Anne which ended with mother sobbing. It was only long after that Anne told me that mother was pressing her to break away from a man she loved because he wasn't a good marriage prospect.

But social climbing begins at a very early age if security is more or less inevitably connected with the "right" neighborhood and the "right" people. This is especially true if one's family's finances are in as precarious a position as ours were. I didn't have any idea about our money problems, but I knew we weren't rich because I didn't get lots of things I wanted such as a bicycle or an air rifle. The Platt yard somehow became a symbol of something I wanted to be sure of being invited to. That need to be asked to join a club or a fraternity or anything to which others belonged began when I couldn't have been older than eight. There was no questioning of why certain people were "in Society" and others weren't. There was simply an overpowering desire to belong – and with that a curious feeling of not being completely "in."

One element in this, of course, was my desire to emulate my brother and sister. Both went to Society dances and parties. Anne was attractive, gay, a real beauty in the Gibson-girl period; there was a family legend that she had shocked father's Massachusetts relatives by riding around Boston on the roof of a handsom cab. And as for my brother Bert, I simply worshipped him. He had played football on the Central High school team. I would rather have been a good football player than anything in the world. There is a photograph of me at five or six with a football under my arm and a sweater with an "H" for Harvard which mother had sewn on it. We didn't have the money to send Bert to Harvard, so he went to Ohio State University and the Law School there, but he always wanted me to go to Harvard. Bert had belonged to a fraternity at Central High, and to another at O. S. U.; he had volunteered for the Army in the Spanish war. Everything he did was right – and I was not going to let him down.

Then too I loved father very much and we had a real companionship. I don't remember his ever whipping me except once when I had said "Damn you!" to mother. I forget the occasion but not the lesson. He was a gentle, friendly man and I think everybody liked him. If he had any ambition, it was to be appointed to the Ohio Supreme Court, but disaster came before that was ever achieved. Father was a staunch Republican. On election nights he would take me to the *Journal* or *Dispatch* buildings where we would stand in the crowd and get the results. I remember father's great jubilation one year when Missouri voted Republican; I think that was in 1904 when Teddy Roosevelt was elected President. When I was older, he would take me to the Ohio political conventions to which he was usually a delegate; once he introduced me to a "Boss" from Cincinnati named Cox who was evidently an extremely important person.

Father loved the theater too. So did mother, and they prized their memories of having seen Joseph Jefferson in "Rip Van Winkle,"

Henry Irving in "The Bells," Mary Anderson and all the Shakespeare that ever came to Columbus. Also all of Gilbert and Sullivan, extracts from which father used to sing while he shaved. I remember the excitement about Eva Tanguay. And there was a wonderful man who made up and sang verses about people in the audience. "There sits a fellow with his hand upon the rail, if he hadn't been so stingy maybe he'd have brought a girl." And always at the end came a Pathé rooster and a short movie. There were only two real theaters in those days although there was a summer stock company at Olentangy Park. The Great Southern was connected with the Southern Hotel at Main and South High; the High Street, the "ten-twenty-thirty" home of melodrama, was between Long and Spring on North High. I was not allowed to go to the latter except when the Al G. Fields Minstrels were the attraction, or Humpty Dumpty, and, one memorable occasion, when Williams and Walker played in "Bandana Land." I think, incidentally, that segregation was taken for granted in Columbus in those days; at any rate, at the High Street the top Gallery was known as "Nigger Heaven." At the respectable Southern my greatest first memory is of Kellar the Magician, who came down the aisle, asked father for his watch, and then returned to the stage where he deliberately smashed the family heirloom to bits with a hammer. I burst into tears but everyone around us was laughing and when Mr. Kellar came down to reassure me and return father's watch unharmed, he took an egg and a chicken from my mouth and I determined to become a magician. The great hero of our family in those pre-movies days was Maclyn Arbuckle who starred in "The County Chairman" by George Ade. Seeing that was a thrilling experience for me, almost as much so, I think, as the Hagenback and Wallace circuses or the Pawnee Bill Wild West show. There was a certain moment when the lights in the theater dimmed and the curtain slowly rose which seemed so magical in those days and still seems irreplaceable by movies or television. But perhaps only those of us who did not grow up on movies can understand that thrill. There *was* a movie theater in Columbus – a nickelodeon called "The Exhibit" at High and Spring, opposite the Chittenden Hotel. I wasn't supposed to go to it, although I sometimes did. There were also occasional "medicine shows" in an empty store, with waxwork heads of celebrated criminals in the window – Czolgosz who shot President McKinley, Tracy the outlaw, Cassie Chadwick, John Wilkes Booth. These ghastly wax heads made me feel queer, and I never dared investigate what went on inside. Somehow I felt guilty just looking at the window. For music, there was the annual visit of Sousa's band; I always used to get a big choked-up lump in my throat at the "Stars and Stripe Forever," especially when the six or eight trombones would come to the front of the stage and let loose. Music was also represented by the steam calliope in the circus parade and (to a lesser degree) by the piano lessons which I took from the unfortunate and patient Miss Kitty Gleason, who did her best against tremendous odds. And father, without cheering anybody up very much, induced a morose Mr. Wills to give me banjo lessons. But my heart, body and soul were concentrated on sport; especially baseball and football.

And the sad thing was that I wasn't ever any good at it. I had no speed and no muscular coordination. I read all the books on "How To Bat," "How to Play First Base," "How To . . ." everything. I would have given my soul to win the right to make the childhood "H" on my sweater come true. These dreams originated, I suppose, with the Frank and Dick Merriwell nickel novels which I devoured. (I wasn't allowed to read "Buffalo Bill" or "Nick Carter" or the Jessie James series.)

A further blow to my athletic hopes came at the age of eleven when, to my horror, I was made to wear glasses because of near-sightedness. This was one of the big tragedies of my youth and must have contributed to my timidity, especially with girls. I was nicknamed "four eyes" and it hurt. Perhaps a lack of confidence in my looks had begun earlier, but with "four eyes" I increasingly came to assume that my face was far from being my fortune. Anne was beautiful, Bert was good-looking, but little Don was the ugly duckling. So much the more reason for becoming a great football hero!

But there came another block, although I fought against admitting it for many years. I wasn't only "shy," I was physically timid. I didn't really like to throw my body at a boy running toward me with a football. I flinched when I faced a pitcher with a fast ball. Fortunately, there were exceptions to my timidity. One fall afternoon in the Platt yard I was playing end and for some reason my fear vanished. I made tackle after tackle as though inspired. And one winter in a snowball fight in Bob Little's yard I went berserk and charged the enemy (six boys loaded with ammunition) all by myself. Nothing could stop me. The fact that at eighty I can remember these two childhood episodes (I can't have been over ten) seems to indicate that they were momentary releases from a deep unconscious fear. And the fear wasn't so damned unconscious, either. One day in the fourth or fifth grade at Douglas a larger, older boy told me he was going to "get" me at recess. I went through a torment of terror waiting for the fight I knew I couldn't get out of. At recess we went around behind the outhouses and the fight began. I can't remember what it was about or how it came out. James Thurber, another Douglas school-tie, told me years later that he always remembered the fight and that I won. That was news to me, because all I have ever remembered is the fear.

So I never became Frank Merriwell, and "How To Bat" usually resulted in being struck out. There were other books of my boyhood which led me into equally unsuccessful fields. There was a period when I felt an urge to get closer to the exciting life of the trappers and the Indians of early American history. This, as I have suggested, presented certain difficulties to a boy living in an hotel. I made figure-four traps as directed by the *American Boy's Hand Book,* but there was only that vacant lot to set them in. I wanted to make a catamaran out of two barrel staves and a log but faced the problem of getting a log, not to mention inducing the Long Streetcar line to transport it way out to Franklin Park lake, the nearest body of water. The book also told me how to make inexpensive underwater telescopes, wigwams, rabbit hutches, dog sleds, and life-size kites in the shape of Chinese mandarins. I tried them all. Even with an underwater telescope there was nothing to look at in the bath tub. The hotel wouldn't let me have a rabbit or a dog. The mandarin kite went up five feet off The Normandie roof and plunged down into the telephone wires. I did get a sort of a wigwam set up in the vacant lot but mother wouldn't let me spend a night in it, and when I tried to bake a potato in the coals of a fire I couldn't get the fire lighted with the twirling stick-on-stick device which (the book assured me) was the favorite method of all Indians. Indian "smoke signals" from The Normandie roof got me into trouble with the elevator man. Once I terrified mother by crawling (on a "scouting expedition") across the glass panels which formed the topmost roof over the central open well around which the hotel was built; if the glass had given way I would have plunged to my death seven stories into the office of Dave the Day Clerk who handed out the mail and the keys. The Night Clerk was Mr. Lawson; every Sunday evening father would call down to him from the corridor around the open well "the exact correct time, please?" After Mr. Lawson had called back the correct time, father would fix up our various timepieces. To this day I feel that Sunday is the only day on which to correct clocks.

Sunday was also the day for the funny papers and church. Father, as a vestryman, was entitled to wear a frock coat and pass the plate. For some reason he thought it a good idea for me to sing in the choir; the reason certainly could not have been my soprano voice. The choirmaster, a wonderful red-bearded German curmudgeon named Karl Hoenig, tried every year at Easter to let me sing one of the solos, and every year he had to pass along the privilege at the last moment to another boy. For four or five years I went one or two nights a week to choir practice in the vestryroom behind the church. I can still smell those black cassocks and white cottas which we kept in our lockers, to be worn on Sundays. I still fear Mr. Hoenig's blazing sarcasm, and his wrath at any foolishness during service. He could watch us in our choir stalls from a mirror at the keyboard of the organ. Misdemeanors such as whispering were penalized by "fines" taken from our wages. I think I got twenty-five cents a week; boys with good voices who sang solos got more. Easters were very exciting: two violins, a trumpet and a trombone were added to the organ music, and the church was full of well-dressed Episcopalians and lilies. Sometimes it was my turn to take the collection plates from the vestryman and, with another boy, turn and carry them to the Reverend Julius Atwood D.D. at the altar, who would cue the choir into "Praise God from who all blessings flow –." One Easter I got caught without a handkerchief and had to receive the plate from father in front of the whole congregation with my nose flowing miserably over my chin and onto a dollar bill. Before church, of course, came Sunday School in the parish house across Broad Street. My teacher was Singleton Outhwaite, brother of the man who, in 1905, married my sister Anne. "Sing" Outhwaite was a Princeton graduate and a remarkably good teacher. In fact, he was a bit of a misfit as a lawyer, and should have been a professor. It was through him that I first got interested in the exciting new science fiction of an Englishman named H. G. Wells and the historical novels of another named Henty.

Not that I didn't derive considerable cultural ambition from my own family. Dickens and Thackeray were well-thumbed household gods, not just half-calf morocco sets. Very early in life I learned the delights of Edward Lear, and knew much of *Alice in Wonderland* by heart. Father subscribed to *St. Nicholas* for me, and there were bound volumes of the same magazine from the days when Bert and Anne had been subscribers. There were also bound volumes of *Harpers Weekly* dating from the Civil War, *Harpers Monthly*, *McClure's*, *Everybodys* and *Munsey's* during the Lincoln Steffens and Ida Tarbell muck-raking period, *Life* (then a humorous weekly featuring the Gibson girls) and *Theater*. Father and mother loved William Dean Howells, Bert preferred Maupassant and O. Henry. Both adored Mark Twain, "Mr. Dooley" and George Ade. One of the Sunday morning breakfast table rites was father's reading of Mr. Dooley's latest. I borrowed books from the Public Library on Town Street and later from the new Carnegie Library at Oak and Grant. I absorbed all of the Horatio Alger "Strive and Succeed" philosophy and feverishly awaited every new Edward Stratemayer heroic tale of American history. I got a Civil War craze and father supplied me with four volumes by E. E. Coffin, beginning with *Drum Beat of a Nation.* My boyish appetite for humor was fed with *Verdant Green,* Anstey's *Vice Versa,* and *The Real Diary of a Real Boy,* which I tried to imitate. Mother at least thought my diary very funny. I already had a bit of a family reputation as a humorist from the time when mother called to father from another room and I, aged six, lying alone in bed, answered in father's rather annoyed tones: "What it is *now*, Clara?" Fortunately, no other examples of my childhood bright sayings have been preserved.

2

In 1904, when I was going on ten, father took me on a real railroad
journey. He had been appointed lay delegate to an Episcopal Church
national convention in Boston. For weeks ahead I quivered with excitement, read books about New England and revolutionary history
– and I wasn't disappointed when the enchanted voyage finally came
off. Every meal in the dining car (my first ever) was "a whiz." The
distinctive smell of Pullman cars and engine smoke became per-
manently connected with adventure. Sleeping in an upper berth, including the acrobatics of undressing, was a wonderful thrill. Negro
porters and waiters were fascinating. And Boston itself was like
dreams come true. We stayed in Cambridge at the home of father's
sister Aunt Belle Whittemore and her husband. There were three
sons, two of whom were real flesh and blood Harvard un-
dergraduates; the third, Bob, was near enough my own age to play
football with me in an honest-to-God front yard of my own relatives.

Father took me to the old swimming hole where he had swum in
the Charles River as a boy. There was Bunker Hill, the Lexington
Minute Man statue, the Old North Church, the Red Sox – my first
Big League baseball game – the newly opened Harvard Stadium.
Aunt Belle told her joke about the Irish groundkeeper who thought
that the Harvard motto "Veritas" meant "To hell with Yale." (Since
I was present, Aunt Belle said "To 'H' with Yale.") Father's older
sister, Aunt Annie, was much more stern Puritan New England than
beautiful gray-haired Belle; she was married to a clergyman named
Dr. Pervear, and "H" was no joke to them.

The next year was even more memorable, for Anne married

Charles Peabody Outhwaite in Trinity Church. Charles was what might be termed a "catch of the year." He was the son of a deceased Democratic Congressman who had had a distinguished record in Washington. He had gone to Princeton, joined his brother in the leading law firm of Outhwaite, Linn and Thurman, and was reputed to be one of the richest young men in town. He owned one of the few local automobiles, a Pope-Toledo, and had taken mother and me for our first auto ride. I do not remember much about the wedding except the champagne breakfast at the Columbus Club after the ceremony and the little white initialed satin box with a piece of cake in it. (I secretly ate the cake and then guiltily slept on the empty box under my pillow for several nights.) For their honeymoon, Anne and Charles went abroad on the "Kaiser Wilhelm der Grosse" and brought me a knife made of "real Sheffield steel." They then settled down in one of Charles's real-estate properties, a newly built two-story house at 924 Madison Avenue in Columbus. He also owned 916 Madison, which we were to occupy two years later.

The Stewart social and financial position seemed to have reached both status and security. There were, however, two facts about this wedding-of-the-year which were known only to a very few people – and certainly not to me, aged eleven. 1905 was not only the year of Anne's wedding but also of uneasiness in Wall Street, in which, two years later, the "catch of 1905" was to be caught short and end up owing so much money that it took him the rest of his life to pay it back. The other fact concerned father – but we didn't know of that until later.

They were, on the whole, happy years – except for unpleasantnesses like having my teeth straightened by a pioneer orthodontist who filled my mouth with wires and rubber bands, and made me feel more than ever like a four-eyed monster. Then there was dancing school, to which I shamefacedly had to carry my patent leather "pumps" in a bag. Presumably, both orthodontia and dancing were necessary steps in my social career, and I bravely accepted them. The dancing school was run by Mr. and Mrs. Randall, aided by their young son Carl who later won Broadway fame in musical comedies. I more or less mastered the two-step, the waltz and the lancers and acquired, as well, an increased lack of confidence about girls. Mrs. Randall was a terrifyingly firm little woman, and when she blew her whistle for us to "select your partners for the waltz" there would be a mad rush of males for the pretty girls and I would end up with the fat one. That she was one of the richest girls in town did not impress me, although somewhere along the line I was acquiring an increasing, if unconscious, repect for names like Vanderbilt and Gould and Whitney, about whom I had read in the papers.

Two girls stand out in my unfortunate pre-puberty memory. One was Mary Ford, who lived at The Normandie when I was five and with whom I used to wrestle persistently, with outstanding lack of success. The other was Bob Little's red-haired sister, Mary, who one day replied to my daily teasing by hitting me on the head with a brick. Several stitches were required; "I learned about women from her."

Father was popular with the other men – "one of the boys" – although he drank very little. It's strange that, with all our companionship, I can't remember being influenced by him, at least by any of his words of advice. Once, when he saw a man take a woman companion by the arm, he whispered to me "A gentleman never puts his hand on a lady." And much later he gave me the explanation of why Socialism couldn't work: "If everything was divided up equally, it would only be a few years before most of it would again be in the same hands." I remember him as a quiet handsome man with a gray moustache. But I never knew about any of his thoughts or his worries. (This was true also as regards Bert and Anne. I suppose this was because of the differences in our ages.)

I certainly had no worries of my own, other than a great fear of being thought "different" from other boys. I hated to wear any unusual clothing, such as overshoes or a bright necktie. Father would embarrass me occasionally by singing too loudly in church. I wanted to conform, and that was that.

I had exciting "crazes" which would come and go – usually induced by books and a desire to do something or be like somebody I read about. One of these was a craze about Scottish history, during which I tried to be a true Stewart with what must have been an extraordinary Scottish accent. This particular craze ended when I discovered that my presumed ancestor, Mary Stuart, Queen of Scots, had, in addition to spelling our name wrong, been a rather immoral person. There was an intense stamp-collecting period, and an electricity craze when I tried unsuccessfully to make sparks leap from a home-made "Leyden jar." The only sparks I ever produced came from scraping my shoes along the rug and sticking my finger into someone's face. There was a short period when I was crazy about "etiquette" and gravely learned about what fork to use with partridge, which we never ate. Aside from that, though, I wanted above everything else to be a "regular" boy. I tried to get mother to let me sell papers or to do "chores" like the boys in books. I didn't want to get good grades in school for fear of a being a "teacher's pet." I was incurably romantic about the past. I wanted to do everything that father and Bert had done when they were boys, or at least emulate mother who had lived on a farm. I was crazy to have a dog, and adopted an awful looking cur bitch which I kept secretly in the vacant lot and called "Bob Son of Battle" after my favorite book. I longed to have sheep with which to train Bob, and once tried her out on Mrs. Collins' cow. No sheepdog she. Winter was wonderful, with hitching on to wagons with one's sled and hopping onto the runners of sleighs racing out Broad street. Once, on Gay Street, I caught hell from Anne when I knocked Charles's hat off with a snowball. He was really furious with me, which I thought rather unsportsmanlike of him.

Then, when I was thirteen, came the wonderful move from The Normandie to 916 Madison Avenue. This was a dreamed-of home with a front and back yard, an attic with a ladder leading up to the roof, an actual cellar, and chores like other boys such as cutting the grass and pumping bath water from the cistern up to the tank in the attic. On our first night Bert noticed the unprecedented joy with which I was practicing "The Happy Farmer" on the piano. "He can't be *that* happy," he remarked. But I was. And at last I had a dog – given me by Anne and Charles who now lived next door. It was a Boston terrier named "Bostie" which they had owned until they unfortunately bought an airdale who had established its immediate superiority by chewing one of Bostie's eyes out. But even with only one eye he was my dog, and he used to sleep every night on my bed.

Douglas school was right across 18th Street, which eliminated the long bicycle ride from The Normandie. Only a mile away was Alum Creek and the swimming pool. And in the next block, on Hoffman Avenue, was John Gager who soon became my best friend – my first real boy friend. John's family were fairly well-off, at least more so than we were. They had an automobile and electric lights, and a garage in the rear of their house where John and I could use carpenters' tools and perform experiments in electricity and chemistry.

Across the street from 916 lived the Persifor Frazer Smiths, who had only recently come to Columbus from Philadelphia. He had been sent by the Pennsylvania Railroad to be in charge of their repair shops – the "Pennsylvania" shops, as they were called. The Smiths had two nice daughters Johanna and Thomasine, younger than me by three or four years. Our families became quite good friends, and Mrs. Smith gave me a summer job as his office-boy. It was my first real job and I was very proud as I left every morning for the shops with my lunch box fastened to the handle bars of my bicycle. Father wanted me to work "so that I would learn the value of a dollar."

I wanted to work as a recognition of my growing manhood. There were other symbols to record this exciting fact. One was my first suit with long trousers, and socks instead of stockings. To celebrate this important event I had my photograph taken at Bakers Art Gallery. This was also to mark my graduation from Douglas School in February, 1908 and entry into East High. I was keeping up the Stewart tradition; the next step was to make Bert's high school fraternity and the football team.

I developed a craze for anything German – perhaps because my German teacher at Douglas was so pretty, perhaps because of a wonderful old German woman named Mrs. Reggett who had worked for us at The Normandie. Germany superseded Scotland in my international favor. France was represented by Alphonse and Gaston in the funny papers, England by a dude named Cholly who said "Bah Jove." The Irish were two comic characters named Pat and Mike who said "Begorra" and sang sad songs at Keith's Theater about a river Shannon which flowed. Then there were "hunkies," "polacks," "dagos," and "wops" from somewhere in Europe. But I never had any idea of ever getting to any of those countries. Perhaps someday I would go to New York – or at least to Pittsburgh and see the great Honus Wagner play shortstop for the Pirates. But not Europe. As I have said, nobody went abroad in those days except the rich. And we Stewarts had never been rich. That didn't bother me at all, except that I occasionally wished we had an automobile. Charles had turned his Pope-Toledo in for a Frayer-Miller (a local product) and then an Autocar runabout. Anne had a Columbus "electric," in which she would take mother for rides. And I had a scrapbook filled with cutout pictures taken from the advertisements of all the other makes of automobiles.

Another event of growing-upness was my Confirmation at Trinity Church. To qualify for this I had attended special Sunday School classes where I learned the right answers to the catechism questions.

I've forgotten most of the answers, but the fact that anything sticks in my memory shows how impressed I was by the ceremony. As a matter of fact, I was deeply moved by my Confirmation. I felt very close to Jesus, and can remember lying in bed one night with the positive assurance that angels were watching me. It was a beautiful feeling of surrender and security, and I was determined to walk in the path of the Lord forever. The family were sympathetic. Anne gave me a gold Confirmation ring and a hundred calling cards engraved with the words: "Mr. Donald Ogden Stewart." I had grown out of childhood. I was ready to take my place in society – and Society.

East High School was out near Franklin Park, and presented many exciting possibilities. In addition to real football (there had been no official Douglas team) and Bert's fraternity, there were now subjects like Latin and geometry. Latin somehow brought school closer to father, who had gone to the Cambridge (Massachusetts) Latin School. And geometry was a mature step ahead of boyish arithmetic. But for some reason or other, I began to be disappointed in East High and gradually came to hate it. Or, rather, I became increasingly convinced that they hated me. Not the teachers, but the boys and girls. Perhaps at first it was what every freshman goes through. I was teased and made fun of. They invented a nickname which gradually came to hurt more and more. "Duck Lip" they called me, because of my slightly protruding upper lip. Nothing I could do would stop them.

There were other tragedies. I was too young to make any impression on the football team. I was not invited to come around to Bert's fraternity. I wanted to be popular and successful, the way he had been, but instead I was Duck Lip. And one night, when a bunch of boys went past the house and yelled that name up at my window, I broke down to mother and told her how unhappy I was at being such a "failure." It was at this low point, I think, that I began to reach for humor as a weapon with which to protect myself; to think up a wounding epithet to hurl at someone before he could throw it at me. Or to call myself "Duck Lip" *first,* with a smile.

As a more hopeful side of this rather gloomy East High School period I gradually and happily became attached to a group of boys and girls of my own age. We called ourselves "The Bunch" and for the next eight or ten years we danced with each other, had "crushes" on each other, enjoyed each other's company immensely during the Christmas and other vacations when we were home from school and college. We weren't the "old" Columbus first-family society, but we were all that there was in our age-group to give dances and ride around in automobiles singing "By the Old Mill Stream." Among the charter members were Josephine Baldwin (my first love, from Sullivant School) whose father was the town's leading surgeon; Adeline Werner, of recent German ancestry, whose father owned a wholesale shoe business; Betty Wheeler (I can't remember what her father did, but they lived on East Broad); Jeanette Neal and Katherine Barcus whose fathers' businesses are likewise forgotten. And the boys were John Gager, son of a manufacturer of sheet-metal coilings, etc.; Stuart Price whose father owned a wholesale drug company; and Burnham Lanman, whose father I think was dead. The only heiress at our parties was the grand daughter of the astute pioneer in the patent medicine field who discovered that by mixing a good stiff shot of alcohol with harmless colored liquid and bottling it under the name of "medicine" you could sell enormous quantities at a rather modest initial cost. The older Columbus families who had made their fortunes in dry goods, real estate and beer, resented this intrusion of the *nouveau riche,* especially as the heiress's German father built an East Broad Street green stone castle strictly out of the Brothers Grimm by Frankenstein. Columbus was changing.

In the summer of 1909, while I was working as a paint-spattered laborer at Mr. Gager's factory, it was announced to me that I had been accepted as a student by the Phillips Exeter Academy in Exeter, New Hampshire. I went wild with joy. A real Eastern school, founded before Columbus Ohio had ever existed – with classes called Lower Middle and Upper Middle instead of Sophomore and Junior. And courses in Greek, just like father. He had, I suppose, been told by mother about my "duck lip" unhappiness at East High. And he and Bert had always had the ambition to send me to an Eastern college.

So in the fall father and I went East again. At first I was a little vexed that he had felt it necessary to come with me, but as the train from Boston neared Exeter I was awfully glad that he was beside me. I got more and more nervous as we came closer and closer to the Unknown. There were other boys with fathers (and even *mothers*) on the train, but there were also loud laughing groups who seemed contemptuous of me, a new boy. Father understood this and tried to encourage me with pats on my knee. I had a moment of panic as we puffed into the small Exeter station, but it was too late to retreat. We followed the other boys through the tree-lined streets of a quiet New England town. I had been assigned to the Porter House, a small one-story frame dwelling which was presided over by a young instructor Mr. Perkins and his family. Upstairs were three little rooms, to be occupied by myself and two other new boys. Father helped me unpack my suitcase, we had a walk to see the school buildings, the playing fields and the town, had a talk with the Registrar, and then father took the afternoon train back to Boston. Childe Rolande took a deep breath and returned to the Porter House. My trunk had arrived. I put away my belongings. My "Sunday" suit, in which I had been confirmed. My small new leatherbound prayerbook which mother had given me. My neckties, the fanciest of which were old ones of Charles's who got them from a place called Budd in New York. My razor, an old "straight" one of father's. Photographs of father, mother, Bert, Anne (with the baby Anne), Charles – and a framed poker hand (a straight flush) which Bert had once held and which he took down from the wall of his room and gave me "to bring me luck." I started to hang it up and Mr. Perkins knocked on the door to remind me that I was not allowed to drive nails in the wall. I sat down at my desk in front of a box of writing paper which father had just purchased for me in the town. At the top of the paper was inscribed the Phillips Exeter Academy shield, with the motto "Huic venite pueri ut viri sitis" – "Come hither boys that you may become men."

3

So, in the Porter House in 1909 there I sat, a fourteen-year-old boy filled at the moment with a deep sense of gratitude for having been given this chance to "make good" at Exeter. I could not have defined "good" except that I was obligated to make the family proud of me. I felt grateful, kneeled down and thanked God for letting me have this chance. Then I picked up my pen and wrote "Dear Mother" – and began to feel homesick as hell.

The homesickness persisted during the first term. It was increased by the disheartening discovery that scholastic requirements were incredibly stiffer than in the Columbus schools. I did not do at all well in my studies; there was even a sickening fear that I might be dropped before the Christmas recess. I had great periods of discouragement, especially in Latin where Mr. Robinson seemed to delight in making me the butt of his sarcasm. It was good for me, I suppose. I learned to study, and survived. But it made for a grim three months, the first really miserable period in my life. Another frightening experience was what is known as a "wet dream." I had been given absolutely no sex education and guiltily wrote father about it as though something awful had developed in me. I didn't dare reveal it to anyone else, and crept about with a dread apprehension that I had something which I had heard about called a "dose" or "the syph." Then came father's letter assuring me that Dr. Moore told him it was perfectly normal for boys of my age, and in my prayers that night I thanked God for my escape. Incidentally, I had been kneeling and saying my prayers every night since I can remember. Church attendance was compulsory at Exeter, but I would have gone anyway. I even volunteered to help the rector with his furnace, and got up very early many cold mornings in the service of my God. The Lord didn't seem to do me any appreciative reciprocal service in Mr. Robinson's Latin class, but it helped make me feel that I was atoning somehow to father and mother for my low grades.

The first term wasn't all unrelieved horror. There were various high moments: a hot chocolate fudge at Wetherell's Drugstore; a huge griddle cake with syrup at Billy's small restaurant. But I didn't have the spending money for much of this, and ate all my meals at Alumni Hall, where the zenith was the Sunday noon chicken and the depths were reached that evening with a thing called "cheese fondu" which we secretly named something quite different. "Scholarship boys" waited on table at Alumni Hall and also at a few private houses. One of the distinctive features of the school was the comparatively large number of these poorer boys which gave Exeter a reputation for democracy, in distinction to other Eastern prep schools. Many of these scholarship boys, by a curious coincidence, were good athletes, but the democratic tradition was indeed greatly helped by their presence.

When the great day of the football game with Andover came around I began to feel that I was becoming a real Exonian. It was, at least for us, the Yale-Harvard game of prep schools. I dutifully bought a pair of red and gray socks and a ditto colored tie. I lined up behind banners with the rest of my class on Front Street to await the arrival of the hated Andover boys who came en masse by train. The suspense was terrific. We heard the whistle of the train, and then, in the distance, a band playing the Andover march. Our spines stiffened. Their voices, singing, came closer, as did the tramping sound of their marching feet. Then – there they were, with their damned blue and white flags. We obediently gave them a cheer, "with three long Andovers on the end." Our own band crashed into "Cheer now for Exeter!" which we had been practicing for several nights, and especially at a pep rally in chapel the night before.

Cheer now for Exeter
And raise high her spirit true,
No line can stah-hop our men
From smashing crashing through the line of Blue!

We felt exhilarated as we started behind the band towards the field.

We couldn't lose. Our principal, "Pop" Amen, had assured us in chapel that morning that, when he woke up and looked out, "the sky was all red." An omen of certain victory. But in spite of that and my red and gray socks there was no "smashing crashing through the line of blue." Andover won by a big score, and there was a gloomy post-mortem meal at Alumni Hall. We tried to cheer ourselves a bit by singing defiantly in a whisper:

Oh Exeter was Exeter when Andover was a pup
And Exeter will be Exeter when
Andover has gone up.
And if any Andover sons-of-bitches
Come wandering round our halls,
We'll paint their tails with iodine
And ostracize their balls.

The reference to iodine came from an old Exeter custom practiced on any particularly "fresh" new boy. There were always one or two at the beginning of each term. It kept us newcomers uneasy, because nobody was sure, but this was the only "hazing." Fraternity initiations were something else, but that was still another world. There were four fraternities, distinguished by their different colored hatbands and called the "Middlewellers," "Bootlickers," "Greasers," and "Ass wipers." I didn't have any hope for one: I was not an athlete, and I had done nothing to merit any attention. I was not even sure that anybody liked me. At least I wasn't "Duck Lip" any more.

My cousin, Bob Whittemore, a Harvard freshman, asked me to come down to the Harvard-Yale game and I joyously accepted (after getting father's and the school's permission). That night Bob and I went into Boston to see a show and I tried to live up to what I thought was expected of a wild cousin from the West. I had heard in school that the bar of the Adams House was the great Exeter hangout, so we went there and I downed my first sloe gin fizz. So far – okay. Then we decided to experiment and followed it with something pink called a "Ward Eight." This seemed to call for another; on the list of drinks I discovered a "Widow's Dream," and daringly took a chance. The unknown dream (also called an "Angel's Tit") came toward us in the form of four different coloured liquors with cream on top. That did it. Bob and I got back to Cambridge somehow or other. I remember diving happily and confidently with outstretched arms into a snowdrift.

I was sure I could fly. I have been drunk many times since but I have never equaled the absolute joyful ecstasy of that first one.

At the beginning of December, there was the school custom of chanting in Latin every morning in chapel the same dirge:

Oh come oh come Emmanuel
And ransom captive Israel
That mourns in lonely exile here.

Not that Exeter could under any circumstances have been identified with Israel. There were four Jews in my class, which was about the average in those days. One of these was Robert Nathan (later to become a leading author); then there was Julius Freund and Paul Godchaux from New Orleans and Bernard Foreman from Milwaukee. The latter was a scholarship student who supplemented his income by arranging with the railroads to furnish a carload of Exeter boys bound for the middle west for the Christmas vacation. It sounded like a good idea, and I signed up. Poor Bernie! What a beating he took on that trip. We were shunted here, delayed there. Worst of all, dining cars avoided us like the plague. One compensation was that in a long stopover in Cleveland we saw a wonderful fire which burned a huge building to the ground. But Bernard couldn't take the credit for that.

Sex, like the hedgehog, was in a state of suspended animation as far as girls were concerned. Nor was there any homosexuality. I had never heard of it, and I don't think any of us had. We all indulged, I assume, in a certain amount of what Kinsey calls "self-induced" sex, but it was not talked about. One poor fellow was caught masturbating in the Gym, was cruelly nicknamed "Jerk" and left school, unable to bear the disgrace. It was universally accepted that such conduct led to insanity or, at the very least, to an excess of pimples and a growth of hair in the palms of hands. An evangelist named Mercer came one spring and attracted a long line of penitent self-inducers after a "frank talk" in chapel. His advice included exercises, cold showers and prayer. There was a town whore, but I never heard of anyone who "knew" her. There was also a Robinson Female Seminary but the standard of charm was rumored to be rather doubtful. There was a Pre-Raphaelite print of Sir Galahad on most of our walls, and beside it was usually Kipling's "If." Those were our ideals and there were no doubters, even if some didn't quite live up to them.

Then came spring and it was wonderful. I whistled Mendelssohn's Spring Song lying in my bed one night until Mr. Perkins came up and stopped me. I took long walks along the river to nearby villages. I played tennis, as I had no possibilities in baseball or track. There was great excitement about Halley's Comet which set the boys in the dormitories to shouting "Comet" every night on the slightest pretext. We went down to Andover and marched triumphantly back to our train after winning the baseball game. A glorious end to a year which had begun so miserably. This was 1910. Taft was in the White House. I was getting the best education possible. I was meeting all the "right" people, or at least their sons. Presumably I would eventually become a Columbus lawyer; I didn't really have any ambition other than that. I believed in all the right things: God, my family, my country, honesty, hard work, purity, the Republican party. The road ahead seemed clear.

In the interest of continuing my education in "the value of a dollar" I worked during the summer for the Citizen's Telephone Company. This was the independent organization competing with the pioneer Bell company. Father had as a client a promoter-capitalist named Frank Davis who took an interest in me and got me the job. I was the "boy" among six other laborers. Every morning we climbed into a truck and were driven to whatever part of the city or surrounding country where new telephone poles were needed or old ones had to be replaced. This meant digging a hole from four to six feet deep, no matter how hard the ground. It was the lowest form of labor, but it was outdoors and I enjoyed it. I especially liked the foreman whose first name was Howard. He had been brought up on a farm and had, like many farmers, become a telephone lineman. At first he had no use for me and my soft white hands – neither did the other men – but gradually, I think, I won Howard's acceptance as a good worker. The others were real "types"; it was unskilled, low-paid, hard work, and attracted the casualties in the struggle for existence. I remember only "grandfather" with a dirty straw hat and a dirtier white beard, and "Johnny Nuts" who was a pathetic stuttering half-wit. I took this job every summer for the next four years and came to be regarded with a certain amount of liking. But never as one of them, which I, romantically, would have been pleased at. They dried up when I tried to talk to them about my school or college. I had the feeling that they didn't trust me. I remember earnestly trying to explain to Johnny Nuts that I worked like this because my father wanted me to learn the value of a dollar. Johnny looked at me blankly and walked away as though to say, "And they call *me* nuts." Once or twice I almost became "one of the boys." We had a pole job at the Hoster brewery on South High Street, and in those days visitors to the breweries (one of Columbus's main industries) were given a large glass of free beer. We disguised ourselves as "visitors"; even Howard had a couple, and the ride home after work was, to say the least, very companionable. And once Howard delighted me by asking me to come to his house for supper and meet his wife.

My second year at school proceeded at first on its normal way. I was an Upper Middler now and roomed in a campus dormitory, Hoyt Hall. Partly at first because of a fear of being classed as a "shark" instead of a "regular guy," but mainly because I did not have a scholarly brain, I never aspired to high marks. I wanted to win my "E" in football or track or anything – but I was not any good at anything. I did, however, play guard that fall on my class team and had a red "1912" sewn proudly onto a white sweater.

Then another Christmas vacation was happily danced away with "The Bunch." John Gager was still my best friend. I do not remember having as yet selected any lucky girl for my concentrated devotion. There was no such thing as "necking" or "petting." A kiss was taken as a very serious step towards engagement. When we were younger we had been trapped into kissing girls by playing "post office," but now we just joked about it. I remember father and mother being quite worried one night when I came home from a small "Bunch" party with my rear shirt-tails out. I was as surprised as they were, but even more surprised when father began to question me as to the truth of my explanation that John or somebody must have pulled them out as a joke. I didn't have the foggiest idea of what he was suspecting – and if I had, I would have been completely flabbergasted. I was seventeen. A year or two later Charles half-jokingly implied that I had paid a visit to a local brothel and I replied very seriously, "I don't do that sort of thing." There was a song at the time "Oh they don't get any tail down at Yale!" And they certainly didn't at Exeter, at least none that I knew about. Nor any alcohol, either. After that first glorious spree with my cousin Bob, the only liquor which passed my pure lips during prep school days was a stein of Culmbacher beer at Charley Wirth's German restaurant in Boston on my way back to school after each Christmas vacation. It was a sort of solemn assertion of manhood, and it made me feel very good.

It was during the 1911 winter term that I made another similar assertion: I started to smoke a pipe. Bert had given me two or three of his older ones, and the tobacco used by all Exeter men was Imperial cube cut (25 cents a can). The great game was to get the proper "cake" in the inside of your pipe's bowl, and the correct shine (by rubbing it on your nose) on the outside. This occupation served to make the long cold winter seem a little less dreary. There were other equally worthwhile extra-curricular diversions; one of these was furnished by "Fat" Mecum across the hall who had developed the extraordinary gift of being able to light his farts with a match, producing an exciting blue flame, on the length of which bets could be made. There were occasional "alarums and excursions" such as could be furnished by a dormitory pillow fight or snowball battle. We weren't allowed to go to the weekly movies which the "townies" could see in the auditorium of the Town Hall, and I can't remember any enthusiasm for the occasional "cultural" lecture there. The school did, however, have a Dramatic Society, and I had a go at acting when the Deutscher Verein gave a play called *Der Neffe als Onkel* in which I was cast as a young lady. My performance was followed by no invitations to act in anything else.

But I did have one major success, which was to mark a turning point. Up to now it might fairly be said that I was a resolutely mediocre young man. There was nothing I did above the average, except perhaps ballroom dancing. I couldn't play any game well, nor any instrument – not even the banjo. And then a piece of luck came my way.

There was a professor of English whose name was Cushwa and whose nickname was "Cush." His fat body moved awkwardly; his one good eye glared from his blotched face as he grunted out in angry judgments. We loved him. His Shakespeare classes were the most popular in the curriculum. His student imitators (and they were legion) could always get a laugh, but it was a sympathetic laugh. One of the things which brought Robert Benchley (Exeter 1908) and me together at our first meeting ten years later was our mutual affection for Cush.

It was Cush who suggested that I enter the competition for the editorial board of *The Exonian*, the school bi-weekly newspaper. It wasn't athletic or particularly in the line of my ambitions. But after I had narrowly succeeded in the competition there followed the completely unexpected. I was chosen to the top position, to be Managing Editor for the next year.

It was luck for me – but it was also something else. The boy who should have been Managing Editor was Bernie Foreman, one of the four Jewish students. He had been elected to the Board long before I had. He was older, more experienced, and a better editor. I don't know who was responsible for this injustice. I should have refused. But – I didn't. I was sorry for Bernie, but if they had decided that I was the better editor, who was I to argue?

4

So I suddenly and undeservedly became a Big Man. And shortly after this came my long-cherished desire: I was elected to a fraternity.

But before I could sport the Middleweller green and black hatband I had to go through the initiation. There was a week of intermittent paddling and a sore behind, of which I was properly proud. And then instruction to me and the other two initiates: we were to walk alone on a certain Saturday night, past the fraternity house and along a country road until we arrived at a gate on which there would be a lighted skull. When the time came I obeyed. It was a long lonely walk in darkness. From ahead came a long, ghostly whistle; this was answered by a haunting one from behind. These whistles came at odd and startling intervals. It was very frightening. Finally I arrived at a gate topped by a lighted skull. Suddenly a ghost beckoned and shrieked, "Follow me!" and I followed until I reached a little clump of trees. From then on all was confusion. I was tackled, thrown to the ground, blindfolded, told to run, and tackled again and again. Finally, still blindfolded, we were marched back to the fraternity house and underwent the final rites, followed by hot coffee and sandwiches. I was a Middleweller, a "brother in the bond" to the captain of the football team and the captain of the track team. The future was bright.

My heritage was even brighter. I found that I was a brother to most of the names I had worshipped in the years before. Football captains at Harvard, Yale and Princeton. Record breakers in track events. I eagerly leafed through the "blackbook" which devoted a page and a photograph to the collegiate triumphs of each former Middleweller. This was a dazzling view of success. If they, why not I?

Of course, ambition didn't come all at once. Nor did the assumption of the responsibilities of a Big Man. There were many things to learn, including the writing of editorials for *The Exonian*. I still hadn't achieved my ultimate dream – an "E" on a sweater. Earnestly and faithfully I tried everything, including throwing the hammer. And to perfect myself in this art I persuaded our pint-sized track coach to let me take a hammer (twelve pounds) home with me to Columbus that summer so that I could practice during the vacation.

Anyway, spring was glorious in spite of no "E" and an epidemic of "pink eye". As a matter of fact, it was a lovely epidemic. The Infirmary was a wonderful place, with the best food, a pretty nurse and no obligation to study. Some genius discovered that by glaring at the sun and pummeling your chest with a hair brush you could produce all the pink eye symptoms. The Infirmary was crowded that spring.

I changed my eating place from Alumni Hall ($5.00 per week) to a private "joint" operated at the same price by a local lady and patronized by some ten of us, including "Pink" Fulford from Providence R.I. and Phelps Putnam, a strange moody bird who wrote poetry. "Put" was later to become one of my dearest friends, but at Exeter he was decidedly not Big Man material and, what's more, I had no interest in poetry. "Pink," on the other hand, was of the Asswiper fraternity and played in the banjo club, and when he said that they needed another player I hopefully sent home for Charles's old dress suit and Bert's banjo and gave it a try. They really must have become desperately hard up, for I couldn't even read the notes of the pieces we played, but I learned enough by heart to be able to fake it. We gave one concert at Bradford Hall, a girls' school near Boston, and both the dress suit and the banjo survived.

Although what this banjo club played bore no resemblance to any music living or dead, music itself was beginning to creep into my consciousness. As a boy my favorite record had been "The Battle of Manila Bay," which began with the American sailors singing "Onward Christian Soldiers." But little by little I found myself appreciating opera, possibly because of Anne. At Exeter there wasn't much opportunity for music lovers. "Cush" and "Robbie" had organized the Amphion Club where chamber music was indulged in by Paul Godchaux, Julius Freud, Robert Nathan and two or three others; I didn't have time for this sort of stuff. But when I found a good phonograph in the living room of the Middleweller house I made use of it. I was also considerably encouraged by the discovery that Tommy Cornell, captain of the track team, liked music. He and I used to sit up after the others had gone to bed and play the three or four "classic" records in the large collection.

This friendship with Tommy was the beginning of my deviation toward Yale instead of Harvard. Tommy was going down to New Haven (as Yale is always referred to by those who "know") the next fall, and he thought that I ought to keep up the tradition of Middleweller success there. What could Harvard, in spite of father, offer comparable to this? Owen Johnson's *Stover at Yale,* which had just been published, determined my switchover. It was just about the only book I read all year, and I read it with intense self-identification. Eight years later, when I got to know really well a then unpublished Scott Fitzgerald, we roared with laughter at our shared confession of the affect of "Dink" Stover on our prep school dreams.

Then I went home for the summer with my twelve-pound hammer and my Middleweller hat to face the task of breaking the news to father that I wanted to go to Yale. Father beat me to it. He had news for me. He was broke. Or, at least as he apologetically explained, he couldn't afford to let me finish at Exeter unless I could help out by getting a scholarship and paying some of my expenses. He had written to Mr. Rogers, the Registrar, and was awaiting a reply which might offer some hope. I was so stunned I didn't mention Yale.

It *was* quite a shock. I knew we weren't rich and I had unquestioningly kept down my desires. It was just that father and Bert had had an unexpectedly unsuccessful couple of years. I accepted the bad luck, was sorry for father and for myself, and went to work once more at my old job with the Telephone Company. I also made one or two attempts to find jobs at night, just like the heroic boys in Horatio Alger novels. I wasn't too disappointed that there weren't any such jobs. Then came a letter from Mr. Rogers. Mother told me that father cried when he read the appreciative things that were said about my character and the value to Exeter of boys like me. A scholarship would be arranged, and I could earn my board by working as a waiter in Alumni Hall. The path to Skull and Bones was still open to Dink Stover Stewart. I unpacked my hammer and threw it around Franklin Park with restored determination.

What a romantic figure I became to myself! The Judge's son was to put on a waiter's jacket. The family were quite proud, as were "The

Bunch." I floated back to Exeter on a cloud of approving good wishes. And the approval was echoed by all my classmates, even the unfortunate twenty at whose table I learned the duties of a waiter. It was glorious, romantic fun, playing at being poor.

The football season started off with a new coach, Gus Ziegler, who had been a famous All-American guard at the University of Pennsylvania. It was hoped that we could break the run of defeats by Andover. Gus did what he could. He taught us what might be described as "good, hard football," and it seemed at times as though most of it was directed at me. Gus apparently wanted to know if I could "take it." I took it, which does not mean that I enjoyed it. My weight was 165 pounds. Playing opposite me, on the First Eleven, was Ben Neale who weighed 210. The other guard was "Pi" Way, weighing 200. I managed somehow to hang onto my job on the second team. The week before the Andover game I was sent in for a few minutes against the Harvard Freshmen at Cambridge. And then came the Andover game, with me there on the bench in the red jersey, ready at any moment to give my all for P. E. A. If anything happened to either Ben or "Pi" I was sure to take their place. That "E" was at last within my grasp.

But the game was not going the way Gus had expected in spite of the fact that we had Charlie Brickley (later an All-American) on our team. Andover was putting up a great fight. On their side was "Ned" Mahan, another Harvard All-American-to-be. Finally there came the sound of the referee's whistle – an Exeter man was lying on the ground. It was Ben. Gus looked along the bench in my direction. And I did an incredible thing. I looked away. I deliberately avoided his gaze. Perhaps in that split second if I had leaped up eagerly Gus would have sent me in. I do not know, but in my own mind, to this day, I failed some kind of test. In another minute it was too late. Ben got up off the ground, the game went on, Exeter lost. And I had lost too, not only the "E." I could not understand what had happened and I did not admit to myself that I had been a coward, but I suspected it.

This struggle with physical timidity taunted me all through the winter term. I was obsessed with a puritanical fervor to do those things I didn't want to do. There was a great need for a conquest of myself, for a forcing of my body to perform unpleasant duties. I had always been afraid to dive head first over a long box onto a mattress. I could make the dive when the box was sideways. Then I could measure the width of the box – and successfully dive over that empty space. But when I would put the box lengthwise between me and the mattress, I couldn't. Time after time. Day after day. Finally I concluded that if I went on looking for things I was afraid to do, there would be no end to it. If a box that long, then would come a longer box to be conquered, and on and on. I was right – but it seemed like an evasion, an unsatisfactory answer to a real problem.

This grim, humorless desire for self-perfection came partly, perhaps, because of a growing sense of my responsibilities as a Big Man. I owed perfection to the school. The younger boys looked up to me. They read my editorials in *The Exonian.* They heard me praised in chapel for having searched all night in the snowy forest nearby for two students who were supposed lost. Mr. Perkins, who had despaired of me in my first term, now nodded approvingly. The school was on my shoulders and I would not let it down. There were awards to be voted for by my classmates at the end of the year: "Done The Most For Exeter," "Most Apt To Succeed." (When Robert Benchley died in 1945 and there was talk of establishing at Exeter an annual Benchley prize, I suggested that it be awarded each year to the boy "Least likely to succeed.")

That winter there were other triumphs to be happily recorded by me about myself in the Middleweller book of records, including Vice-President of the "Christian Fraternity." This last honor involved a trip one bitterly cold Sunday to our Mission where I addressed some ten or twelve of the "less-fortunate" in the town. The average age of these miserable creatures was well over fifty and the average desire to hear my message was considerably less, especially as I chose at the ripe age of seventeen to cheer them up with the comforting information that "the greatest lessons in Life come to those who have the hardest knocks." At least they got hot coffee and sandwiches.

The final spring term arrived with the usual glorious outburst of birds and trees and outdoor athletics. The New England winter is always so long that its end comes as a well-deserved radiant miracle. Another miracle, neither deserved nor radiant, was that I was elected to write the Class Poem. I had never written a poem in my life. I didn't understand or like poetry. I think that "Cush" was appalled at my election to the poetic obligation, and the only explanation possible was that there was nobody else. Of the leading literary lights Robert Nathan had been in our class only one year, Charlie "Doc"

Walker had been selected as Class Orator, and Phelps Putnam, who should have had it, wasn't as 'popular' as I. So I got a rhyming dictionary from the library and grimly invoked the muses.

There were, however, many more important priorities, and the muses didn't get going for a long time. Most important of all, there was the hammer throw. My competitors included one perfect athlete and one giant, so my chances weren't too bright, but I finally succeeded in gaining the coach's (George Connor's) approval as the third representative in this event in the Andover meet. This kindness got the Academy no points, but got me an AEA on my sweater. We won the meet, and with the rest of the team I was dragged through town in an old coach while the Chapel bell pealed triumphantly.

The class poem still awaited me and, although the results don't show it, I put down my hammer and picked up my pen. I read several previous ones to see what the problem was. I discovered from the dictionary that more words rhymed with "men" than anything else. So the muses nudged me into the brilliant idea of using as my leitmotif the Exeter motto "Come hither boys that ye may become men."

The poem itself began:

Autumn it was, Autumn in late September,
When the Squamscott wandering slowly mirrored rays
Of gold and green and much we still remember
With thoughts of joy and many words of praise.

Of course I didn't write that all at once. It took a lot of looking up in the dictionary. And after I had composed those beautiful words, the muses yawned and went to sleep. This worried "Cush" but not me. Didn't I have the example of Coleridge who layed off for a long time after the opening of "Kubla Khan"? Anyway, I had the ending of my poem, which went:

Be men, be men, be men!
Honest and straight and true!
Ready to help a friend!
Ready by deed to do!

All I had by deed to do was to fit in something between the beginning and that impressive conclusion.

At the same time, all the other preparations had to be made for Commencement. I invited Jeannette Neil, one of the "Bunch," to come from Columbus to the June Ball (at her father's expense). I had to arrange for my scholarship at Yale, and for my fellow Exonians to agree to eat at the Exeter table in one of the boarding houses from which I was to receive free board. Pi Way, Put Putnam and Doc Walker accepted, not only for meals but also rooms. I had to have my dress suit put in order, and a cap and gown rented. The "Pean" reported that in the class election I had been voted "Squarest." I'm not quite sure what that meant, but it pleased me and the family.

To my joy, Bert came as the family representative to Commencement, and stayed at the Middleweller house. He made a big hit with my friends, although I had to warn him that his whisky breath was rather embarrassing. Liquor was strictly taboo at school and I had this desperate fear of being with anyone who was "conspicuous." I certainly wasn't ashamed of Bert: during the preceding Christmas vacation he had got tight at a charity ball in Columbus and I had helped him home and put him to bed; he thanked me in the morning and it made me feel very manly and very close to him. And I think he was quite proud of me – even after the Commencement exercises at which I read my Class Poem. Later I discovered that after hearing "Be men, be men, be men!" he had hurried down from Chapel and bought up all the copies of the "Monthly" in which it was published, so that no one could ever know how awful it was.

The June Ball passed pleasantly and perspiringly. I had developed into an enthusiastic and tireless dancer with a number of tricky whirls and counter-revolutions of my own invention. Jeannette was an attractive, graceful girl and a lovely partner. She was accompanied by her mother as a chaperone but, as she wasn't pretty enough to kiss, I satisfied my urges by dancing. I had come to enjoy dancing more and more, especially as the old two-steps and waltzes were being superseded by fox-trots, bunny hugs, etc. And I responded excitedly to the new rhythms, beginning with, I think, "Alexander's Ragtime Band." All music brought to me an almost uncontrollable urge to dance – except of course opera, which existed for me only on phonograph records.

It is strange that at that time the music of words, as in poetry, never opened itself equally to me. Like Latin and Greek, poetry existed as something to be learned in order to pass the college entrance examinations. I can still remember "Arma virumque cano" at the opening of the *Aeneid,* and we used to divide poems into appropriate feet, but any connection between that and the beauty of music remained completely unrevealed. The only bits I remember from all of Greek are "Entheuthen exelaunay" ("From there they marched") and, also from Xenophon's *Anabasis*, the word "sungignomi" which is what Dr. Leacock explained to us in confidential tones as what Cyrus is said to have done to the beautiful Sicilian queen.

The main criticism one might make of our classroom education was that most of it never had any real connection with the world we lived in. Ancient History, Latin, Greek, French, German, Physics, Chemistry – there were mainly "to discipline our minds" and to pass the dreaded College Board exams. And probably, for our age group, this was the best that could be demanded of the faculty. We had entered as boys. Now that we were men, it was up to the colleges to direct these well-trained minds into a real understanding of the world about them.

So I packed up my diploma (in which I was referred to as "Donaldus Ogdeniensis Stewart") and with real tenderness bade farewell to my professors and my companions. I loved the school, and still do. It had done its part in forming my character and I think that on the whole father had made a wise investment. "Learning how to study" had not by any means been the chief benefaction. When I became editor of *The Exonian* I suddenly became responsible for something other than myself. I also acquired confidence in myself. I had achieved something. I could "take it" – I had in the first term been confronted with sickening failure in my studies and had fought and overcome. I had made a beginning toward being a Success. I had acquired status. It was, so far, in a small field, but larger than Columbus, Ohio. And there were promises of even larger fields and more impressive portents of that still undefined "Success."

5

The summer started quietly. I was in a hurry to get the vacation over with, to start my life at Yale, my real life. Columbus didn't seem to understand the importance of what lay ahead for me. No one had read *Stover At Yale,* especially among my fellow employees at the Telephone Company. I had been given a job in a badly ventilated storeroom, and I was bored. In the evenings there wasn't much excitement, either. The girls were away at summer resorts. John Gager and I would occasionally go the roof-garden on top of the Southern Hotel where we would drink beer and eat popcorn. John wasn't impressed by either Exeter or Yale; he was going to enter Ohio State in the fall, and that didn't interest me at all. I found myself drawn more and more to Bert who was thirty-two. He knew about my life; he had actually seen Exeter. He was proud of me. We would go together to the Arlington Country Club on the Scioto River and play tennis. He told Anne that I was a lot of fun to be with.

So I wasn't surprised when one noon he came round to the Telephone building and asked me to have lunch with him. I was delighted. We went to a nearby saloon, but Bert didn't want anything to drink. He didn't eat anything, either. And when he told me what was up my appetite vanished.

Father was about to be charged with the theft of two thousand dollars. It seems that when he was a judge he had had a lot to do with organizing the County Law Library, and had served for some years as its president. A salary was to have been voted to him; father should have been paid for all his work, and expected it. In fact, he was so sure of getting the money that when in 1905 Anne was married and he needed additional cash for the expenses of the wedding, he dipped into the Law Library funds rather than ask Charles to help him out. Then the unexpected happened. The vote to reimburse him was never passed. Father's law business barely made expenses. And now an ambitious young Democratic district attorney had discovered the deficit and was threatening to have father indicted unless the funds were restored. We had three days in which to raise the money. Charles couldn't help out. He had lost his fortune – and a great deal more – in the 1907 panic. Father and mother didn't yet know of the crisis; they were visiting Anne in the country near Columbus. Bert came to me about it in desperation: he thought we might be able to borrow the money from Aunt Annie in Boston who was rumored to be fairly well off. Or perhaps I might get a loan from one of the fathers of my rich Exeter friends. If we didn't succeed, father might have to go to the penitentiary. And certainly there would be the disgrace of publicity and a trial.

The disgrace came all right. Bert and I didn't have any luck with last-minute appeals for help. That night there was a frantic frustrating long-distance telephone call to Aunt Annie. All of our Madison Avenue neighbors must have shared in our secret, as did the nearby grocers; next day several long-overdue bills were presented at the kitchen door. I had to yell into the telephone several times at the top of my lungs, "Fat"Father is in trouble. Can you hear me, Auntie Annie? Operator, she can't hear me. Father is in trouble. No – financial trouble. We need money. Right away. No, Aunt Annie, he isn't sick. It isn't – it's – we need money!" It went on like that for half an hour at least. It was a miserable hot August night; perspiration was rolling off my face onto the desk blotter. Moths were flying around the gas Welsbach lamp. Aunt Annie wanted details and I remember screaming, "He may have to go to jail." Finally she said she would telegraph in the morning but that she couldn't provide any money, even if I came East to explain. Her telegram next day offered the thousand dollars she had been going to leave father in her will. Nothing more. We were sunk.

Those three days of trying desperately to "save the family honor" were an unsuspected lesson. It didn't seem possible to me that father's friends would let the disgrace happen. He was an honored citizen, a former judge, a member of the Columbus Club. There may have been other factors, but Bert's story was accepted by me. I believed father was the victim of an ambitious Democrat who was using father's misdeed to pillory an esteemed Republican and advance his own political fortunes. Who had ever heard of this man, this district attorney? He did not belong to any of our clubs. If he had any children they did not go to our parties. Never for a moment did I blame father. He had believed that the money was deservedly his; he should not have "borrowed" it, but it was not for himself. It was for us that he did it, for his family. There was no problem of ethics. It was a clear case of political ambition and father's bad luck . . . .

And yet, it was the beginning of doubt. A little machine began ticking inside me. Things were not what they seemed to be; people were not either. I hadn't lost my faith in people, but I was jolted out of a groove. Father was indicted. The story and his picture hit the front pages of both the afternoon *Dispatch* and the *Citizen.* I bought a copy of one of them and read it as I walked home. From then on I was on the stage and I was going to give a good performance. "That's Don Stewart," I could hear the whispered voices saying. "You know – Judge Stewart's son." Everyone in every automobile that drove past was looking at me. I was properly and heroically defiant.

When I got home, father was in bed, ill. He smiled and I kissed him. He seemed dazed, and there was no communication.

Bert and I sat down to dinner, awaiting mother who was upstairs. Suddenly there was a commotion on the stairway. I ran out. There was mother sitting on the floor at the foot of the stairs. She smiled at me. "I'm all right," she said, without trying to get up. I couldn't understand that she was drunk. I couldn't believe it. Bert and I helped her to her feet, and to her chair in the dining room. I was worried that our cook would discover the truth.

I needn't have worried. I was, it seemed, the only one who didn't know about mother. I soon learned that this had been going on for some time – ever since the doctor had recommended a bit of whiskey as a way of helping her over her "change of life." Mother had found that whiskey helped her over a lot of things. Father, Bert and Anne all tried to break her of the habit. But she cunningly learned to hide her pints of Columbus Club rock and rye ("for colds"). It had never occurred to me that my mother could be an alcoholic, just as it had seemed impossible that my father could do anything wrong. And now, in one week, both these sheltering roofs had come crashing down about my head.

But externally there was no change. The Bunch treated me as though nothing had happened. The subject of father's guilt or innocence was never discussed. I was invited to all the parties. Dancing, seemingly unconcerned, I perspired just as much as before at the Country Club parties.

But then arose the question of whether I could still go to Yale. Charles was firmly opposed. He didn't share Bert's optimism about my future. He wanted me to come down to earth, and earth meant the Columbus Gas Company where he could get me a job. Bert fought this bitterly, and got his friend, Warren Higgins, a Yale graduate, to lend me part of the money necessary for Freshman year. Father persuaded another friend to complete the loan. I had already been awarded a scholarship and had arranged to get my board for nothing. Yale had won.

I went to college more grateful than ever that I was being given this chance, and more than ever determined to "make good." I now had the additional obligation of redeeming the family honor. But I wasn't frightened as the train puffed into the New Haven station. I was entering the battlefield with a prep-school reputation; another former managing editor of the *Exonian* was arriving to carry on the tradition. I didn't have many doubts about my eventual success.

Four of us from Exeter roomed at a small boarding house run by a Mr. and Mrs. Elliot. I would get my meals free in return for keeping the "Exeter" table at full strength and collecting the bills each week. Mr. Elliot, an Italian whose name was really "Alliotte," spoke practically no English. His wife was Irish. I shared the upstairs rooms with Doc Walker, Pi Way and Put Putman. Pi was the only one who arrived before me because he and I had received letters during the summer informing us that Freshman football practice began two or three days before the term officially opened. My letter made me feel quite important, especially with the impressive blue letterhead "Yale University Football Association." Pi, being a really good athlete, hadn't been so impressed.

A streetcar took the various teams from the old Gym out to Yale Field. We Freshman from different prep schools looked each other over nervously. Prep school sweaters were not supposed to be worn, but I recognized three or four men who had played for Andover the year before. None of us spoke or laughed except the coach, who was joking in the front of the car with a Sophomore assistant whom I later came to know quite well. His name was Archibald MacLeish.

Doc and Put arrived, and the class of 1916 began happily to experience what the anthem calls "Bright college years – The shortest gladdest years of life." That anthem which ends:

Then let us pray that ever we
May let these words our watchword be,
Where'er upon life's sea we sail:
For God, for country, and for Yale.

– a final line which has been cynically termed "one of the great anticlimax sentences in American literature."

But cynicism about Yale – or anything – was not possible for me. Realities about father and mother had shocked but not changed my fundamental attitude toward life. The manner in which my Columbus friends had stood by me in my family disgrace made me appreciate more than ever the "goodness" of people. I believed that the world was good and that Yale was the best of universities. My only problem was to be a success in that world and receive my just rewards.

My roommate Doc was of the same hopeful and ambitious mold, with certain important variations. He had much greater intellectual inclinations than I, and much less social conformism. Doc used to embarrass me terribly by the way he dressed and the people he ran around with. He wanted to be a writer in the tradition of Emerson and Goethe. At Exeter he had won instant recognition and had edited the literary *Monthly,* which of course was considered much less important by the students than the *Exonian* since *Monthly* writers were held to be rather strange birds. Even though Doc had also won his "E" on the track team, he wasn't "regular." But I respected him as a genius of some sort, and was perpetually picking up his shirts, his books, his underwear, and the scattered papers of his essays on subjects like "where Bergson has left us."

Put was literary, too, but not embarrassingly so. Put just didn't have the energy to "make good." His fierce asthma kept him from sports and he wasn't an eager joiner of organizations. He was neither ambitious nor competitive. What he did have, I only slowly appreciated, was a mocking cleansing spirit, a keen critical mind, and an imaginative poetic gift. But in that first year I was sorry for Put. He was a sort of weaker brother to all of us Big Men. We liked him, but. . . .

Pi was what might be called "earthy." He had no literary or social ambition. He was a year or two older and had learned about life from a rather rough battle with poverty. He was the only one of us who had any perception of what life was like "out there" in the struggle for existence. He had learned from his father certain shrewd cynical Yankee-trader appraisals of human nature which made good funny stories about business deals but seemed as foreign to my own world as did Doc's philosophical and poetic abstractions.

Life was wonderful in those first weeks. There was freedom compared to Exeter. Beer in the room, brought up from a saloon Saturday nights; new acquaintances were made in the classrooms, on the football field, in the dining room downstairs. There were strange, rather forbidding classmates called "Grotties" who had "prepped" at the exclusive (as compared to "democratic" Exeter) Groton school. The groups from the various big prep schools tended to stick together. Those unfortunates who came from small schools and high schools led a rather lonely existence.

Freshman studies didn't seem to be much different from prep school: in our first year we grimly faced more Latin, Greek, physics, chemistry, etc. Unexpectedly I discovered, in Freshman English, a professor who began to make me appreciate the aesthetic side of life. Larry Mason was an inspired teacher; he had a way of smilingly slipping little drops of poison into our well-protected skulls, so that before we were conscious of what had happened we were looking at paintings by Giotto, and listening to Wagner operas sung in German. The poison had begun to work; a counter-irritant had been set up against the ambition for success. It was a new elite and, characteristically, I wanted to join. I had no ambition to be a writer or an "aesthete." It was just that Professor Mason had given me a glimpse of something which suggested that the reading of Shakespeare or Carlyle might be connected with satisfactions other than the passing of an examination. It may have been that father's tragedy had prepared me to see the imagination as something which was in its essence a counterbalance to my planned ladder to success.

That ladder got another jolt when, in mid-November, Anne telephoned me that Bert had died of bronchial pneumonia. "Father is not well; mother is all right. It would be unwise for you to spend the money to come home for the funeral. Charles and I are taking care of everything." She was crying. I can't remember crying. Bert was the person I loved more than anyone in the world. I may have gone into a sort of state of shock. I don't know. I remember that Harold Pumpelly won the game at Princeton that week with a sixty-three-yard drop kick.

Three days later Anne telephoned again. Father was dying and I had better come home. I informed the Freshman dean. He was sympathetic. "Was I coming back?" I didn't know. Put was very upset and came with me to the station. I told him the whole story of father's disgrace. It was the first time I had told it to anyone. Put insisted that I ought to return to college.

Father was unconscious most of the time after I arrived. He had Bright's disease, and died on November 28th. Mother, Anne and I were in the room. Mother was on the bed whispering "Gil! Gil!" Anne, sobbing, threw herself on her knees beside the bed. I tried to feel the appropriate death-bed emotions, but nothing happened.

The funeral afforded a great many people the opportunity to express with flowers how fond they had been of father and how sorry they were about the indictment. Actually, his death must have come as a relief to everyone. Bert had assured me in September that the indictment would not be carried to trial and that father would never have to go to prison. Perhaps not. Anne told me that the disgrace had killed Bert. We buried father beside Bert in the family plot in Green Lawn on a miserable, cold, windy afternoon.

Father must have been glad to get out of life, especially since Bert had already gone. Bert's career had been a failure, too – and there had been so much of life still to come. He deserved so much better than he got. I was bitter about Bert's death. My first bitterness. For God, for country, and for Yale. Well, I couldn't get angry at my country – and certainly not at Yale. So God had to take the rap. I began to doubt my faith. At the funeral service as I was repeating the words which I had been saying mechanically since Trinity choir boy days, I found myself thinking: "I don't really believe a lot of this." I became especially angry at the insistence on humility. They wanted me to bow down and humbly worship. "Blessed are the meek." I didn't feel meek. I wanted to stand up and defy somebody. I wanted to shout, "God damn it, Bert got a raw deal!" There wasn't anyone I felt I could safely talk to about this, but I had a hunch that when I got back to New Haven – if I got back – the person to go to was Put. He would understand.

My loss of faith left a vacuum, but nothing rushed in to fill it. At eighteen I was rebelling against certain sections in the contract which I had accepted at my Confirmation without really understanding what they implied. It was as though I had been initiated into a fraternity without knowing what the rules really meant. It was my

first rebellion, but I didn't throw the baby out with the bath water. I
continued taking "the body and blood" of my Savior at the commu-
nion service without any question. I did become aware of a discrepancy between what people were professing on their knees every
Sunday and what they were actually doing in the world. This didn't
get any deeper than a contemptuous smile at the hypocrisy of women
who chanted "blessed are the poor in spirit" while wearing expensive
hats. It was as naive and innocent a rebellion as that. I had been
hurt; I was, in the spirit of the Exeter football field, not going to be
humble about it. I would fight back.

Clara Stewart, Donald Ogden Stewart's mother.

Anne Gray, Anne Stewart Outhwaite, Clara Stewart.

DOS and Adeline Werner, 1915.

The Normandie Hotel, Columbus, Ohio.

DOS at Yale – "the letter I never won."

6

What might have happened if I had gone to work for the Columbus Gas Company which Charles strongly felt to be my unquestionable obligation? Charles had a point, but his motive was not entirely that I might get a deeper insight into the realities of life. Mother was very definitely a great problem, not only her drinking but her day-to-day maintenance. Father left not a penny; his insurance only barely covered his debts. Bert had left his insurance to me; he wanted to be sure that I was given my chance at Yale. This gave me just sufficient money, if I continued working my way. I finally persuaded Charles and Anne – and myself – that it was worth the gamble.

Mother's drinking: that was a gamble, and she held all the cards. It was a rough experience, knowing of the problems, to open the door to her room with the fear that she would be sitting with that awful fixed smile and glazed eyes. Our doctor couldn't offer much hope. The situation wasn't helped by our having to sell everything in the house. Poor mother! The furniture she had lived with all her life: the bed she and "Gil" had slept in since their marriage; his favorite chair; Bert's desk. All the books, all the bound magazines that she and Bert and Anne and finally I had read and re-read. Mother's life had been her home and her children. "Gil" had loved her. She didn't need anyone else. And what was her future now? She begged me to let her apply for entrance to the Old Ladies' Home. The thought froze me with horror. I couldn't think of my mother living in an "institution." Everyone would know about it. It would be a criticism of me. So we sold the furniture and paid the grocery bills and made plans for mother to take a room in a nice respectable boarding house

– on East Broad St., of course – where she would be near her friends. What friends, God help us – especially if she went on drinking?

And then God did help us, in the form of the Rev. Theodore Irving Reese, the new minister at Trinity Church. Anne went to him about mother, and the miracle happened. Not that Mother doesn't deserve the major credit – she was a strong tough fighter – but Mr. Reese somehow supplied that little extra essential encouragement. We held our breaths. The clouds around both Past and Future were lifting. The Franklin County Bar Association held a well-attended memorial service to honor father and Bert. I sold the furnishings in their Wyandotte building office and paid more bills. In Bert's desk was a packet of letters from the only girl he had ever wanted to marry; I returned them to her unread, since those were Bert's instructions on the envelope and she had married someone else.

I spent a great deal of time the next weeks sadly listening to opera records on Anne's phonograph; Charles only protested once or twice. A real companionship between my mother and myself was begun. Christmas came. Charles gave Anne a new phonograph and I happily grabbed the old one to take with me to New Haven. I called on The Bunch to say goodbye. Josephine and Betty had entered Smith College, Kay Barcus was at Vassar, and Adeline at Bryn Mawr. Anne and Charles were a little sarcastic about this: "in their time, girls didn't go to college." In spite of this I held Adeline's hand (after her stern German mother had gone to bed) and we kissed each other goodbye. A gentlemanly embrace, of course.

On New Year's Day mother and I left for Boston. Anne and Charles had decided that she needed and deserved a change. I would take her first to see father's Cambridge relatives, on to Yale.

It worked out beautifully. I became "head of the family" and she became "Clara." She would consult me before spending any money or reading any books. It was quite flattering to have someone dependent on me; later on it became at times irritating. Girls and young women in those days were expected to control their men by playing a game in which the poor male never suspected what his woman was really after (mother loved "Bunty Pulls the Strings" and all of Barrie). If Clara wanted, say, a ribbon for her hat or a bottle of cologne, she would begin circling the target from a distance of two or three miles in the air, making little diversionary darts here and there, until finally I would cry out "For heavens' sake, mother, what *is* it you want?"

My friends without exception adored Clara. Put and Doc and Pi made me realize what a lot of fun there was in the person I had always sort of taken for granted. I began to glimpse the Clara with whom father had fallen in love. It may have been that I had never seen her with strangers. Certainly it did her a lot of good to have this new audience. When I put her on the train back to Columbus, I felt very proud of her, and very grateful for the fight she had put up against liquor. This pride, and my appreciation of her, were to increase steadily.

That winter I had to make up for the important lectures I had missed. I studied, I played my phonograph, I took examinations. In one of them I cheated for the first time, and felt compelled to go to "Tute" Farr and confess. This self-righteous act was phony. I was almost certain that "Tute" would not punish me. He didn't. He passed me without another examination, and I felt rather hypocritical.

Thanks to a friend and my phonograph I was being affected by music. I went to my first opera, *Aida*, sitting in the top gallery. The cinema and theater entered my life more and more: I remember one snowy night when Pi came home raving about a funny little movie character with a mustache and a cane. Another night he begged all of us to go to the "Hype" to see a man named Jolson in *The Honeymoon Express*, and played the hit song "Waiting For the Robert E. Lee" on his banjo.

Then came the Main Event: the struggle for the board of the *News*. Two of my classmates had already been elected in the first competition which I had missed because of father's death. It was my last chance of becoming a Big Man. Any possible athletic glory for me was sadly fading. It was still the era when the Head Coach of the football team was always a former captain who could seriously say to the team before the Harvard game that they were about to have an experience greater than they would ever have the rest of their lives. There was still the tradition of the football player who had committed suicide because he had become universally known as the man who lost the game by fumbling a Harvard punt. It was the *News* or nothing. Fifteen of us started out, including, to my surprise, Put. The grind was to last twelve weeks under the supervision of the Assignment Editor, "Baldy" Crawford, a Junior. Points were scored by covering one's regular assignments successfully, but the competition was really decided by suggesting and securing "scoops" such as special articles, interviews with visiting lecturers, celebrities, etc. Also by getting trade advertisements, usually done with the help of one's father and his business associates. The *News* was a student-operated business, with the profits distributed each year to the current Board. I was, therefore, not entirely working for dear old Yale, although I am sure that we would have competed just as furiously for the honor alone as did the majority of the athletes.

So I rented a bicycle and started eagerly chasing my assignments. There was very little time for anything else, especially studies. I climbed dormitory stairs to the rooms of crew captains and baseball managers. I went to Vanderbilt Hall to interview a Senior named Cole Porter about a new song he was writing called "I've a shooting box in Scotland." It was eleven in the morning and he was asleep. God, I envied him. I survived the various "cuts" by which they narrowed the competition. Put stuck until almost the end, then his health broke down. Finally we were in the stretch and I landed a big scoop. There was a disastrous flood in Ohio (the same which later provided James Thurber with his "The Day the Dam Broke") and I discovered an Episcopal clergyman I knew who had just come from Dayton. His story hit the front pages not only of the Yale *News* but also of the New York papers. I got another scoop by interviewing a distinguished visitor to New Haven on the secret of his success. He was an old financier named Henry Clewes. I can't remember his secret, but I remember his extreme irritation at my bothering him with questions which showed that I didn't have the slightest idea about anything. He was right, but I was elected to the Board.

The summer passed uneventfully in Columbus. I lived with Clara at her boarding house and worked for the Telephone Company on their pole-replacement gang. We went to movies, to church, to Greenlawn Cemetery, and out to have Sunday dinner with Anne and Charles. Charles was supplying the money for Clara's living expenses. I danced with The Bunch at the East End Country Club and brought the Middle West up to date on what the East was dancing. Adeline and I held hands, and kissed on departure. She was going to Bryn Mawr, and she invited me to come to their Lantern Night in the Fall. I eagerly accepted. Our romance was progressing. I was definitely in love.

So Sophomore year started with me traveling to Bryn Mawr full of anticipation. It didn't quite work out that way. I didn't see Adeline alone at all. There was no dance. We visitors were ushered out to an open space. After quite a while there was the distant singing of a Greek hymn and a number of Sophomore girls in Grecian robes came slowly forward chanting "Pallas Athena Thea." They carried lanterns which they solemnly presented to members of the Freshman Class. That was it, Lantern Night.

In the autumn of Sophomore year at Yale the five Junior fraternities had their "calling week" in which delegations from each fraternity visited the sophomores' rooms at night in order to select ten new members, the "first ten." It was a week of increasing excitement and suspense. Almost everyone got a visit the first night; then the selective process began until, on the final night, the lucky ten were definitely asked to join. In cases where two or more fraternities were after the same man, there would be a mad rush for his room and he would have to choose. Pi and Put and I were rooming together in one of the dormitories on the campus. Put knew that he didn't have a chance for the first ten. Pi and I were sorry for him, but that was life. On the first night we had a lot of visitors, many of whom we didn't know. The conversation was a bit on the dull side. "You're from Exeter?" "Yes, we're all of us from Exeter." Silence. "Red Brann over in Sheff is Exeter, isn't he?" "No, he's Andover. His brother Dutch was Exeter." Silence. "Well, I guess we'll be going." Smiles. Handshakes. Exits and exeunts. Actually, it was all nonsense. No one could possibly "sell" himself to the visitors. The graduates from the big prep schools each had their candidates and the fight was merely as to how many would be chosen from each school. Only occasionally did a high school boy make the first ten, and then only if he was an exceptional athlete, or had made the *News* (which wasn't easy for him, either, since the big schools did what they could to help their proteges). Towards the end of the week the suspense mounted. Steps coming up the stone stairs; one pretended to study; Pi plucked at his banjo. Then the steps hesitated; they were looking at your card on the door. Damn it – they were going up the floor above. But other footsteps mounted; a knock on the door. "Come in!" It was the top delegation, in derby hats and wearing the fraternity carnation. Dark red for "Deke," Ranny MacDonald, Chairman of the *News.* That was a good sign. Both Pi and I wanted Deke. Put nonchalantly studied a book; he knew that they hadn't come for him. On the final night of decision, there was singing down below on the campus. Each fraternity was parading with torchlights, dressed in their monk's robes and hoods, waiting to receive their selected candidates. "A band of brothers in D. K. E. we march along tonight –'' The hour struck on the Chapel chimes at the corner of the campus. Noise. Scampering feet. Shouts. Someone coming up the stairs. The door bursts open. It's Deke – for both Pi and me. We've made the First Ten. Put congratulates us. We are rushed downstairs to join the procession of the Elect.

The First Ten elected the Second Ten; then "running week" and after that the formal initiation. This merely involved delivering dark red carnations early each morning to the Junior and Senior Dekes, and performing any other more or less ridiculous services which their humor might dictate. It was the last remnant of "hazing" which at Yale was now considered "collegiate" and worthy only of those crude Middle-West and Western State universities. I think I was called on once or twice to sing a song or recite a poem, but there was no pad-dling as there had been at Exeter. One of the early morning recipients of my carnation was a "Deke" named Dean Acheson whom I remember only as a very superior Groton type whom we from democratic Exeter scorned.

The "Grotties" were my first experience with something perplex-ing at Yale. They didn't seem to care about having my friendship. This bothered me, baffled me. I am cursed with a need to have peo-ple like me. The cold, unsmiling stranger has me right where he wants me and, miserable, I want to try to win him over. This began at Yale. Anyway, I did not charm Dean Acheson or any of those who had come from the exclusive schools such as Groton, St. Mark's, and St. Paul's. I cannot say that they did not like me but they gave me the feeling that they were living in a world which I could not hope to enter. I had not been born in the right place or in the right family. I did not for a moment admit such a thing, but there was something about these unknowable fellows which intrigued me. They seemed so sure of themselves. They had a security toward which I was climbing. It was like the Platt Yard on East Broad Street in Columbus but much more inaccessible. It was the *real* High Society – New York, Philadelphia, Boston, San Francisco. *That* was an Elite beyond Skull and Bones: the next step. I now had two new aspirations: High Culture and High Society. It was like leaping onto a horse and urging it to gallop in opposite directions. And no one could warn me.

The motto on the Yale shield is *Lux et Veritas*. But the faculty could not be blamed that the Light and Truth which they were trying to teach was overwhelmed by the lights and truths which were pouring in from the world outside the campus. The curriculum was constantly being sabotaged by the extra-curriculum. Fathers had sent their sons to Yale to "make contacts." The way to do that was to make a fraternity. The competition was for a "success" that had nothing to do with the truth.

Summer of 1914 in Columbus was unchanged from the preceding year. Outdoor work with the telephone gang; movies with Clara; dances at the East End Club. In August the war broke out in Europe but it did not seem to have much to do with me. I was rather for Germany, partly on account of Adeline. I was hunching for them to take Paris, but only because of the excitement it would cause. Anyway, I refused to believe the atrocity stories. They did not jibe with the Germany I had learned of through Goethe's *Faust*. Anne and Charles took the English periodicals and I was sorry for the young officers who had died "for King and Country." But young Germans were being killed too.

Junior year started busily. Put and I were still rooming together, but I hadn't yet been able to get him into Deke. I rather patted myself on the back for sticking to Put; there were so many other more successful men I might have roomed with. Put had missed the boat. The fraternities didn't want him. He hadn't learned to "contact" people. At times he was damned irritating, especially when he would make fun of my bids for popularity. We would be walking to a class and I would be greeting everyone, "Hi, Bob," "How'ya, Bunny." Put would walk silently beside me, a cynical smile on his face. "You know 'em all, boy," he would mutter. Once we approached a classmate who had been injured in football practice. "Hi ya, Frank" I smiled and then added solicitously, "How's the leg?" That was too much for Put. "Jesus!" he burst out, and for the rest of our lives "Hi ya, Frank, how's the leg?" was always good for a laugh. He became, in a way, my other self – that little man standing out there watching me. I was sorry for him, but I feared and resented his criticism. He was more honest than I, clearer, more probing, more sure of himself. At times I bitterly resented this self-assurance from someone who hadn't even made a fraternity. But for some strange reason I had made him my best friend. We roomed together, and I enjoyed being with him – except when he would embarrass me by failing in public to observe certain Yale proprieties. For instance, he would be walking past the Skull and Bones "tomb," a somber stone ivy-covered building on High Street. For an ambitious Yale man, Skull and

Bones was the ultimate goal. The honor of being admitted was so great that no one was supposed to admit that he wanted it; and if one was accused of "working for Bones" it was disastrous for his chances. Put would suddenly turn and walk toward the huge iron door at the entrance as though he were about to enter. My stomach turned over. One just didn't do things like that – especially with Tap Day only months away.

Studies were becoming more interesting; as Juniors we could begin to specialize. I majored in English, which opened new delightful fields, but there were others not so delightful – such as Economics, where I plowed through two volumes of Taussig from which I remember only one bit of information: socialism could not possibly work. As most of us were preparing to enter banking or the security-selling professions, this was particularly comforting to know, and cannot be said to have come as a great surprise. I had heard of an odd somebody named Eugene Debs, and I think that perhaps there was a college Socialist Club. Among my friends there was very little interest in politics. Ex-President Taft, a Skull and Bones man, was our hero; it was inexplicable and most unfortunate that he had been defeated in 1912 by a Princetonian, but on the whole the field of politics was one of which we washed our hands. I was too busy getting out the daily *News*. I had been grieviously disappointed when our Board had failed to elect me Chairman, but was chosen to be Assignments Editor. This turned out to be a very agreeable job, in that I became a sort of "benevolent overseer" to the fifteen or twenty Freshmen who were competing for the Board. I was their wise old adviser and their friend, even though I also had to be their executioner when the competition narrowed.

Another job in my Junior year was that of Treasurer of the Deke finances. In those days the "tomb" (it was never called a "frat house"; that collegiate stuff was for places like state universities) was a narrow brick building to which no one but members and the wonderful Negro janitor were ever admitted. It was my fraternal duty as Treasurer to collect the dues and insist that the janitor run his department on a strictly "no credit" basis. It all seemed easy at first, but there were two distressing factors which slowly began to emerge. One was that the brotherly bonds of fraternal obligations did not seem to extend to financial matters, and the other was that my family financial disaster had given me pathological terror of unpaid grocery debts. Bill, on the other hand, had no complexes on the subject of money at all. He lived in a state of childlike purity which was helped by the fact that he could neither add, subtract, multiply, divide nor spell. His was a happy soul and he wanted everybody else to be happy – especially those nice Deke gentlemen who couldn't pay cash. The merchant world outside the "tomb" didn't share his faith. There came to be such a discrepancy in my books between Plus and Minus that I decided in desperation to take stringent measures. I announced that brothers who did not pay their dues and their restaurant bills could not enter the sacred precincts until they did. This was logical and just – and completely unenforceable. As the struggle grew, I became a stubborn righteous watchdog. It gave me a horrifying glimpse of the effect of money on human relations and I resolved never to be treasurer of anything again. Years later when Robert Benchley first gave his burlesque "Treasurer's Report" on the stage of the Music Box theater I fell into the aisle screaming with laughter. But it had not been so funny at old Deke.

In mid-winter came the annual Deke–Psi U "German" in New York and I decided to show the brothers that their grim Treasurer from Columbus had his social side too. These dances were then held at Sherry's, a romantic building long since departed, to make way for bigger and better mid-town banks, from the south west corner of Fifth Avenue and 44th Street. This was my first entry into the enchanted territory. The impecunious young man in the dress suit found himself standing in his first stag line (Columbus dances were still "program" affairs, with no cutting in), listening to the marvelous outpourings of a Markel orchestra led by a young genius of a violinist who, toward four in the morning, would substitute a resined cane for his bow and lead the orchestra and enraptured dancers in a file around the ballroom to the delirious strains of Sousa's "Stars and Stripes Forever." There was an abundance of new dance rhythms, and new orchestrations were bringing in strong things like saxophones, massed banjoes, steel guitars. Turkey trots and bunny hugs were settled down into the one-step and cheek-to-cheek waltzes in a secluded corner far from the rapacious stag line. The war was on in Europe and a dance craze swept America, headed by Maurice, Florence Walton, the Castles. And here I was, right in the heart of it. It is impossible even now to recreate the thrill of hearing that Markel Orchestra (or Eddie Wittstein's in New Haven), the excitement of joining the competition of the stag line, the superiority of appraising the field as the dancers swept past, the recognition of an appeal for help from a marvelous-looking girl who is "stuck" with an older man, the rescue, the opening gambit, the "Well, how are you?", the despair at being immediately cut in on by someone else to whom she may *really* have been appealing. Those were the days of famous "prom" girls who were fought for by stags and did not consider the night a success if they could dance three feet without a cut in. The days when one danced the night through without any need for liquor or any refreshment until the scrambled eggs at sunrise. It was a pleasure world in which the sheer joy of dancing took precedence over everything. After the ball, I walked happy and dazed through the early morning streets from Sherry's to Grand Central Station to take the "milk train" back to New Haven. I got my suitcase but did not bother to change from my wilted dress clothes. As the train left the station I sat alone and still enchanted by a strange, wonderful world.

7

Inevitably, Tap Day was coming nearer. This was the May afternoon when the three Senior Societies (as distinct from the Junior Fraternities) issued forth from their tombs to notify fifteen Juniors of their election by "tapping" them on their backs, at the same moment shouting "Go to your room!"

Even then, efforts were being made to discourage this over-dramatization of "success" to such a small proportion of students, but in those days there was still a great deal of excitement connected with the occasion, mostly among the fifty or so "eligibles" for Skull and Bones, Scroll and Key, or Wolf's Head. As the day approached lists were made, bets were placed; the most respected list was that of a marvelous unshaven character known as Rosey. If you were on Rosey's list you were a pretty good bet. I was on his list for Bones; so was Doc Walker. Pi, who had won his "Y" in football and baseball, was on the Key's list. Put, of course, was on nobody's list. Among the clubs and groups there was an endowed organization called the Elizabethan Club whose members formed a cultural elite toward which I began to cast my ambitious little eyes. Put had been elected; Doc was a member; so were Archie MacLeish and Douglas Moore. Why not I? The love of music had become my leading private cultural passion. Alone, I went rather regularly to concerts by the New Haven symphony orchestra; I can remember my self-conscious pride and astonished joy at discovering that I could sit through a whole symphony and even enjoy some of it. I went to the Metropolitan Opera House in New York to listen to the Good Friday performance of *Parsifal,* and wrote a long theme on Wagner's theories about opera, greatly to the bewilderment of my professor who understood that he had asked me to cover the subject of the Monroe Doctrine.

When the day finally arrived, Put decided that he wasn't going to dignify the Roman Holiday by appearing on the campus at all. He had, in the course of the year, found a fellow spirit named Fred Manning whose brilliant analytical mind had likewise not been diverted into any of the extra-curricular paths to glory. These two outsiders formed a masterly team of mockers; I was afraid of them, especially when they would get a little drunk in public places. It could be very embarrassing, so I wasn't particularly sorry that Put wasn't going to be on hand for my glorification.

Actually, I wasn't as sure of my election as all that, but there was that list of Rosey's and it looked as though most of the very Big Men were going to Keys, so I thought there would be room in Bones for me. The hours dragged by interminably and Don Shepard, who was also on Rosey's list, decided to pass the time before the appointed five o'clock at a movie. I went with him. We had bad luck. Put and Fred were also at the movie, and when we came out they pretended to be taxi drivers. "This way to Skull and Bones, sir," called Put. "Take you there in five minutes." They then wanted us to have a drink with them and laughed loudly when we nervously glanced at our watches. It was ten minutes to five. "What's the matter?" asked Fred. "Got another engagement?" "Don't worry," added Put. "Lots of time. They'll wait for you." Finally they entered a bar and we hurried to the campus. Most of our class was there. We exchanged nervous greetings, forced smiles. Then there was a hush. The chapel chimes began to sound. Toward us, from different directions, came three Seniors wearing derbies. Somewhere in the crowd a slap on the back, a cheer. "Who was it?" Another "Go to your room." More hand clapping. More cheers. Don was tapped, and went away smiling, followed by a Bones Senior. An excited murmur from the crowd. Alec Wilson, the football captain, had turned down Bones and taken Keys; Harry Crocker had gone Keys. So had Pi, and Ross Proctor, chairman of the *News*. Doc was taken by Bones. Only five places left. Then horror! Put and Fred had shown up and were following me around, pointing the way to me for an advancing Bones man. "There he is," encouraged Put: "Old Don Stewart, the peoples' choice!" He was right behind me. It was disgusting. Put was drunk – and here, now, on Tap Day! Suddenly the Bones man who had been coming toward me stopped, wheeled, and brought his hand down hard on Put's shoulder. "Go to your room!" I caught Put in my arms as he staggered and almost fell. "Jesus Christ!" he whispered, unbelieving. Nobody believed it. But it was true. Put marched off toward our room. I gazed after him. I pretended to be happy, but I was furious. What sort of a double-cross was this? A minute later I was tapped myself, but as I walked away through the crowd in front of my Bones Senior my bewilderment grew. This was the moment I had been working for ever since Exeter, the culmination of my hopes, my dreams. And Put had made Bones without trying; he had even mocked the effort. Where was the justice of that? Put was my best friend. Why wasn't I happy? Was I really such a heel? This wasn't the way a member of the Elite was supposed to act. Three years ago my image of my father had become a bit dented. Now my picture of myself fell off the wall. I picked it up but I didn't put it back. I didn't know where to put it.

Strangely enough, it was Bones itself which helped me solve that problem. The curious discovery was that the external image of the organization was completely different from the internal reality. Put would never have been elected to the Skull and Bones which existed in the minds of those who viewed it solely as a reward for virtuous achievement. Put was a perfect choice for the reality in which we Happy Few spent our last year at Yale. He had an inspired insight into the minds and motives of his friends. He was singularly honest with himself, and he could be devastatingly so with others. Around this keystone of integrity were grouped fourteen very different characters held together by loyalty, trust and affection. It was a year of adjustment without competition. We had no reason to struggle against each other. We had no reason to use each other to our own advantage. We could examine each other, and ourselves, with affection and laughter, with mutual respect and trust. It was a magic year, a fantastic year; fifteen young men suspended fraternally in time and space until they would be dropped – more or less valuable commodities – into the Market Place.

The same magic truce made Senior year an enchanted one for most of our class. The classroom lectures were strictly from an elite. By now I had become a devoted "appreciator" of the arts and somewhere picked up the satisfying formula that whereas at engineering and scientific colleges they were learning to make a living, at Yale I was learning to live. I was also beginning to look for a philosophy which would give me the Absolute Answer as to what life was about. John Cowper Powys came to college with a dramatic lecture on "Nietzsche or Christ?" I chose Nietzsche. This seemed so obviously The Answer that for several weeks I had a crack at being a Superman. Between classes, or alone in my room, I fancied that I became hard and in my inmost mind burned with a gem-like flame. The object of life was Power. After graduation I was not going to let anyone stand in my way. God was dead, Christ was a pale Galilean, and I would be cruel, like Napoleon. Then the sight of a poorly dressed working girl threw a monkey wrench into my Answer. She was sitting alone on a bench in the New Haven Green, and she was crying. I had never seen her before, I didn't stop to ask her what was the matter, and I never saw her again. It was just one of those moments. It rang some kind of distant bell, and I realized that I could never be a Superman. For a while I gave Goethe a chance to prove something. Reading the second part of *Faust* is pretty tough going, even in an English translation. I was intrigued but I couldn't grasp the profundities of Goethe's philosophy, so I temporarily abandoned the hunt for the absolute philosophical Yea.

I'd been making extra money from the *News* and from selling corsages to students who were taking girls to football games or dances. I hated this work and would be overjoyed if there was no answer when I knocked on a dormitory door. I managed anyway to save enough money to bring mother to New Haven for my twenty-first birthday. Clara and I officially celebrated my arrival at political maturity (or, rather, at the age at which I could vote) by a gay dinner at the Hof Brau restaurant, during which we each drank a tall stein of beer and promptly went on the wagon. Years later, when searching in the volume I had used at Yale for a quotation from Tennyson, I came across this solemn notation in my handwriting opposite Lord Alfred's poem about some besotten drunk (a farmer I think): "Nov. 30 1915 – I gave up alcohol." This is ironically amusing in view of my later drinking career, but it also shows how seriously I viewed myself. There was no reason for my going on the wagon: no liquor was served in Bones and I drank very little outside. The truth is, I had become a Dedicated Man. I had quite an important future ahead of me, and I owed it to myself to develop all my capabilities so that I could fulfill my destiny. What shape that exalted future might take was unknown and the details were only vaguely speculated about. But whatever was to happen, nothing like alcohol was to be allowed to interfere with the flowering of this promising young candidate for . . . President of a New York bank? Editor-in-chief of a great newspaper? Chairman of the board of some company? But a *cultured* bank president, editor-in-chief, chairman of the board. One who went to symphony concerts, knew about Sudermann and Synge, had read Conrad. Somewhere there undoubtedly was a brilliant aristocratic world of the Cultivated Rich. That seemed to be the next Tap Day to work toward.

There was the Me who wanted, above everything else, the Security of a job and money in the bank; there was the super-imposed collegiate Me who wanted Culture in order to understand and appreciate this secure life. And now another Me was coming into being: a mocking devil afflicted with an uncontrollable urge to stick pins in the other two. This last Me existed mostly in my mind. I found myself making fun of all those climbers struggling to get to the top. Though conceived as a defensive weapon, this other Me was showing signs of being strong enough to take the offensive. A slightly mad young sense of humor at first welcomed by the other Me's was greeted as a junior partner. The ability to create laughter seemed to present added possibilities for making "contacts" both in the financial and the cultural fields. I set out to enjoy the final months of the shortest gladdest years of life. There was the Prom to which "Ad" came from her own Senior year at Bryn Mawr; we danced all night and, still in our evening clothes, I took her to the morning train and fell into my bed to sleep the clock round. At the New Haven Lawn Club I danced with a real movie star; her name was Anita Steward and I only danced three feet, but it was a thrill.

There were other proms. At Vassar, Harriet Skidmore and I were asked to leave the floor because we were dancing cheek-to-cheek, a startling innovation which I had brought from New Haven. Dancing in the very latest fashion was a serious obligation; one could almost tell what college a man came from by the way he held his girl. And the music was getting better and better. This was the year of "Goodbye Girls, I'm Through" from Fred Stone's show, of "Babes in the Wood" from Ernie Truex's "Very Good Eddie," and the Castles dancing to "Columbus Discovered America."

There were more serious cultural activities. John Masefield came to New Haven, the Elizabethan Club gave him a tea, and there was a run on his books at the new bookstore. I had been elected to the "Lizzie" club, largely, I imagine, on Put's and Doc's guarantees of my cultural reliability and determination. Masefield took a great shine to Put, praised his poetry, said he looked like Rupert Brooke. When I tried to talk eagerly to Masefield about Tennyson he seemed amazed that I should be interested in *that* poetry at this date. I bought Rupert Brooke's poems, asked Masefield to autograph them. Billy Phelps urged all of us in his "Contemporary Drama" course to see Galsworthy's *Justice* starring John Barrymore at the new Taft Theatre. I thought it was terrific, but didn't connect it with any contemporary sociological problems – at least not in America. My interest in sociological problems anywhere was what might be classified as an "abstention." I hadn't taken any course in the subject and, besides, I was majoring in English Literature.

But in spite of this, the war in Europe, although far away, kept getting closer, and Wilson was keeping us safely out of it in spite of the Lusitania. Ex-President Theodore Roosevelt began to demand that America become excited about what he called Preparedness. A Yale battery was organized, to begin training at Plattsburg N.Y., after graduation. Many of my Bones-mates enlisted. I took the opposite side. Norman Angell, who had written against war in *The Great Illusion*, came to lecture and I was greatly impressed. An "International Club" was formed, with the backing of Billy Phelps, and I became president; this was my first and only political activity in college. My interest in keeping America from entering the war against Germany was due to a romantic feeling about the country of my hero Goethe, and about "Ad" whose grandparents were German. But there was still no understanding of what war was like or what it was about. Not that we didn't have lectures . . . but the reality of war in Europe, like most realities, was far away. The important problem was life after graduation.

Various possibilities for a career suggested themselves. A president of a New York bank had an interesting plan for training a selected few. This was tempting, especially as many graduates had succeeded rather quickly at large financial institutions. Another recent graduate friend, Charlie Merz, had made an equally spectacular start by becoming almost immediately the managing editor of an unknown (to me) publication called *The New Republic*. I bought a copy or two, but didn't think it was in my line. One job which I did seriously consider was an offer which involved going to China as an assistant administrator of the Yale-in-China Christian university there. This tempted me largely because of the romantic possibilities of further cultural education in China and, somewhat hypocritically, as a Dedicated Man's opportunity to do something helpful for God, for Country and for Yale. I avoided facing the "Christian" aspect of my qualifications; my little fling with Nietzsche had confirmed my agnosticism, but I figured that when I got to China I could straighten that out to the benefit of God, the Chinese, and myself. Especially myself. Look at Marco Polo! But then, while I was looking at Marco Polo, Anne and Charles came down with both feet on this romantic attempt to avoid my responsibilities for taking care of mother. Mr. Frank Davis of the Columbus Telephone Company had a definite job in mind for me. That was that.

So, on a hot June afternoon, dressed in a rented cap and gown, I received a parchment confirming the fact that I was now a Bachelor of Arts. This was a gala week, led by the antics of alumni in car-nival-like reunion costumes who had come to drink, to recollect, and to march to the Bowl for the Harvard Baseball game. There were the Class Day exercises at which Doc Walker was deservedly the Orator and I luckily was not the Poet. It was a most portentous moment in history, according to Doc. He was certainly correct. And we 450 bachelors of arts didn't have the slightest idea of how portentous. *Lux et Veritas* were the golden words on the college shield. Lights were going out all over Europe, but the Yale light didn't even seem to flicker. Truth remained obediently constant – since it was lighted by the same unchanging flame. The forces which controlled the Light controlled the Truth. It was not part of a liberal education in 1916 to search for the sources of this control.

What then had I learned in four years? If I say that I learned little, I should also say that I was very young. "Only connect," advises a very wise character in one of E. M. Forster's novels, and I would place those words on the crest of any university. If I could go back to Yale now I could connect all the disparate facts from the disciplines I studied there. Light and Truth are nouns which need a verb, an ac-tive verb. As it was, Yale gave me a few keys which might unlock a few doors in the search for a real education; and for that I shall be forever grateful as I am for the fact that truth was not presented as an Absolute, but as something to be continuously sought. The need to compete for a living and the American emphasis on Success made it impossible in those years for an ambitious young man to get more than a few drops of truth. What is important is that I got a thirst for more. The disastrous effect of my Yale extra-curricular "education" had transformed me (in my own mind) into a superior sort of person somehow above the ordinary college graduate – except, of course, Harvard, Princeton and, perhaps, Williams. The rest of the world was to be treated kindly; one should not allow one's superiority to show; just as the Bones pin was always worn on the undershirt, instead of flaunting it immodestly; I knew that it was there, and took it for granted that others would find out about it and be properly impressed.

My general superiority did not extend into all areas of human knowledge. Compared with today's sexual understanding and experience, I could not have passed a single question in an examination. I was not an exception here, either. Freud had not entered the Yale *Veritas,* let alone the Yale subconscious. I talked rather intimately about sex with many of my classmates. Those who had lost their virginity had done so at whorehouses, and were often quite ashamed. A man was supposed, God help our wives, to enter the marriage bed with his amateur standing completely untarnished. As for homosexuality, it simply didn't exist at Yale. Its existence was an extremely rare phenomenon which might possibly occur occasionally at, say, Harvard, but it was never anyone you knew. One Spring day a "fruit," as we called them, appeared with painted cheeks on the campus, and was subjected to cruel mockery until the police took him away. We were equally ignorant of politics, except of the Republican vs. Democrat variety. Marx was as unknown as Freud. Ours was truly a world of innocence, or, at least, of ignorance and taboo.

The farewells to this world were, as they had been at Exeter, sincerely affectionate. We all had great fondness for our president and most of our professors. I said goodbye to Gil who was going into the bond business in Chicago; to my other Bones-mates; my room-mates Don Shepard and Larry Tighe, both of whom were starting in New York banks; to "Far" Knapp of Hartford, who was entering the Harvard Law School in the hopes of some day becoming a Supreme Court judge. Other Bones-companions on their way to Harvard Law were Kinley Tener of Pittsburg, and President Hadley's son Morris. I bade farewell to Doc, who was taking a job with Charlie Merz on the *New Republic,"* and to Put, who was happily engaged to be married to Ruth Peters. There are many, many others whom I was loath to part with and whom I still remember with great affection. My college years were indeed "bright" and "with pleasure rife," although fortunately they were neither "the shortest" nor "the gladdest" years of my life. Indeed, these words in the anthem are a rather critical commentary on a Yale education if they imply that the four years of preparation for life are never to be equalled by any gladness in life itself. Or perhaps they are merely a judgment on the American way of life as experienced by Yale men – although I doubt that that was the intention behind them.

8

The second farewell that year, when I left Columbus, was not marked by any ceremony or display of grief. Back home in Columbus Mr. Davis, who had helped finance my education, now managed to get me a job with the American Telephone and Telegraph Compnay in New York. I rather gleefully thought it was to be New York but after they had looked me over at 100 Broadway they promptly sent me to a district office in Birmingham, Alabama, where, like all Horatio Alger heroes, I was to begin at the bottom and work my way to the top. I was never quite sure about what they had in mind as the "top," but Birmingham was certainly the bottom. My salary was $15 a week, my duties were those of clerk. I lived as a boarder in the home of my boss. The life was simple and good for me. No one had ever seen a Yale man before, and what they saw didn't seem to impress them. I ate my "grits" for breakfast, walked to work through part of the Negro section and got my first smell of life in the South. It was a nauseating smell and and it wasn't deodorized by the incredible attitude of my landlady and the other two boarders toward "niggers." I didn't argue. I read books every night after dinner. I became enthusiastic about Dostoyevsky and can remember the excitement, after finishing *Crime and Punishment*, of anticipating the rest of his work, then Tolstoy, then Turgenev. There wasn't much else to be happy about – except that early in November Woodrow Wilson was re-elected President on a "He kept us out of war" platform, and then later in the month Yale beat Harvard. The boarders didn't understand the true importance of the latter event and so, with no other Yale man in town, I celebrated alone on the favorite local drink: a "coke" spiked with ammonia. I was quite lonely. My Yale jokes were unappreciated; my reading of "highbrow" books scorned. I started writing critiques of the books I was reading so that I could send them to Put and Doc. Also to Clara and to Ad, to whom I considered myself engaged. At any rate, we began our letters with "Darling," and receiving hers provided me with great happiness. Then in December Billy Phelps came to town on one of his lecture tours, and for one evening at the Tutwiler hotel I was Somebody again and to hell with the alien corn. Billy called me Don and talked to me about Dostoyevsky; the lady chairman asked me to come to dinner to meet a local man who had gone to Yale – "or was it Dartmouth?" But before that could take place in December, I received orders transferring me to the Pittsburgh office for the next step in my training.

The Pittsburgh district office was a long way from the center of the city. I found a cheap boarding house nearby and settled down for another period of inexpensive cultural activity. My wages had been raised by three dollars a week, so I could send more to Clara, and the work was a little more interesting, partly because I had a friendly Chief Clerk who wanted to help me become a good loyal organization man.

On April 6, 1917, America entered the War and I found my Purpose. Grandfather John Ogden had fought in the Civil War, Bert had been a soldier in the Spanish-American one, and now it was my turn. Bands were playing. Flags were flying. The Pittsburgh Symphony Orchestra canceled a program of Wagner's music. Frankfurters became "Liberty sausages." There were indications that Congress would pass a conscription act, but I didn't want to wait to be drafted. All my classmates were rushing to Officers' Training Camps. I wanted to get back with them, with my Elite, as quickly as possible.

Anne and Charles, sensible as always, reminded me that I had a mother to support and intimated that I was behaving like an ungrateful selfish fool. So I stayed at my desk, hating it. There were compensations. I consoled myself by reading *War and Peace.* I found *How To Listen To Music* by Krehbiel, and discovered at a concert of Dvorak's "New World" that I could pick out first and second themes in the first movement. Shortly after that I decided to take piano lessons. My landlady's ten-year-old daughter "took" from an old German, Herr Weber. Weekly lessons were only fifty cents which I could just about afford. So Herr Weber found himself with a twenty-two-year-old pupil, his only adult. Occasionally the poor old man would get confused and say: "Now, Herr Stewart, remember: the white notes are the 'papa' notes and the black notes are the 'mama' notes." I didn't get to papa or mama Chopin but I could play the first five bars of the "Moonlight" sonata by the time I was transferred in the fall to Chicago.

This was a definite promotion and an important stage in my training. Chicago was a Division headquarters; Birmingham and Pittsburgh were merely district offices. I was evidently satisfying the Big Shots in New York. After Chicago, presumably, I would be graduated to there, and I could start my real career in that tall building on lower Broadway, working my way up floor by floor until one day ... who knows? The only smudge in the picture of my own bright future was that I was finding myself much happier *after* office hours, even if I was just reading books. Shouldn't I be enjoying work itself? God knows I was trying to, and I had reason to believe that they were pleased with my efforts, but something was wrong in a life where work itself was somehow not my consuming interest.

Anyway, Chicago was exciting. The office was in the heart of the Loop. I lived in a small room on the South Side, went to work on the Elevated, and ate all my meals alone at cafeterias. My Chicago Yale friends were all away in Officers Training camps, but I wasn't particularly lonely at first. As my salary had been upped another three dollars, I could afford a better piano teacher, who also found me a place where I could practice. But living expenses were much higher, my budget balanced on a very slim margin, and twice my pocket book was stolen. Once more I discovered the fearsome fact of poverty. To be broke a day or two before pay day, to have no one to go to for a loan, and to be standing outside a restaurant window watching a cook tossing pancakes was an experience I could never forget. I had read about the hungry poor, but here was hunger itself, and it was in me. Most vivid of all was the feeling of isolation, of having no one to go to. Another emotional shock came that winter in a letter from Ad telling me that she was engaged to be married. Although I had never been what might be called an ardent suitor, I had come to think of Ad as engaged to *me*. After all, she had knitted a red and gray tie for me when I had first gone to Exeter; I had faithfully worn the tie and her Columbus School for Girls pin, and eventually taken her to the Yale Prom. What more did she want? As far as I know, all Columbus took it for granted that she was *my* girl. What to do? I didn't know, so

I did what I thought was romantically expected of me: I went into the Loop and fell off the wagon I had been on since my twenty-first birthday. I got grimly drunk, all by myself. Then I took the El back to my little room and sank sobbing onto my bed. That was the way to play the part – only I played it a little too well. When I lay back on my pillow and closed my weeping eyes on a monstrous world, a moment of reality crept into the performance and I had to rush to the bathroom down the hall before I threw up.

Meanwhile my education in the clerical paper-work of a huge public-service corporation continued. I began to get little glimpses into the rivalries, jealousies, jockeying-for-positions of the other clerks. They felt that I must have influence in New York, or at best wasn't competing for their jobs, so they would come to me with "frank" talks about the others. I also discovered, to my innocent incredulity, that one or two of my fellow employees were spying for the Chief in connection with a rumored "unionization"; in fact, I was asked to do a little pussyfooting myself.

The even tenor of my lonely way was interrupted by two events of major importance. The lesser of these was the arrival in Chicago of Harry Crocker, voted "most popular" by our class at Yale, and everyone's boon companion wherever there was a gay time to be had. Harry had become an Ensign in the Naval Reserve and was assigned to a training station for officers in the Merchant Marine which had been set up at the Chicago Municipal Pier. In charge of this small school was a wealthy middle-aged Chicago Yale graduate named William Derby, who had donated his yacht "Gopher" for naval educational purposes and had been commissioned a Captain. Captain Derby had a beautiful daughter, Dorothy, who had "come out" into Chicago Society. Dorothy had a number of equally attractive friends. Owing to the war, there was in Chicago Society a great dearth of eligible young men. It seemed almost as though God had sent Crocker and Stewart to fill this nature-abhorred vacuum. Crocker and Stewart did not hesitate a moment. For God, for country and for Yale – that was us. I sent to Columbus for my tuxedo (or rather, Charles's old one). Life was picking up – at the expense of the Harvard classics and my piano practice.

But then, early in 1918, came the second major interruption. My draft number had come up on the Columbus conscription list. My claim for exemption had been turned down and I was requested to report on a certain date for physical examination – or else. The joke was on Anne and Charles, and I laughed my head off. I had done my duty. I had reluctantly claimed exemption on the grounds of having mother as a dependent, and my claim had been rejected. I was to get into uniform at last – even if I was to be nothing but a private. The only problem was: could I pass any physical examination, being as near-sighted as I was? There were sad stories in the papers of poor fellows who had been kissed goodbye by weeping parents, presented with knitted scarves and bibles by local committees, and then returned home in shame by discoveries of flat feet or hay fever. But there were also tales of those true knights who had managed to cheat the examiners by various devices. Then Captain Derby came up with a brilliant idea: he would get me an appointment to his Officers' school on the Municipal Pier. So before my due-date in Columbus I took a physical exam in Chicago. The examiner removed my glasses, asked me to read the chart posted on the opposite wall. I couldn't even see the wall. He asked me to walk forward until I could read one of the lines. I obeyed and when I was less than three feet from the chart I reported the top letter to be "A". He looked at me, then said "Wait here" and left the room. While he was gone, I studied the chart and learned it by heart. He was gone quite a while. When he returned, I suggested that he give me another shot at the chart, as I had been nervous. On my second trial I read every line but the bottom one. He grunted, "that's better," and I was in the war. Clara proudly put a service star in the window of her room at the Columbus boarding house. I had not let grandfather and Bert down.

There was no ship except the "Gopher," which was reserved for Captain Derby, Ensign Crocker and another officer, and it very rarely ventured from its moorings. In order to accustom the students to life on the bounding waves they slept in hammocks above the cement floor of the pier, kept their "gear" in sea bags, ate their "chow" in the "mess," and used all the correct seagoing expressions such as "topside" and "corking off." Watches were kept along the pier in rotation by men with loaded rifles. Time was announced by the ship's bell. It was all very romantic to me, especially as I had never been to sea or fired a rifle. I can still remember the thrill of my first night in a hammock (after I got into the damned thing) and the even greater excitement of being awakened at four bells in the morning in order to walk in the darkness along a cement path with a real gun in which were real bullets, ready at any moment to shout "Halt! Who goes there?" Luckily, nothing ever went there.

My shipmates were all from around Chicago, and the uniform made it very difficult to appraise anyone by Brooks Bros. standards. There were certainly no Eastern College graduates except Harry and me, and my friendship with him had at first to be carefully subservient to naval protocol. I saluted him solemnly, and he gravely returned the salute. In the early weeks of the training it was forbidden to leave the pier. The cold winds blew in from the lake, and some of the romance began to wear off. The day was devoted to classes and drill, the nights to study. The climate was not cultural. Some of the petty officers had served in the regular Navy and were loudly contemptuous of us "land sailors." Many of the students were small businessmen, without college degrees. I even discovered men who had come to the pier because they didn't want to do any real fighting if they could help it. I couldn't believe it. I was getting a glimpse of a strange, un-Yale-like world.

In the spring we were ready for the next step in our training which involved "practical experience" on board the huge boats which carried cargoes of iron ore and coal to the various cities on the Great Lakes. After a month or so of that, the successful candidates were to be sent on to the "finishing school" at Pelham Bay, N.Y. for further practical experience, this time on real salt water. They would then receive their commissions as Ensigns, followed by service aboard various merchant vessels carrying troops and supplies to Europe. So I duly packed my sea bag and embarked on the William F. Smithers (I can't remember the real name) with an energetic young businessman named Bill Neighbors who had been in my classes. The captain of the Smithers was a gloomy old character who resented our cheerfully unskilled and useless presence, as did most of the crew. We voyaged as far East as Buffalo on Lake Erie and North to Duluth on Lake Superior with loading and unloading stops at Cleveland, Toledo, Detroit, and Sault Sainte Marie. We stood watch, took our tricks at the wheel, learned about compasses, charts and lighthouses, and kept worthless notebooks. Bill was a good companion. When we went ashore, it was fun being treated like real sailors by the patriotic young Society ladies in the canteens. But on the boat, time dragged interminably and I can remember lying in my bunk despairingly wondering what had happened to the hopeful Yale "me." I had no ambition to read, no curiosity about anything. I felt at the bottom of the barrel.

When the cruise ended, I discovered that the barrel was seemingly bottomless. I was given another physical exam and disqualified, because of my eyes, for any commission. But I was ordered to stay on as an instructor. Bill Derby's friendly little amateur navy had become important in the increasing showdown with the German submarines. Candidates were pouring into the school from all over the Middle West. The Derby yacht had been replaced by an old Spanish-American war "battleship," and Derby himself superseded by trained professional officers. The war was beginning to bite into the American consciousness. Casualty lists were now on every morning's front page. All my room mates except Put were officers in France. Put was ineligible because of his asthma. I tried in every possible way to get transferred, but it took a seeing-eye dog to lead me to an oculist's chart. I was out of luck. "What did you do in the War, daddy?" "I was in the Chicago navy, son, and shut up!"

There were compensations. I was given a Quartermaster First Class rating, with the privilege of occasional nights away from the pier. Families of my college classmates gave me greatly appreciated meals on the rare occasions when I could get away. Even though I was only a "gob," the very exclusive University Club was open to me, thanks to Captain Derby. My relations with my "shipmates" were also becoming more congenial. I was even selected by the Commandant to be one of the squad of men six feet tall to escort Mary Pickford when she came to Chicago on a Liberty Loan drive. This was a great occasion. Mary's speech was to be delivered in the Marshall Field store which was absolutely jam-packed with excited patriots. The duty of us escorts, carrying our rifles in the appropriate position, was to force a way for the film star through this mob to the speakers' platform. It was a task for which I quickly found myself completely inadequate by nature and previous training. I began with "Please, if you don't mind stepping back" and ended in a crowded corner, hatless and rifle-less, trying to get back to my squad which had disappeared in the direction of the platform. The fans very kindly gave me my rifle back and I was saved from court martial. We had Liberty Loan drives among ourselves on the pier, with cheers to the Company which went "over the top" in subscribing 100 per cent. In my Company we had gradually almost reached the top; one man said that, because of wife and children, he could not afford to sign up. He was honest, stubborn, and completely justified in refusing, and yet we went to work on him with jeers, taunts, and with patriotic mass pressure until he finally yielded. This was the first time I had so clearly seen a group in action against an individual in the name of patriotism.

By autumn the pier had become important enough to have its own monthly magazine. A Chicago newspaperman named Lloyd Lewis was given a Chief Petty Officer's rating and the responsibility for publishing *Shipmates.* He asked me to contribute and I sent in a naval version of Edward Streeter's best seller *Dere Mabel* called *Dere Queenie.* It was the first public humorous writing I had ever attempted and it made a hit with Lloyd and with my shipmates on the pier. Lloyd even suggested that I take up a writing career after the war. It was a startling idea, but I laughed it off. I knew where I was going. And besides, there was Clara to support. But in Lloyd I had found an exciting friend. He took me to see my first artist, in a real studio, and told me fascinating tales about strange Chicago literary birds named Ben Hecht, Carl Sandburg, Edgar Lee Masters, Vachel Lindsay. I told him about Tennyson and Browning.

Then in November came the shrill exultant whistles announcing the Armistice. First the fake, then the real. As with everything I took it personally. The War was over and I hadn't done anything I had expected to do. But in the universal joy I shamed myself out of my disappointment and decided that the least I could do for my victorious country and her allies was to fall off the wagon again. I found a Navy officer from New York (Yale, 1917), and we started at the University Club with a quart of Scotch and made many friends. I woke up on the bed in my room at the Y.M.C.A. with an unknown derby hat in my hand. The war in Chicago was definitely over.

9

The war, to me, had been unreal and, like my college days, it had been lived in a dream world. There followed a two-year period of even greater romantic unreality. The immediate problem after the 1918 Armistice was to get out of the Navy and this did not happen for six months. It was in that period that I took a good whiff of the lotus and saw marvelous beatific visions of graceful living as enjoyed by the Rich.

Shortly after the end of the war the Navy decided that now I could not possibly do any real harm so I was given the rank of Chief Quartermaster, which entitled me to stop showing my long neck in my cute little middy blouse and to wear a collar and necktie (black). With this welcome change also came a substantial wage increase and the privilege of sleeping every night in my Y.M.C.A. bed if I wanted to. I wanted to, very much. I had become acquainted with the wonderfully congenial brother of one of my Yale classmates, Jack Cowles. His close friends included four superb girls. One was Janet Pauling, whom Jack was in love with; another was Dorothy Keeley, whose father was a famous newspaperman; the third, Sylvia Shaw, was the daughter of the architect Howard van Doren Shaw; the fourth I shall call Diana. Janet was tall, graceful, moved like a stately Viking queen. Dorothy, was witty, intelligent, well-read; Sylvia was a charming warm-hearted companion. Diana was the one I fell madly in love with.

Why? Well, love is not an easy disease to diagnose. I suppose that in the twenty-four odd years I subsequently enjoyed in Hollywood I have written some two hundred variations on the theme. In most of them I tried to give some believable reason for Cupid's havoc other than that Norma Shearer or Clark Gable was playing the part. In my romance with Diana, it would be possible to point with a cynical shrug to the fact that her family was one of the wealthiest and most socially prominent in Chicago. My previous history (up to this point) would indicate that I almost pathologically equated High Society with security. I also felt incredibly happy in the social elites who had given me a non-resident member's card. There I was – an entertaining young man who used the right fork. So far it's a B picture, with David Niven's stand-in playing the lead. And yet – it wasn't quite like that. Any connection between these girls and the Hollywood image of "Society Women" was purely accidental. Diana and her friends were serious, intelligent, well-educated, as were their families. Diana was in Society, but she wanted none of it. She wasn't in the Scott Fitzgerald flying prom-girl circus, although she had gone from Chicago to Westover "Finishing" School in Connecticut. She was a strange and "different" person. She had an aloofness in her which at first intrigued me, then gradually drove me to depths of frustrated desire to solve the riddle of this sphinx. She was so beautiful, and so untouchable. She would smile – and the smile came from On High. Music brought us together. She knew more about it than anyone I had ever met. She played Debussy, Ravel, Schumann, Chopin superbly. We went to Chicago Symphony concerts in the family seats with her mother; I would close my eyes in breathless awe at the sight of her glorious mass of heaped-up light brown hair. We went on long walks together. Once we tramped in a snowstorm from the Lake Shore Drive apartment to their place in Winnetka. It was ten or twelve miles and I was absolutely exhausted. She wasn't, and laughed at my weakness. I figured that it was one way of keeping me in my place, for she was by now afraid of my mind (or at least of my mockery). And then gradually I came to understand what I was really up up against. I had suspected it, but I had no idea how deep it went. Her intriguing, exasperating, insurmountable "out-of-this-world-ness" came not from any "superiority" but from her religion. She was a devout Christian Scientist. She walked every moment with her God, lived every day in His presence. I was competing with Him, and it was too late to get the hell out. I couldn't possibly accept her belief. It was my love against His.

God won, of course, but it was a tough fight. And at the moment of greatest crisis, He played me a rather unfair – or at least unexpected

– trick. It was in April, and I had finally got my discharge from the Navy. Diana and I had battled it up and down, around, and from all sides. I was groggy, but still coming in fighting. Then the Telephone Company decided to transfer me to the Minneapolis office where they needed a Chief Clerk. I had expected that the next stop would be New York, but this was quite a promotion. So I had my last walk with Diana, our last concert together, and then the final showdown in her family's apartment. At midnight I was to take the train to Minneapolis. I hoped desperately that I was making progress with her, that she was genuinely distressed that our idyll was coming to an end. It was now or never. She was sitting on the couch, looking more than ever like a divinely beautiful goddess. And then, unexpectedly, I was completely overwhelmed with a new emotion. It was as though everything I had felt up to then was nothing, that I now knew love for the first time. I can only approximate it to a religious ecstasy as described by those who have "found God." It had elements of the surrender which I had mocked in the Christian ritual. It wasn't ex- actly that, but it was not concerned with me or what I felt any more. I didn't want to possess her. I was hers – if she wanted me. And she was presumably to be mine – in some sort of uncompetitive blessedness. The struggle was over. This was the deepest emotion I had ever had. Perhaps the first. It was time for the train. Diana kissed me tenderly and I left, still under the spell of my strange new-found peace and inner security.

When I got to my hotel in Minneapolis I came down with influen- za. 1919 was the year of the terrible epidemic and I almost died, greatly to the annoyance of the hotel manager. I couldn't have picked a more unfortunate time or a worse disease, for the after effects produced an emptiness, a lack of vitality which made it very difficult to struggle against the despair of realizing that I had lost Diana forever. Gradually I came to realize that while my blinding flash of revelation had given me a profound insight into what might be called love, it was not the way to win a girl. Such love is not for the battlefield of the sexes, and the object of it is better left up on the pedestal. It was a bitter truth, and the process of rising from my knees and building up my protection against ever again exposing myself to such an overpowering emotion took a long time.

The process of returning to the world was greatly helped by my Minneapolis and St. Paul friends. Larry Tighe and his sister Katherine insisted that I leave my grubby little room and my cafeteria meals, and come across the river to a St. Paul boarding house. The river happened to be the Mississippi and the distance considerable, but Mrs. Porterfield's homelike establishment and the several cheerful fellow guests (in Birmingham and Pittsburgh they had been "boarders") was exactly what I, in my sunken, lonely state, needed. The daily streetcar ride across the Mississippi to the office in Minneapolis took an hour, but I had recovered my hunger for books and read as eagerly as I had in my cultural dawn in New Haven. As soon as I got settled I sent to Columbus for Clara and she was a great addition to the general gaiety, especially at meals. It was a happy life – except for the emptiness where there had been the beauty of Diana. Everything seemed to be a bit unreal.

And then, as though on cue, there arrived shortly after a young, blonde, good-looking Princeton graduate named Frances Scott Key Fitzgerald. Kay Tighe had said, "You'll like Scott" – and I did. He had just come up from Montgomery, Alabama, where he had been unsuccessfully trying to get Zelda Sayre to marry him. I told him about Diana and we became commiserating "rejects" under the skin. He still had hopes, however, of getting somewhere with his girl. Zelda sounded wonderful. Scott told me of one incident just after they first met. They had gone swimming in the river and, like me, he was a bit timid about diving from even moderate heights. While he stood hesitantly rather far above the water on a rock from which he had intended to impress her with his daring, a body suddenly shot past him in a perfect dive from shudderingly high above him. It was Zelda. He made up his mind right then that she was the girl for him. But what interested me particularly was that he had just finished a novel. I got him to lend me his cardboard box full of *This Side of Paradise,* written in pencil. I approved of it, with my Yale reservations. I didn't know enough to appreciate his style and form, but the content was exciting. Scott was really a godsend at that time, and filled the educational void left by my separation from Put and Doc. We were neither of us interested in political happenings at home or abofabroad. From Scott I first learned to love the poetry of A.E. Housman; to him I owe my delight in many novelists, Compton McKenzie's *Sinister Street* and the Catholics like the English Benson and the French Huysmans. I myself was flirting a bit with mysticism and the reality of Satan, and Scott was watching me with that green-eyed Mona Lisa smile, as though he were taking notes. Actually, it was that note-taking watchfulness of his that kept me from ever feeling that he was really a friend. And I too kept somewhat aloof, but this was due more to my Yale conformism; when Scott got drunk he embarrassed me, although in those early days of Prohibition there was very little drinking. Scott had an outrageous way of asking the wrong (actually the right) quesions about one's most private feelings – questions which one just didn't ask. Or so I had been taught.

Also he was very curious about my humor. "How did I go about making people laugh?" Part of my answer to that one lay in a technique, which I had slowly been developing since Yale, of imitating "funny men" who were so popular at parties and as ushers at weddings. George Chappel, for instance, had endeared himself to his New Haven generation by a mock bedtime story recited in a childish voice which began with " 'Just the day for a picnic' said Teacher, and all of her bright eager happy pupils clapped their little hands in glee." As George delivered it, it was gloriously funny, and in every succeeding Yale class there were one or two who performed "Just the day for a picnic" at the drop of a hint from an eager hostess, or without any hint at all. I myself developed a mock circus act in which I was both ringmaster and two trained seals named Otto and Minnie. I would crack my imaginary whip and then in a German accent ask Otto "whether he liked the ladies or the gentlemen best?" I would then become "Otto" by crouching on a chair and waving my head in seal-like fashion from side to side; after several promptings from myself as whip-in-hand ringmaster, Otto would come out with a loud bark which, I explained to the audience with a triumphant bow, signified that "Otto liked the ladies best."

In addition to these "stunts" I was developing another source of entertainment for social occasions. In the first period of Prohibition it was almost impossible in the Middle West to get anything alcoholic to drink. But whenever I did happen to hoist one or two too many, a wonderful sort of release would take place within me, so that I would find myself explaining things in "Alice-in-Wonderland" non sequitur. In that respect, liquor was not a curse to me at all, and it did miracles in helping me to overcome my basic fear of people. Later when I began to depend too much on it, especially on occasions when I was expected to live up to my Life of the Party reputation, I was, I suppose, in danger of needing Alcoholics Anonymous, but that never quite came to pass.

I was lucky with Scott, because I first knew him intimately in that comparatively calm period before he sky-rocketed as a novelist to somewhat unapproachable heights. He and I had one thing in common: we were both impoverished and ambitious "outsiders." I think that he was almost as obsessed as I with the magic of great names, both in Finance and Society. We were both products of Eastern upper-class universities, and both insecure and unprepared for sudden success. My 1920's and 1930's were, on a smaller scale, the Fitzgerald 1920's and 1930's. And when, just before his death, we had one final blessed month together of a return to our 1920 relationship, I was able again to be understandingly grateful for those few months in St. Paul "at the beginning."

In the autumn I had earned a week's vacation from the office and I was seized by a strange desire to go away, to be alone. I had met many people, and had undergone one tremendous emotional experience. I wanted "to connect" what I had experienced, to do what a French girl I knew four years later called *arranger mes pensées*. So I put some clothes in a knapsack, tucked A.E. Housman's poems into my pocket, and set out for a solitary walk along the Mississippi. Nature was at her best, and in Minnesota, in the autumn, that is thrilling. I would walk, sit under a tree, read for a while, then continue. When my feet and legs began to rebel, I would hitch hike. At night, in whatever town I had reached, I would wander the streets, looking into the homes, wondering what those people were like. I never got to know. I have never been able to be free and easy with strangers, and of course I was a strange subject to them. Once I went past a hall where some high school dance was in progress. I wanted very much to dance, but I just couldn't bring myself to ask any girl. On the last night of my walk I got into conversation in the dining room of a small hotel with a scholarly-looking middle-aged visitor and discovered to my joy that he knew Housman's poetry. He seemed well-educated and widely read, but his occupation was in what he called the "labor movement." He told me stories of how the so-called Bolsheviks in America were being persecuted in a Red scare, and after he had satisfied himself that my ignorance was real he asked if I'd like to go with him that night to a school house where the local farmers were having a meeting. Off we went into the darkness in a young Swedish-American farmer's Model-T Ford. The school was a long way from town and when we got nearer we were challenged twice by farmers carrying lanterns with which they closely examined us. With some difficulty my new friend was able to assure them that I was not a police spy. I was beginning to get a bit nervous. The farmhouse was also carefully guarded. Some ten or fifteen farmers eyed me suspiciously as we entered, then sat down at the school desks to listen to my friend talk on the benefits of organizing themselves into a Non-Partisan League farmers' union. I had read in the papers about this dangerous Bolshevik menace, but had thought it was confined to farmers in North Dakota. Then suddenly there was a sharp whistle outside. All the lanterns were doused and we sat in suspenseful darkness. I wondered how in hell I was going to explain to the American Tel. and Tel. that I had come along only in the interest of talking about Housman's poetry. There was soon an all-clear whistle, but the men were too skittish to go on with the meeting and we drove silently to our hotel. It was my first and, for many years, last contact with what are now called un-American activities. It didn't present much temptation to interest myself further, especially as my organizer-friend turned out to be a homosexual and I had to lock my door. I was more embarrassed and disappointed than angry. I had enjoyed talking to him, and he had spoiled it.

That solitary trip on foot in the autumn of that year had a curious symbolic significance of which I was not in the least aware. It was a quiet interlude, a breathing space between two periods of history, and between the first and second stages in my own life. The era of belief in the steady sure progress of mankind through enlightened liberalism and God's watchful love had ended. St. Paul, Minnesota, as I knew it, represented that to me as had Columbus, Exeter and Yale. The men and women who were my friends were still living in that hopeful security – or at least their parents were. They were – and still are in my sentimental memory – "good" people with established values which they and I respected. I was in a safe job in a huge public utility corporation. I had had nothing to do with its creation and no responsibility other than that of carrying out someone else's plans, someone who was somewhere at the top of a tall building in New York. If I made good with him I would be tapped for a higher job, etc., etc. But I had begun to worry about my job. Something was wrong in a setup where my real sense of living came after I had left the office. My life should be my world. Perhaps this problem was why I had taken this lonely trip as my vacation. But I certainly did not come back with any right answer. I did not even know any right questions.

Then occurred a small revolution in my own affairs. A dark and dynamic Yale grad named Harold Talbott, Jr. had been up to St. Paul on a visit to his fraternity brother Lou Ordway, and Lou had sold him on me as an up-and-coming young man. Harold and his father had made huge profits during the war by manufacturing airplanes for the government, and the problem for the Talbotts was now the investment of that money. What Harold had in mind for me in this dazzling Tycoon-ery was not clear even in his own mind, but he took a liking to me and offered me the giddy sum of $4000 a year if I would care to come down to Dayton and "see what happened." It didn't take me long to decide, especially as this was double my salary and I had discovered that, due to power shifts in the upper floors of the New York Telephone executives, I was no longer on anybody's priority list. "They" – whoever they were way up there – seemed to have lost interest in me. And I had certainly lost my interest in reports to the Division Office. This new opportunity seemed like something strictly from heaven.

Clara and I arrived in Dayton in the spring of 1920, and quickly found an excellent boarding house run by two amiable sisters. As an adjunct to my financial career I bought my first golf clubs, knickerbockers and Scotch woollen socks. Golf had always been connected in my mind with my brother Bert's Arlington Country Club in Columbus, and therefore with Society. Harold put me up at the Dayton Country Club, I began to take golf lessons, and Fore! My usual companion on the golf links was a young lawyer named Murray Smith, who lived at my boarding house. Murray was the most civilized and intelligent person I met in Dayton, and his loyal friendship and quiet humor helped a great deal to make this difficult period less miserable.

The misery did not lie in the work, but in the insecurity of my position at the "Talbott court" and in Dayton Society. I had no close friends as I had had in Chicago and St. Paul, and I didn't seem able to make any. There were no "Puts," no "Docs," no Scott Fitzgeralds, no one even slightly interested in books or music. I am sure that after a while Harold began to wonder whether he hadn't been sold something out of the wrong catalogue, especially as none of his family or his friends evinced any enthusiasm for the strange bird he had brought down from the North. I was finding myself in a world I didn't care for and yet in which I had to survive by living up to what Harold and the Chief expected of me. But what was that?

Harold just didn't have anything for me to do. I sat at my desk and studied Accounting, Factory Management, Economics, Banking, Investment, Shipping and Merchandising in a series of volumes entitled the *Alexander Hamilton Business Course*. I could have passed any paper examination, but I didn't really have the slightest idea of what business was about. I tried to learn. I faithfully followed the stock market, high and low mean average in rails, industrials, oils; I compared the freight car loadings with the total bank deposits; I drew graphs and charts. Then on the way home I would pass the library and fight off my desire to borrow a book by James Branch Cabell which I had read about in the *New Republic*. That was the mistake I had unwittingly made in St. Paul – reading books – and here I was doing it again. In spite of the *Alexander Hamilton Business Course* I was slipping back. If Harold had had any work for me, if I could have been of the slightest use to him or the Chief, I might have been saved. But fate was against me. I began to investigate the literary and musical recommendations of James Huneker and of a new critic, H.L. Mencken. I smuggled their books into the office and hid them behind the front covers of Alexander Hamilton. I secretly took up my piano lessons again, and stole off to Cincinnati to hear a symphony concert. It was my one-man rebellion against the values of the Alexander Hamilton Road to the Top.

10

My dream of success in the world of High Finance lasted about a year. At the end of November 1920, on my twenty-sixth birthday, I came to a decision about my life. It was partly due, of course, to the increasingly obvious failure of my Dayton venture. Harold Talbott had given me no indication of this; indeed, he continued to encourage me and even to apologize that he had not been able, so far, to fit me into the organization. But my own ambition to "succeed" had died, or, rather, had changed into a rejection of any climb to the summit which involved a competitive effort along the lines of Big Business. Even had I "made good" with the Talbotts I gradually came to realize that that kind of Elite does not bring either security or self-fulfillment. It depended on making oneself *persona grata* within a hierarchy; and I had watched myself losing self-respect in a struggle to deserve four thousand dollars a year. I became aware that a visitor's card to a club was not the same as a fully paid-up membership. If anyone were to "tap" me for any Society in the future it would be I myself. It wasn't Harold's fault; he treated me very decently, even though he was losing money on his investment.

Scott Fitzgerald had read me a poem of Masefield's which began: "Be with me, Beauty, for the fire is dying." That was what I was now determined to seek, even if it meant taking a job in a book or a music store. I also wanted somehow to get to Paris. I suddenly felt free of a great weight. I had found an Answer. It encompassed the Answer which had come to be in my love for Diana; it transmuted the beauty and the pain which that love had brought; it opened a new window from which I might catch glimpses of the radiance which was the

Beauty of the whole world. That was what I would now seek, as before I had sought "success." Aesthetes of the world arise! You have nothing to lose but your jobs.

I lost mine just before Christmas. Harold explained, and with some truth, that the Depression, necessitated financial retrenchments. He also suggested, with even more truth, that I might be more happy in a different kind of work, and with great generosity gave me three months advance salary to enable me "to look around." So after settling Clara temporarily in Columbus I decided to begin this looking around in New York. The Depression was still raging, but I wasn't depressed. I was unbelievably light-hearted. As I packed my suitcase, I felt that I had exchanged my Brooks Bros. suit for the robes of Pan, although Clara insisted that I also pack my long woolen underwear. I left behind my golf clubs and my tuxedo. I was ready to join the angry young men of 1921.

Disillusionment was the aftermath of the war which was to make the world safe for democracy. I was disillusioned. The new slogan was "Down with Puritanism." It was those mean old Puritans who were to blame for all our frustrations, and as my train pulled into Penn Station in New York I started out to find a recruiting office where I could enlist in the war to make America safe for Paganism.

I directed my steps away from the Yale Club and down to Greenwich Village where, to my entranced delight, I found a Columbus friend living on Morton Street in a real studio with real artists. He was Hubbard Hutchinson, a recent Williams graduate who was talented both as a musician and writer. Sharing the studio with him were three young painters one of whom was Harold van Doren, also from Williams. It was all strictly from *La Boheme.* The studio was a loft, high-roofed and freezing cold. No one had any money, or any prospect of same. And it was fascinating. Easels held half-finished paintings of the modern persuasion. There was a grand piano on which Hub and Gene played Bach. There was talk of Cubism, of a new book called *Main Street,* of a new conductor named Mengelberg whom the Philharmonic had just brought over from Amsterdam. There was a dinner at a nearby Italian restaurant with dirty tablecloths but real red wine (if you knew Angelo the proprietor) served in coffee cups. They let me buy them a meal, and invited me to share the studio. I was flattered and delighted to accept. This was where I belonged; at least, it was where I wanted to belong. This was as far from the Miami Valley Hunt and Polo Club as it was possible to get, and I was very happy.

Clara, incidentally, had unexpectedly staged a surprising personal revolution of her own. She decided to become a Roman Catholic. I'm not sure what she was rebelling against; her own explanation was that she wanted to belong to a church that was sure of itself. Perhaps this was her reaction to the general spirit of unrest and disillusionment.

But I still had a job to find, and Clara to support, and it didn't take me long to discover that getting a job wasn't going to be easy. The Depression was at its height; men were being fired, not hired. My dismissal pay from Harold Talbott wouldn't last forever. La Vie Boheme was beginning to look a bit insecure – and then Scott Fitzgerald came to my rescue. *This Side of Paradise* had been published while I was in Dayton, he had married Zelda, and they had exploded brilliantly into the sky over New York. They were living in an apartment on 59th Street, convenient to a drug store on Sixth Avenue where Scott could get pure alcohol made into gin. I had not kept up with their exploits and the first time I called, expecting to have a quiet dinner, I found myself eventually swept along dinnerless with ten or fifteen others to a ball at the Savoy Plaza given by the Daughters of the Southern Confederacy.

It was not the same Scott I had known in St. Paul, and I wasn't sure that I was as crazy about Zelda as everyone else appeared to be. She seemed much more interested in her own conversation than in mine; so did Scott, and I felt like some embarrassed spectator caught by the unexpected rising of the curtain on the stage of a comedy in which the two stars were competing for the spotlight. Neither then, nor in the years to follow, did I ever have any sense of a relationship between Zelda and myself. I just couldn't get through to the real girl, and God knows I tried, especially on that first acquaintance. At one point that evening, however, the gin gave out, Scott took me with him to the drug store for a refill, and I had a chance to tell him what had happened in Dayton and why I had come to New York. He was immediately sympathetic and told me to go to Frank "Crownie" Crowninshield, the editor of *Vanity Fair,* who might have something for me in the advertising department.

On my first trip to the *Vanity Fair* offices I found that Scott had prepared the way for me with "Crownie" as well as with the two assistant editors, Edmund "Bunny" Wilson and John Peale Bishop, who had been at Princeton with him. "Crownie," white-mustached, suave, elegant, soft-voiced, listened with benevolent courtesy to my plea for "any kind of work" and shook his head. "Unfortunately, my dear boy, there is nothing." I asked if he could suggest any possibilities; perhaps on a newspaper, as an assistant music critic, or in the *Vanity Fair* advertising department. He smiled sadly and I rose to go; I too had good manners. He offered to give me letters of introduction to other magazines, but it would be better if I could let him look at something I had written, so that he could judge what sort of position he might recommend me for. Well, Scott had done his best. The Depression had obviously hit culture, too. Tomorrow I would try a Yale friend at the Bankers Trust. On my way out I heard Scott's laugh. He had dropped in on Wilson and Bishop. I shyly poked my head in to thank him for his help, then continued on my way to the elevator. I could hear the laughter behind me. I felt very envious, and very out of it.

When, next day, the Bankers Trust unhesitatingly declined the offer of my slightly less than valuable services, I was relieved, and yet I began to panic a bit about the future. I tried to figure out what sort of sample of my writing might induce Crowninshield to recommend me, and telephoned Edmund Wilson for advice. One humorous possibility which occurred to me was a parody on Dreiser, for whose novels I did not at all share Mencken's enthusiasm. Wilson's advice was "Let's see it," so two nights later I timorously rang the bell of his apartment in the Village. I found that he was living with two of my Yale classmates; one was Larry Noyes from St. Paul who was studying architecture at Columbia, and the unknown other was practicing on the oboe in preparation for a possible symphony orchestra career. Somehow this seemed very courageous to me, even though his doleful notes from the next room didn't exactly make an encouraging accompaniment to Wilson's reading of my attempt at humorous parody.

Watching someone read something which is supposed to be funny is never an enjoyable experience, especially if your hopes for a job are desperately based on it. Wilson read the first page with a frown. I hated him and all Princeton men. I pretended to be interested in the books on his shelves, and was about ready to say, "Well, it was just an idea," when a beautiful sound arose over the wail of the oboe. Edmund Wilson was laughing. He liked it. I immediately liked him, and could see what a splendid critical intelligence I had come in contact with. When he had finished, we discussed Dreiser, parody and

Max Beerbohm, of whom I had never heard. Then he surprised me by asking if I could write a parody of James Branch Cabell, whose *Jurgen,* I told him, had become one of my favorite books. "I think so," I replied "but why? Don't you think the Dreiser one will be enough to persuade Mr. Crowninshield that I might get a job on some newspaper?" His reply knocked me off my feet. "If it's good enough, we'll publish both of them," he announced. I couldn't believe it. "In *Vanity Fair?*" I asked. He nodded, and I walked home in a state of suspended credulity. It just couldn't be true.

But it was. They accepted the Cabell parody, and then another one making fun of *How To Listen To Music.* And not only that but they paid me for them. If my luck held out, I might as a writer be able to support Clara. It frightened me considerably at first, and I couldn't adjust myself to a life without a weekly pay check. I kept saying, "Well, it won't last." But "Crownie" encouraged me, tried to make me feel that he was as lucky as I.

Just before I had arrived on the scene his assistant editors had been three young persons, none of whom had as yet made any name for themselves: Dorothy Parker, Robert Benchley, and Robert E. Sherwood. Mrs. Parker was the dramatic critic, and in one of her reviews she had suggested that "Billie" Burke as a serious actress was not so much wearing the buskin of Eleonora Duse as the socks of the clown "Poodles" Hannifield. Since Miss Burke was the wife of "Flo" Ziegfeld this brought the all powerful producer in a rage to Crownie's office asking, "Who is this Dorothy Parker?" and demanding that she be fired immediately. Crownie, always the gentleman, tried to appease The Great Ziegfeld (and the Conde Nast business offices) by suggesting that his inexperienced drama critic would undoubtedly atone for her mistake in a later review, but refused absolutely to entertain Ziegfeld's demand for her dismissal. Peace seemed to be established until Crownie discovered that Dorothy would resign rather than retract anything she had written. In fact, her anger mounted so high at the very suggestion that she did resign. At which Benchley and Sherwood reached for their hats and followed her out of the office. Inasmuch as none of them, all in their twenties, had any money at the time or any other jobs, this grand gesture for cultural freedom was greatly appreciated by all except Crownie. Fortunately, the three rebels were immediately hired by *Life,* which was still at that time a humorous and liberal magazine. *Vanity Fair* replaced Harvard's two top humorists (Sherwood had followed

Benchley in college as editor of the *Lampoon*) with Princeton's two leading young literary lights, Wilson and Bishop. Check and double check, with me arriving at a time when Crownie was in considerable need of help in plugging up the enormous gap in the humor department left by the departure of the Big Three.

I didn't know about any of this at the time. I was equally unaware of the significance of that moment in Edmund Wilson's library when he burst into laughter at my parody. An Act One curtain had come down to the sound of that laughter, although the climax to the act had been reached in Dayton when I definitely climbed off the "success" merry-go-round and abandoned the competition for the gold ring. The curtain to Act Two rose to discover me sitting at a desk in a small room at 51 Barrow Street. The green painted walls, black ceiling, purple closet door, orange closet interior showed that it was a room in Greenwich Village, rented from a "free verse" poetess who also dabbled in "interesting" interior decorating. The only other furniture was an army cot at the window where I slept (in spite of a street lamp just outside the window). On the walls were the framed photographs of father, Bert, Anne and Charles which had seen me through Exeter and Yale. I was particularly happy because I had just sold my first short story, and the editors who had purchased it were named Mencken and Nathan. It was because of this that I had finally come to accept the possibility of my making a living as a writer. I had rented this three-room "apartment" and sent for Clara. She slept in a bed in the second room which had been painted in the more conservative colors of scarlet and orange. The third room was a very small combined kitchen and bath. Clara was almost as thrilled by the Bohemian life as I was, or at least she bravely pretended to be. She cooked all our meals except those which we occasionally took at a nearby Italian speakeasy. There was a Catholic church around the corner on Sixth Avenue, and Clara soon made friends with all the Italian neighbors, including the kids who played ball in the street outside our house.

It was a romantic life, completely satisfactory. I was actually a New Yorker, a Writer, living in my own apartment. A short walk took me to Washington Square where I could take a double-decker yellow and green bus up Fifth Avenue to the *Vanity Fair* offices to discuss my next humorous article or to earn additional income by thinking up captions for drawings by "Fish" or Ralph Barton or other famous artists who contributed to their pages. There had been the terrific thrill at the appearance of my name for the first time in the magazine, and the thought that all over America people were reading my pieces – in Columbus, Dayton, Chicago, Minneapolis, St. Paul – and sometimes even on top of the bus in which I was riding. There was the thrill (occasional as yet) of taking Clara to the theater, not as out-of-town visitors but as sophisticated natives who traveled to Times Square and back in the Seventh Avenue subway, changing expertly to the Local at 14th street. It was exciting to read the reviews of the plays the very next morning after they had opened, and to be able to discuss Alexander Woollcott or Heywood Broun as though one knew them personally – not to mention F.P.A. or Don Marquis or Christopher Morley. But most thrilling of all was the feeling of being actually a part of all this, of being a fellow-contributor to a magazine which published articles by the best critics, articles about foreign writers named Joyce and Proust and Cocteau, about a Russian composer Stravinsky, critical articles with photographs of paintings by Picasso and Braque, of strange sculpture by Brancusi. I wanted to meet these critics some day, to let them know that I too wrote for *Vanity Fair.*

It wasn't long before I began to wonder if I weren't capable of much more important work than humorous pieces and parodies of other authors. I didn't let anyone in on this secret ambition, but I began to read novels and short stories for the purpose of seeing how it was done. I had certain favorites, headed by Anatole France. Scott had introduced me enthusiastically to France's philosophy of "irony and pity," and I became equally a devotee. I couldn't share Scott's interest in Dreiser. Nor was I able to go all out for *Main Street* which was becoming the bible of us anti-Puritans. I was looking for subtlety and beautiful writing such as I found in *Jurgen,* such as I would hope to find perhaps in my cultured elite, perhaps in Paris. I was turning away from America – at least from the Main streets of the Middle West. I devoured Van Wyck Brooks' *The Ordeal of Mark Twain* and began to visualize myself as Twain's successor, but as a humorist who would not permit himself to be wooed away from devastating satire by any of the temptations which had turned Twain from the path of Truth. I was to be the new Mark Twain, fearless, uncorrupted. I conceived a great contempt for successful humorists like Irwin S. Cobb and Christopher Morley, who, to my mind, betrayed the great cleansing power of humor by using it to smooth over the difficulties in life. I hated the kindly laughter of smug contented people, and I hated humorists who pandered to this. "Well now," I could hear those jesters saying, "Life has its ups and downs but let's not get bitter about it. Let's just draw up our chairs around the warm fire and have a few laughs to help us over the bumps." I wanted to blast them out of those comfortable chairs. I wanted to toss dynamite into that cosy fire. I remember saying something like this to Clarence Day, who had read one of my *Vanity Fair* pieces and invited me to his Riverside Drive apartment. Clarence listened to me approvingly and as I left remarked, "Stewart, you're a battleship."

But the battleship wasn't yet ready to fire any of its guns, and it still didn't really know where the enemy was. And New York was doing its best to prevent the future Voltaire (or was it Swift? Sometimes I wasn't quite sure) from raising the spyglass to his eye. Scott had told Crownie about my success in St. Paul as a Life of the Party and after I had unsuspectingly given the *Vanity Fair* editorial staff a sample of my trained seals act, Crownie delightedly presented me one night to a club of writers, artists and musicians known as the Coffee House. The performance was a huge success, due partly to the fact that liquor could be obtained by club members, and I was launched into cultural circles as a public entertainer.

This, of course, had its advantages. Many "names" were members, and I would find myself having a rather awesome lunch at a long table with celebrities whom I would hurry home to tell Clara about. There were occasional evening parties in honor of visiting lecturers such as Margot Asquith and Claire Sheriden, but mainly the Coffee House centered around fun and laughter, with Crownie acting as ringmaster to his cultivated clowns, chief among whom was Charles Hanson Towne, whose burlesque Wagnerian operas began and ended the evening's gaiety. It was at the Coffee House that I first met some of Crownie's other contributors, including Hendrick Willem van Loon, Deems Taylor, and Heywood Broun. Van Loon lived near me in the Village. When I called on him he was charming (he liked my stuff), and happy over the prospect that his *Story of Mankind* was showing signs of being his first popular success. I also met my Yale hero, the fabulous George Chappell who had originated "Just the day for a picnic." It was at the Coffee House that George sold the energetic publisher George Putnam the idea of a burlesque on the best-selling "returned explorer" books, and the publisher promptly enlisted Crownie's circus as George's shipmates on the mythical cruise of a ship called the "Kawa." Charlie Towne,

Heywood Broun and I were photographed in sailors' costume on various "desert islands" with various "native" head-hunters and their naked daughters. When the book appeared we accompanied Captain Traprock (as George called himself in the tale) to various bookstores for publicity purposes, and when I couldn't appear Heywood would do the trained seal act with, I was told, much greater success that I had had. I wasn't envious of Heywood's acclaim. In fact, it was impossible to be envious or jealous or anything else unkind of him. He was so friendly, so like a lovable overgrown shaggy dog, so seemingly unprotected – until you said or did something he didn't agree with. Then the shag would bristle slightly, there would be a seemingly innocent growl, and it would be wise to look quickly for your nearest exit. I also got to like and admire Heywood's wife Ruth Hale, even though I made the mistake on our first meeting of calling her "Mrs. Broun" not knowing that she was a most militant Lucy Stone Leaguer with a most sharp tongue. No shaggy dog she.

My greatest "contact" in these early days, however, was Robert Benchley. Bunny Wilson had brought us together at lunch at the Algonquin Hotel, and shortly after that I visited Bob at the *Life* office where I met Dorothy Parker, Robert Sherwood and the idol of my Columbus youth, Charles Dana Gibson, who had become the owner and publisher of the magazine. Benchley lived in Scarsdale with his wife Gertrude and two small sons, Nathaniel and Robert Junior. Dorothy had married good-looking young Lieutenant Parker from Hartford, Connecticut as he was leaving for France. She and Bob always addressed each other as Mr. Benchley and Mrs. Parker, and this practice continued for many years after I first knew them. Bob was the drama critic, Sherwood took care of the movie reviews, and Dorothy was sort of a roving imp-at-large. She was absolutely devastating: petite, graceful, black bobbed hair, keen startling black eyes. We four had lunch at the Plaza, then Bob Sherwood returned to work and Benchley, Mrs. Parker and I wandered down Fifth Avenue in the June sunshine. It was an enchanted afternoon. I felt I had found two people who understood me completely. I didn't need to explain my ideas, or even to finish my sentences. Benchley was the soul, the essence of humor, and Dorothy that of wit. And they were warm, friendly, sympathetic. I fell in love with both of them, and remained so the rest of my life. Finally, after crossing town, we came to the Metropolitan Opera House, where they had their "office." It was the smallest of holes,

with only room for a desk, a chair and one occupant. On the door was
a sign reading "Gents."

I was making friends and my writings were becoming known. The
"Smart Set" published an article of mine on Yale for their college
series, of which the last line read "and in the direction of Henry Ford
the Yale graduate smiles cynically as he presses his thumb to his
nose and gently wriggles his four fingers" – or words to that effect –
the general idea being that an uncouth creature like Henry Ford,
even with all his employees and his manufacturing know-how, could
never really understand the quality of the cultivation and the
friendships found at Yale. Even though Mencken and Nathan
published it, I knew it was not Voltaire at his best, to say the least. It
showed how far I still had to go before I would have the slightest understanding of my country or of the real target for a satirist. I wasn't
Mark Twain. I was the cultivated Don Quixote with "Beauty" on his
shield, looking for giants. My chance along those lines came when I
ran into John Farrar at the Yale Club. Johnny had been a Sophomore at Yale when I was a Senior; he and Stephen Vincent Benet
were the Yale counterpart in the new literary upsurge to Princeton's Scott Fitzgerald, "Bunny" Wilson and John Peale Bishop,
and to Harvard's John Dos Passos and e. e. cummings. Johnny
Farrar had just been made editor of the *Bookman* and, although
he was quite properly astonished that I, of all people, had become a
writer, he delightedly accepted my proposal that I do a series of
parodies for his magazine in which American history would be retold
in the manner of the leading popular writers. The first was to be the
Christopher Columbus narrative in the manner of James Branch
Cabell, to be followed by *Main Street* as the Puritan fathers would
see it through the eyes of Sinclair Lewis. Then would come other
historical episodes as they would be written by Scott Fitzgerald,
Ring Lardner, Edith Wharton, Mary Raymond, Shipman Andrews,
Eugene O'Neill, a "bedtime story" of the Whiskey Rebellion by
Thornton W. Burgess, and "How Love Came to General Grant" by
Harold Bell Wright, whose novels of pure love among the noble inhabitants of Kansas had led all best-seller lists for years. When these
parodies began appearing in the *Bookman* they created quite a stir,
and the publisher George Doran asked me if I would consider letting
him bring them out in a book. I jumped with joy into his arms, and
into the even kindlier arms of Eugene Saxton who was the head of
the Doran office. I was to have a book published – in November! And

only five months ago I would have gratefully taken any job in a bookstore.

So Clara and I found increasing joy in our little purple, orange, blue and vermillion home in the East. The Village continued to be constantly stimulating. One night I was sitting on a bench in Washington Square when a face went past which was vaguely familiar. It turned out to be that of Charlie Ellis, who had lived as a boy near The Normandie Hotel in Columbus. The boy Charlie played pool and smoked cigarettes, so Father had turned thumbs down on my friendship for him. Now he was an artist, living in the Village, and married to Edna St. Vincent Millay's sister Norma, who was acting in plays by Eugene O'Neill. Charlie took me to a cellar on MacDougal Street where the Provincetown Players were putting on *The Hairy Ape* for the first time. I thought it was terrific and met O'Neill in Frank Shay's bookshop. This was what I was looking for – writers who were tearing away at the smug hypocrisies of my Yale Tennyson and Browning world. When *Three Soldiers* was published I looked up John Dos Passos, and became increasingly an admirer of his sensitive rebellious spirit. I couldn't admire, however, his interest in socialism and communism, in things happening in Russia. I couldn't understand how they had anything to do with me. I had the same lack of curiosity about the labor movement. Charles Walker from Exeter and Yale days had gone out to Pittsburgh after the war, worked as a common laborer in a steel mill; he had gone through the 1919 strike at the Carnegie plant and had come out with great admiration for a man named William Z. Foster. This was far away from Carnegie Hall where I now sat twice a week in the top gallery listening in closed-eye ecstasy to the "Pathetique." Tchaikovsky was my hero, not Lenin.

And when I heard Debussy I no longer thought of Diana. I had a new girl. Or, at least, I undeservedly had a wonderful girl who loved me, and with whom I "necked" shamelessly in the best *This Side of Paradise* tradition. The fact that she really loved me quite desperately was hard on her, but very good for my own *amour propre* which had never experienced anything like this before. I was getting over my shyness. Or, let us say, the 1920's were enthusiastically letting down the bars everywhere, and by playing the role of a Fitzgerald character I found the girls were willing to listen to my suggestion of a romp in a taxi without becoming insulted – or (which was my worst fear) laughing. But the romp never crossed the borderline, perhaps because of my old-fashioned Yale ideals, but more because of my fear of rejection. I had, however, discovered a wonderful hotel on Broadway where you told a Negro elevator boy that you had come to call on Mrs. Haviland, and up you went. Mrs. H. had an intricate maze of rooms with elaborate exit and entrance signals which would occasionally go wrong, with interesting consequences. And she was a most charming and intelligent woman: on my first visit I just by chance happened to have a copy of *Vanity Fair* with me and she had liked my contribution.

In the fall we moved to another and nicer Village home, this time at 6 Minetta Lane. Our landlord was a young interior decorator named Hobe Irwin; he lived downstairs and we happily occupied the two rooms above him. Shortly after we moved in, the editor of *Life,* Tom Masson, came down and photographed the building, explaining, to my intense delight, that "perhaps some day you might be a well-known writer." I didn't argue. My *Bookman* parodies were attracting a wide audience – at least I had met a lot people who had liked them. I had started a new series entitled "Contemporary Alfreds," each one a satirical profile of a writer who had the same birthday but not at all the genius of his namesake. "Alfred Lamb" was a rather savage attack on Christopher Morley for what I thought was his whimsical aping of Charles Lamb. But the most bitter was my "Alfred Swift" which, since my birthday was the same as the Dean's, was really a fearful probing of what I dreaded might become of my own fate as a satirist. It was the old trick of laughing at myself before someone else did, but my fears for my own integrity as a writer were not entirely laughable. Life in New York was already becoming too pleasant; my popularity as a trained seal was detracting more and more from the serious business of learning my trade as a writer. And everything was coming too easily: every piece I wrote was accepted and editors were crying for more. George Doran had introduced me to a club of the leading publishers and editors known as the Dutch Treat. Ray Long, the chief Hearst magazine editor, asked me if I could write the book for the club's annual comic show, explaining to me that it would do me immense good and create an immediate demand for anything I wrote. He cited the example of an obscure John Reed who had won fame by writing the show a few years previously. He didn't, however, give the Dutch Treat Club credit for the fact that John Reed was now buried in the Kremlin as a reward for his help to the Russian revolution in writing *Ten Days*

That Shook the World. I myself had no aspiration at the time to be buried in anything; on the contrary, the chance to have my name brought before the top-drawer figures in the publishing and magazine world appealed to me immensely and I leaped at the chance. This was an understandable but unfortunate return to the fallacy that one made good by knowing the right people. However, it did no immediate harm. The show was a lot of fun to write, and the rehearsals brought me more friends – or at least acquaintances – among artists, writers and musicians. Marc Connelly played the part of Mona Lisa in my Dutch Treat show, Bob Benchley and I were German soldiers, and the uncensored production was a moderately raucous success before a well-lit uninhibited audience.

Furthermore, the abhorred vacuum left by Diana was unexpectedly rushed into by Nature in the form of an amazingly beautiful blonde with intriguing black eyebrows whom I shall call Connie. She was perfect. That is, she thought my writings were very good, knew a great deal about music, played the violin superbly, danced divinely, had been a great Prom favorite of my Yale generation. There was only one slight drawback. She was married and had a small male child aged four. But the husband was an old man of forty-five (she was a blooming twenty-four), and I soon began to visualize myself in the heroic role of St. George on his way to rescue the princess from the dragon. I never actually saw the alleged monster, but it wasn't difficult to imagine his smoke-belching nostrils, especially as he was a wealthy and successful corporation lawyer who read detective stories and didn't dance. They lived on an estate in Westchester County, about an hour by train from New York, in the midst of the country-club world to which I had once aspired and which I had renounced forever after my Dayton disillusionment. Connie too was disillusioned – about marriage, about life among the successful. She too had dreamed of a world of the cultured rich, but had settled for the Rich in the hope that the Culture might somehow follow. She was – or so I imagined – sinking into the Slough of Well-Manicured Despond when suddenly on the horizon appeared young Donald Quixote, fresh from his triumphs at the Coffee House and the Dutch Treat. Donald emerged from the rough, galloped across the fairway, leaped the bunker at the eighteenth green, swooped the bored maiden from the bridge table on the porch and triumphantly disappeared in the direction of Carnegie Hall. It was the beginning of a most romantic and educational experience. Flaming Youth mocking Respectable

Middle Age. It was glorious to enjoy a stolen evening dancing with her at Gilda Gray's night club. It was exciting to telephone the next morning and, if The Husband answered, to make no answer except to say in lover's Chinese "Solly, long number, pleeze," and to hang up on a supposedly furious Rich Lawyer. There were delicious hidden moments in the dark cocktail lounge of a 32nd Street hotel, known to all illicit romancers. There was no actual adultery. Sir Galahad was restoring life to a despairing Beauty and for the moment that was all the thrill he needed.

In late November came the additional thrill of the publication of my book *A Parody Outline of History.* I had dedicated it to my brother Bert, and proudly sent inscribed copies to Anne and Charles, to The Bunch in Columbus, to Put and Doc. The publication date was exactly one year after the sleepless night in Dayton when I had decided to drop out of the race for money and success. The reviewers almost unanimously praised it, and to the literati of that day it must indeed have seemed the work of a young man who showed much promise of things to come. A Yale professor of history assigned my Ring Lardner chapter on "The Spirit of 1775" to his students as a notable contribution to historical realism. The celebrated Professor Copeland at Harvard read chapters to his English classes. For myself I felt that in my mocking of American hyprocrisies and shibboleths I was digging deeper than the good-natured harmless fun of many preceding humorists, and in my bitter Eugene O'Neill parody especially, I felt that I was getting closer to Voltaire and Swift. The Edith Wharton parody seemed to show that I was also being subtly faithful to Anatole France's irony and pity. The book was an unexpected financial success, too. For a moment I became outstanding in the "younger generation," with my photograph in magazines and speaking engagements at bookstores and symposia. I would walk several times past stores which had my books piled in the window; I would then enter and, after slyly inquiring how it was selling would modestly let them know who I was. I was most cooperative in autographing copies. At Christmas came the triumphant return to Columbus. "Local boy makes good." The family and The Bunch were proud of me although I shocked some of the natives by pulling out a hip pocket flask at a dance. Columbus still took its Prohibition and its Puritanism seriously, but I was a New Yorker in the Jazz Age.

11

The next step was, of course, Paris. The writer dreamed he might be free there of the New England Puritan heritage which had shackled Mark Twain, freed of the overwhelming Main Street Babbitry with its anti-cultural Normalcy. A symposium of bitter protest by American writers against their own civilization had been compiled by Harold Stearns, and the flight to France was in full swing. I felt compelled to join in that flight for two reasons. One was Connie, the other was myself. The acclaim for my first book had increased my feeling of obligation to live up to my promise as a writer, and yet I found myself enjoying my success too enthusiastically, perhaps, for my own good. My friendship with Bob Benchley and Dorothy Parker was a constant delight. There was a group of wits, writers and critics who gathered for lunch every day at the "Round Table" in the Algonquin Hotel, and I was made welcome to this circle which included Franklin P. Adams, Alexander Woollcott, Harold Ross, Heywood, Marc, and his fellow playwright George Kaufmann. I was never really at ease in this company, partly because of the constant strain of feeling obliged to say something funny, and partly because the atmosphere seemed to me to be basically unfriendly, too much that of dog-eat-dog. I don't enjoy exchanging barbs, principally, I suppose, because my own never seem to come out of their quiver at the right time. Most of my ripostes occur to me three or four hours after I have been attacked – an unfortunate defenselessness which leads to too much dependence on alcohol before entering the lists. But it was pleasant to feel that I could sit down at the Round Table any time I wished.

This was part of the great excitement of being a New Yorker in those days. Prohibition also added immensely to the *joie de vivre*. To be able to claim first-name acquaintance with the proprietor of a speakeasy, to have him nod approvingly to your waiter, to get your cup of wine, all this made you feel that even in a tea cup you were defying that damned Puritanical law, and consummating a rebellious act of independence and self-affirmation against the power of the reformers and their spies. And when thirsty visitors came from Columbus or other Middle-Western deserts it was with such superiority and pride that one ushered them to the not-so-hidden oasis where one had only to display the right card and the magic door would swing open on what were probably the vilest alcoholic beverages ever manufactured. A year or two later the worst aspects of the drought had been largely circumvented but in 1922 drinking was still a happy high adventure. Bob and I discovered a "Jimmy and Eddy's" on 45th Street where we were delightedly initiated into a *specialité de la maison* known as a "pink one", after three of which we would beamingly board the train for Scarsdale for a weekend with his wife Gertrude and his two small sons. On some evenings Gertrude would come into town to share Bob's critic's seats at the theater and fearfully sample a "pink one" afterwards. Another exciting "drop-in" place for me was the studio of Neysa McMein, a beautiful golden-haired illustrator whose drawings were greatly prized and whose company even more so. Neysa lived on 57th Street opposite Carnegie Hall. Dorothy Parker and her husband Eddie, who worked on Wall Street, had an apartment in the same building, and in the late afternoon there could be found in one or the other of these meeting places most of the Algonquin Round Table as well as young up-and-coming actresses such as Helen Hayes, Margalo Gillmore, June Walker, Peggy Wood and Mary Kennedy. It was here that I listened to Jascha Heifetz play on the piano what he laughingly called "Just a Japanese Sandwich," but most of the jokes were better than that. Occasionally there was a visiting celebrity such as H.G. Wells.

Helen Hayes was playing in the second Marc Connelly-George Kaufman hit *To The Ladies*, and it was from another big success of the season, the *Chauve Souris*, that the Neysa McMein Studio habitués, under the name of the "Algonquin Vicious Circle," devised a review of our own called *No Siree*. One of the numbers planned for this was a bit from my Dutch Treat show featuring Marc as Mona

Lisa, with me acting Dante or, perhaps, George Washington. George Kaufman was to write a sketch called "If Men Played Cards as Women Do," with George Heywood, F.P.A., and Alex Woollcott. Bob Sherwood was to have a musical number in straw hat and cane with a chorus including Tallulah Bankhead, Helen Hayes, and June Walker. Bob Benchley was supposed to get up some kind of a speech to be delivered in front of the curtain. We all rehearsed faithfully, mostly in Neysa's studio, and the only doubtful number seemed to be Bob's speech, which he, with characteristic modesty, was most reluctant to attempt. One night, in a taxi, he began jotting down some notes on the back of an envelope, and then read to me the opening of what he described as "a sort of treasurer's report." "Do you think that will be all right?" he asked. I encouragingly said I thought it would be all right. This was a bit of an understatement. When our *No Siree* was presented to a packed theater, Bob's "Treasurer's Report" stole the show; next year Irving Berlin used Bob and his speech as a feature of *The Music Box Review*, with tremendous success; when, six years later, the movies became "all talking," Bob's treasurer's talk immediately became the leading box-office hit for short subjects.

It was after the *No Siree* show that I said goodbye to Connie. The joke had turned out to be on me, not on the husband. In the course of the winter I had fallen so much in love with her that the fun had gone out of my life-saving venture, and as she couldn't see her way clear to give up her son and ask for a divorce, we agreed that when I sailed for France there would be no looking back. Clara and I booked passages on a small one-class French Line boat named (rather appropriately, considering my previous seafaring) the "Chicago"; John Dos Passos gave me a list of good cheap Parisian restaurants and the intriguing names of three or four wines, such as "burgundy"; there were a few farewell parties with my Algonquin and *Bookman* friends, and one hilarious one in the Village with Dos and Bunny Wilson ending with a midnight drive up Fifth Avenue in an open carriage. Then *voilà!* I was being rocked in the cradle of the vasty deep, waiting for the crossing of the ten-mile Prohibition limit and the legal opening of the bar.

It was a wonderful experience, that first-ever crossing. I shared what might be called a modest cabin with three other men; one of Clara's cabin-mates was Lucita Squiere, a pretty little bright-eyed girl who worked in Hollywood as Mary Pickford's secretary and who was on her way to join her husband Rhys Williams, a journalist in Moscow. I was very much interested in Hollywood and Mary Pickford, not at all in Moscow and Bolsheviks. There were other lovely girls on board, especially an enchanting young sculptress who had read *A Parody Outline of History*. Meals were thrilling, with free bottles of white and red wine on every table. *Vive la France!* I took my first saltwater baths and spoke my first Yale French – at least, my first with a real Frenchman.

The crossing took ten days, and then, at last, Paris. I wanted to thrill Catholic Clara, so I whispered to the taxi driver to stop at Notre Dame before we went to the hotel. He finally understood me, and when we stopped in front of the great cathedral I quietly and impressively announced to Clara, "that church is Notre Dame, mother." She wasn't gazing in the right direction, so I repeated, "Look, mother – Notre Dame!" And then, instead of paying any attention to the cathedral, she pointed gleefully to a nearby tree and said "There's an English sparrow – just like the ones in Columbus!"

Our month in Paris was perfect. There was much sightseeing, including a trip to Chartres with Clara and, of great significance to me, to Verdun and the battlefields with Edna Ferber and Alex Woollcott. Paris and Chartres had been an education in the history of the past; here, not far from the German border, was the site of the tragedies of my own times. Woollcott, as editor during the war of *Stars and Stripes*, was full of anecdotes and information; he was also much more "human" than when I had lunched with him surrounded by the Algonquin Round Table wits. Edna Ferber also was extremely helpful to me as a budding writer. The important emotional product of this battlefield tour was an overwhelming rejection of any remaining romanticism on the subject of war. Verdun was a desolate blasted heath. We visited the spot where a line of French *poilus* had been buried under the earth by the explosion of a German shell, with the tips of their bayonets still visible above the ground. We spent a night at a farmhouse which had been directly in the line of the German advance. When I awoke in the early morning and looked out over the hills and fields, now green and filled with blood red poppies, I was tremendously moved by the thought that behind those hills had been stationed batteries of enemy artillery. It all seemed desperately impossible to believe on such a beautiful June morning. War became the number-one enemy which I must fight with my gift for humor. I had been fooled, everyone had been fooled, by the bands and the flags and the cheers. I began to plan a book in which Donald Ogden Battleship would blast away at this evil.

But when I got back to Paris I had other work to finish first. Before leaving New York I had signed with Henry Sell, the editor of *Harpers Bazaar*, for a series of articles to make fun of the various Etiquette books which shared with H.G. Wells' *Outline of History* the top of the best seller lists. I postponed my savage satire on war, and aimed my typewriter at the safer target of High Society Etiquette. I also sat alone at the Deux Magots and the Rotonde, sipping a *demi* and watching French life pedal by on bicycles.

Neysa McMein arrived; we went to the opera with a handsome white-haired young editor of *The Masses* named Max Eastman. He had no interest in me or my humor; he was on his way to Russia. I was told of *Ulysses* by James Joyce, dutifully bought a copy at Sylvia Beach's bookshop, and became an enthusiastic reader, although I didn't understand large parts of it. The artist Harold van Doren and the writer John Mosher appeared out of my early Village days. They were on their way to Vienna where life was said to be incredibly inexpensive for an American with dollars. I decided to join them and devote myself singlemindedly to the writing of a Major Work. Paris was too distracting and too expensive.

Clara and I stopped at Munich on the way, without, of course, any particular interest in political happenings or any knowledge of the post-war events in which young Adolf Hitler was then playing a role. It was much cheaper than Paris, my German was much more effective than my French had been, the beer was better than even at Charlie Wirth's in Boston. I loved Germany. We journeyed to Oberammergau for the Passion Play which impressed us immensely; I remember wishing I had thought of that plot. Deems Taylor and Mary Kennedy joined us for our last week in Munich. He was then the music critic for the New York *World* and had come to interview Richard Strauss. I was sorry to see them return to America, but I was impatient to isolate myself in enforced creativity.

Vienna in 1922 seemed to have been much harder hit by the war than Munich. For a ridiculously low price Clara and Hal van Doren and I rented an apartment, complete with old family cook, from a sad-eyed young baroness whose husband had been killed in the war. We were in the nineteenth *bezirk*, far from the center of the city, and I at last settled down to work.

Nothing now stood between me and the creation of a masterpiece.

I took a deep breath, sharpened six pencils and happily confronted myself with reams of blank white paper. The happiness had its qualifications. I don't know about other writers but for me the process of getting started on a piece of writing is absolute agony, and it was particularly so in those early days when I had had no experience. I would write a few words, then get up and look out of the window. If I was lucky, some bit of Viennese daily life would give me the excuse to remain at the window under the pretext that I was observing life in Austria which I might use in some future novel or play. It went without saying that a writer should always be prepared to note life in all its manifestations, and the delivery of the milk by a fat man in short leather breeches was certainly worthy of careful observation. After the milkman had disappeared, however, I started obediently back to my blank white page, only to be diverted by a mirror on the wall which demanded that I examine the condition of my features. This examination took a bit longer than usual due to the fact that I had decided to grow my first (and last) beard, which seemed to be developing a reddish tinge. Right next to the mirror was a bookcase filled with German volumes, including a fascinating pictorial history of the war as seen from the Austrian viewpoint. This would often postpone any further facing of those sheets of paper on my desk until lunch time. But in spite of these obstacles I did manage to get started on a play. I also found time to be a tourist, to investigate the palaces and museums, to see Schiller played at the Burg Theater, and to fall in love with Maria Jeretza in *The Girl of the Golden West*, and particularly in *Der Rosenkavalier*. I took a week off to return alone to Munich for the Wagner Ring cycle at the opera house where I sat spellbound for hours each afternoon and evening, following the music as best I could in my pocket-size score.

Soon after my return to Vienna Clara and I and my dark red beard moved on to Budapest, partly because our lease had expired and partly because of the romantic mystery which attached itself to that city. Somehow it seemed incredible that we from Columbus, Ohio, should actually be living on the Danube, in the midst of people who spoke a completely incomprehensible language. Not that French hadn't been fairly incomprehensible, but in Paris there were Americans. Even in Vienna we had been visited by Edna Ferber and her mother, also by John Mosher and a friend of Connie's named Helen Porter who, incidentally, reported to my momentary dismay that Connie seemed to be successfully surviving my absence. But in

Budapest I hoped to be away from any human contacts, free from any excuse for talking to anyone but the characters in my play.

And, to a degree, I succeeded. Clara and I found a marvelous hotel on the Margaret Island in the Danube. It was situated in the midst of a most gorgeously flaming autumn forest, an hour from the city. What intrigued us (in addition to the absurdly low cost of everything in dollars) was a horsedrawn tram car which took us slowly and with dignity through the forest to the bridge where we could get the trolley car into Pest on the left bank or to Buda, with the palaces, on the right. Clara quickly made friends in a neutral language with chambermaids, waiters and guests, and we enjoyed a superb month. My writing progressed in spite of two temptations, to both of which I yielded with alacrity. On one of my trips to town in order to change a travelers check I had indulged, at a cost of forty-eight American cents, in a superb lunch at the Ritz, which with other hotels was preserving the spirit of gay old Budapest in spite of daily disastrous plunges in the currency. During lunch I was exposed for the first time to the marvels of a gypsy orchestra and a wine called Tokay, so that shortly thereafter I found myself, upon the advice of the Ritz door-man, in a rather luxurious bedroom at an address which I still happi-ly remember as the Kirali-palutza. As I was gazing a bit doubtfully at a large mirror which was situated in the ceiling above the bed (I couldn't remember having seen anything like that in Columbus), the door opened and a most bewitching red-haired Hungarian girl appeared.

The other tempting side path from the hard road of literary crea-tion was equally educational, although in a slightly different way. My tourist visits to the churches, museums, palaces and battlefields of Europe had aroused in me a fervor for historical knowledge, and I began to read the book which had given the title to my volume of parodies. Wells' *Outline of History* became my bible; as reviewers in-sist on saying, "I couldn't put it down." For the first time in my life I began to get a comprehensive picture of my world – a fascinating pic-ture into which I could fit my own search for a philosophy. The Answer which I had by sheer luck found in New York was writing, but apparently that was merely the first step, a reason for rejecting the struggle for financial success. That rejection had had an amazing and ironical result. I had given up success only to find it. I was living where I wanted, as I wanted, doing what I most desired. It was as though I had discovered a gold mine. I was free. But with that freedom came a growing sense of obligation. Once more, as at Exeter and at Yale, I became a dedicated man. But dedicated to what? Obligated to whom? This is where the *Outline of History* rushed in and supplied the answer. The selfish creation of more-or-less belles-lettres was not enough. I must take my place beside those writers who had helped people in their struggle for freedom, the history of which Wells had outlined from its origin right up to the disaster and betrayal of the Great War. I had been given a gift, I must not betray it.

I finished the second act of my play, and postponed any further writing until we could settle down somewhere. My mock-etiquette contributions to *Harpers Bazaar* and *Vanity Fair* were to be published by Doran under the title of *Perfect Behavior* with illustrations by Ralph Barton. In November of 1922 Clara and I decided to move South for the winter. Shortly after Mussolini had marched on Rome we traveled to Venice for a week of museums. Venice was cold and seemed to be uneasy. I knew nothing of Mussolini, but when I was confronted with small boys in black shirts, marching arrogantly as they sang "Giovinezza!", I groaned to Clara that it looked as though Youth could always be fooled by uniforms and flags. We had just come from the miserable cripples and beggars of Austria and Hungary – and here it was apparently starting all over again. We had an intensive whiz-through of a guide-book tour of Florence, Rome and Naples, and then one afternoon on the south shore of the island of Capri we discovered a small pension run by a white-bearded German named Weber with a gentle smiling Italian wife and two teen-age daughters. The sea was blue, the sun was warm, and the complete cost for each of us was fifty cents a day. "If it's all right with you . . ." I asked Clara. It was, as usual, very all right with Clara, and we moved in for the winter.

It was an ideal winter for a writer seeking seclusion. The only other boarder in the pension was Miss Lucy Flanagan, a middle-aged artist who had come to Capri fifteen years before from New England and never gone back. Old Herr Weber likewise had come to the island as a young "Wandervogel" and found it so much the land of his dreams that his wanderings came to a happy and immediate end. Clara went for confession each Sunday to the local priest, who was Signora Weber's brother. Clara's relations with the Catholic churches of Europe were triumphs of ecclesiastical diplomacy and understanding. She spoke no language other than her own, and considered herself old enough to make her own rules on certain nonsensical matters such as genuflecting and crossing herself. The Capri Fathers couldn't understand one word of her confession, but they must have figured that her sins weren't really very unabsolvable, and happy intercontinental smiles of blessing were exchanged. Most days the sun also blessed us, although once in a while a steady unrelenting sirocco would blow my nerves into wasted days of workless frustration, and I would climb the narrow paths through the vineyards up to the main square in the hope of finding an American tourist. I can't say that I was exactly lonely or homesick, but I was once almost brought to tears by hearing two Brooklyn voices arguing about the Giants and the Cubs.

From then until spring there was some loneliness and a great deal of work. I finished my play and decided to see if I could write a Joycean-type novel, using the same theme and characters as in my play. The theme was Youth, and embodied a rather sad lament for its gradual corruption and death. I was romantically glorifying my Senior year at Yale; the hero was Put who had (in the play) been compelled by illness to spend the first few years after graduation in a western sanatorium where, presumably, he was not exposed to the disillusioning process of war, Wall Street and marriage. He had remained "pure" – which indicates that six years after graduation I was still looking back to that enchanted out-of-this-world year in Skull and Bones. A Yale professor of English composition had once taught me: "Don't worry about style when you write. If you have anything sufficiently important to say, God will provide you with the style." I knew nothing about playwriting, but I did feel strongly about shedding tears over the loss of some of that arrogant defiance to the world which one felt at the age of twenty. The ideal of "Bright College Years" still held me.

But I was also beginning in Capri to develop another theme which led to the writing of my next book, *Aunt Polly's Story of Mankind*. The success of *Perfect Behavior* was all very good, but I felt that it was far short of the mark which I had set myself as a satirist. Clarence Day had called me a battleship, and *Perfect Behavior* was only good-humored popgun practice at an easy target. I wanted to declare war on something more important. H. G. Wells and Hendrik van Loon had clarified my vision, and one morning I woke up with a very exciting idea for another story of mankind. This one would be told to children by their Aunt Polly, a self-righteous matron who assumed that this was the best of all possible worlds and that history was merely the record of the happy evolution of all life toward the creation of herself and her circle. "For this happy product the amoeba had emerged from the primeval slime, cavemen had invented the wheel, Greece had fallen before the might of Rome, Christ had died, kingdoms had risen and fallen into dust." According to Aunt Polly, this was all part of God's wonderful plan, and as proof of His divine purpose we had only to contemplate her husband, the impeccable president of the First National Bank. The audience for this tale of historical progress were to be Aunt Polly's priggish ten-year-old David and the three children of her younger sister Susan. Sam, the oldest, would represent the questioning type of courageous liberal. His sister Mary could be the common-sense down-to-earth female, and the youngest, Genevieve, was to typify the "artist" as contrasted to Sam's scientifically oriented mind. Aunt Polly's son David was to be the "safe and sound" Calvin Coolidge normal American type. What appealed to me about this satire was that it might give me an opportunity of exposing the hypocrisies of the last war and the dangers to the next generation if they allowed themselves to be fooled by the patriotic self-righteousness and religious cant which had enveloped us in the war and the return to Normalcy. The young Italian lads in Capri were now drilling in black shirts; their fathers who protested were being silenced with beatings and the "castor-oil treatment." Fascism meant nothing to me but I didn't like to see these young kids starting the whole horrible business all over again. So I laid aside the few pages of my novel and set to work to contribute my bit to the "it must never happen again" chorus.

By this time, however, it was spring of 1923. Clara and I had had about enough of separation from people who spoke our language, even in such an ideal spot as Capri. Clara wanted to see something of England before returning to America, I wanted more of Paris. So she stayed at the pension while I had my Parisian fling.

It was a perfect fling. On my first night there I found myself occupying Ernest Hemingway's lodgings. John Peale Bishop had suggested, in a letter to Capri, that I do two things:
(a) read a new poem by T. S. Eliot called *The Waste Land,* and
(b) look up an interesting young writer in Paris named Hemingway.
I had got a copy of the Eliot poem and found it fascinatingly expressive of my own feelings at the time. I have never felt at home

with much poetry, but this one seemed (as had *Ulysses*) to strike some deep-lying bell within me in spite of my inability to understand the difference between it and most other poetry. I could only say that *The Waste Land* seemed to have been written for me, and I felt extremely grateful to John Bishop for having sent it my way.

I was even more grateful to him for Hemingway. On my first night in Paris he happened to be at Mme. Lecomte's, the restaurant on the Ile St. Louis which John Dos Passos had told me about, and I liked him immediately. I didn't know anything about him as a writer, but he seemed to be my kind of a guy, which meant, among other things, that he liked good food and lots to drink and he understood my kind of humor. He was going to take an early morning train for Switzerland where his wife and baby son were staying, but we got on so well that he insisted, with characteristic enthusiasm, that I occupy his rooms until he brought them back. I was to learn later that when Ernest was enthusiastic about something it was extremely dangerous to resist anything, especially friendliness, and I woke up the next morning in his room, very happy, with a note from him telling me where I could get eggs and milk.

That happiness grew during a glorious month of May. I was no longer a tourist poking around Paris with a guidebook. When Hemingway's wife Hadley and son "Bumby" came back I moved to the Venetia, a small hotel at 159 Boulevard Montparnasse which had been recommended because Edna St. Vincent Millay stayed there. Elmer Rice must also have been one of the guests, for years later, when the curtain rose on a play of his about Paris, I cried out, "That's my room." The walls were a horrible dark green, the window curtains heavy red velvet. There was a huge clothes cupboard (no coathangers) and a beside lamp which didn't function. I loved it. I was living in Paris, on the Left Bank. John Dos Passos was in town. So was Gilbert Seldes, editor of the *Dial,* who was writing his *Seven Lively Arts.* Every day was full of excitement. Just to walk the streets, to take a bus, to sit at a sidewalk cafe was a joyful experience. I loved everything, even the underground smell of the *Metro.* Through Gilbert Seldes, who was an "intellectual," I met "modern" writers like Tristan Tzara of the Dada movement, the poet Drieu de la Rochelle, the composer Milhaud. My French was hopelessly inadequate, I didn't understand anything very well, but I felt that I was part of a creative ferment. Gilbert kindly encouraged this by trying to explain my "crazy humor" to Tzara as the American equivalent of Dada. Milhaud, as one of the *Group des Six,* was enthusiastic about "le jazz," and I certainly knew about that. I had danced to it from the very beginning. I began to see America through the eyes of Europe. Our skyscrapers! Our hot trombones! Our throbbing mechanization! And I was part of it: a Columbus Ohio representative of the breaking down of old forms, the creation of new exciting rhythms. I shall never forget the ecstatic moments of my first introduction to the Diaghilev ballets of Stravinsky's *Sacre du Printemps* and *Les Noces.* There were the rival ballets of a Swedish company, with music by the *Group des Six,* decors by abstract modernistic painters, and a wonderfully crazy satirical number by Jean Cocteau called *Les Mariées de la Tour Eiffel.*

For my introduction to much of this I was indebted to an American a few years older than I who had been living in Paris since his graduation from Yale, or at least since he had decided, as I had, that the business life was not for him. His name was Gerald Murphy, and he was intelligent, perceptive, gracious, and one of the most attractive men I have ever known. His wife Sara was the perfect complement to these virtues. If this sounds like a child's table beginning "Once upon a time there was a prince and a princess...", that's exactly how a description of the Murphys should begin. They were both rich; he was handsome, she was beautiful; they had three golden children. They loved each other, they enjoyed their own company, and they had the gift of making life enchantingly pleasurable for those who were fortunate enough to be their friends. That they included me in this circle was one of the blessings of that month in Paris – and of many years thereafter. It was as though I had found at last that elite of the cultured rich of which I had dreamed in the days of my college ambitions for "success." But now it was a wealthy elite outside of the struggle for power. If Gerald had any ambition, it was to be an artist; but his primary concern was to live as he and Sara wanted to live, and their money gave them the opportunity. They had an apartment overlooking the Seine near the Place St. Michel. When they entertained at home their guests might include Picasso or Leger, Cole Porter or Douglas Fairbanks, or some struggling young artist they happened to like. They gave a party for the entire corps of the Diaghilev ballet, and rented a Seine river steamer one evening for another of their galas. With Sara and Gerald I came closest to enjoying what might be termed "gracious living." It was a closed circle, it was privileged, but within those narrow limits it was immensely stimulating and I treasure the memory of those two rare spirits as one of the most blessed experiences in my life.

In June the first Parisian idyll ended. Clara came up from Capri and we met in London; we found a small Bloomsbury hotel as a basis for sight seeing and had ten days of it, interspersed with an occasional dinner with Marc Connelly and his mother. Sinclair Lewis enlivened – or, for my taste, over-enlivened – one or two parties. (A life-of-the-party always resents a louder ditto and "Red" in those days was certainly louder and *not* funnier.) Full of Murphy-Paris and my exciting vision of a Stravinsky-Picasso-Joyce-surge toward a new creative rhythm, I found the Tower of London a bit uninteresting, and at Oxford I became very depressed by the imprisoning influence of ancient ivy-covered walls. "How can a young spirit avoid sinking beneath the weight of all this old Beauty?" I groaned, and there were no Murphys or Gilbert Seldes in London to introduce me to any answers. Clara and I sailed for Halifax on a cabin-class Cunarder. Clara wanted to go back to Columbus to tell them about Europe, and I wanted to resume work on *Aunt Polly's Story of Mankind*.

12

I hadn't done a stroke of work since Capri, and as Gene Saxton of Doran's wanted the manuscript for fall publication, he wisely suggested that I stay away from the Algonquin circle etc. until the book was finished. He managed to get me enrolled in the MacDowell Colony, which was a great break for me since it had a reputation as the best place for an artist who wanted to work without any distractions.

The reputation was absolutely justified. I found myself on a large estate in New Hampshire spending the entire day alone in a small cabin with nothing between me and madness but my typewriter and those blank sheets of paper. At noon my lunch would be left on the doorstep. I would try to talk to the local girl who performed this service, but the rules of the Colony were very strict. There was not a damned thing one could do but watch spiders making webs or listen to birds in the tall surrounding pines. At night, however, we all had dinner together and that was fun. Among the other prisoners of creation were Elinor Wylie, William Rose Benet, Mary and Padraic Colum, Alfred and Dorothy Kreymbourg, Douglas Moore, Edward Arlington Robinson and Maxwell Bodenheim. One night Max and I stole away to town because we had heard there was to be a dance. Max, who had picked up a pint of bootleg liquor, was not exactly the Yale Skull and Bones type of drinker, and when he passed out cold at the dance hall I took it upon my shoulders to get him back to the Colony, which was a walk of some two or three miles. I had never carried a poet on my shoulders, and half-way there Max woke up, wanted to go back to the dance, and swung a couple at my jaw.

Finally he passed out again, and I managed to carry him back without being caught. But he never forgave me for having helped him.

That was the only real night off I had, and I was able to finish the manuscript before Doran's deadline. I had worked and thought about it almost continuously from early morning until night for two months. I felt that I had achieved what I set out to do. I had no doubt as to the greatness of my product and was satisfied that when it appeared America would recognize a major work by a new satirist who had dared to attack many sacred cows which Mark Twain had somehow overlooked.

There was a certain justification for my enthusiastic belief in my work. The original idea, conceived in Capri, had involved Aunt Polly's glorification of her own social group as proof of the triumphant historical progress of mankind. I was aiming to deride the belief that the existence of the United States in 1923 justified God's ways to Man – a belief which was considered a reasonable assumption for any patriotic American. But as Aunt Polly's optimistic tale reached the period of Hellenic greatness I got the idea of enlarging her theme by having the dear old lady organize her son's school-mates into a band of Spartan Scouts, with a veteran from the local American Legion to make proper little soldiers out of them. Then, after Aunt Polly has graciously explained the birth of Christ, the scouts become Christian Soldiers and are given the blessing of organized religion by the kindly clergyman of Aunt Polly's church. The next problem for the Christian scouts is, of course, guns, and these are purchased by Uncle Frederick's bright little son David with a loan from his father. David then sells the guns to the scouts at a slight profit for himself, an operation which proves so successful that he organizes a rival troop of Christian soldiers in the other fifth grade at the school and supplies them with guns on the same profitable terms. Aunt Polly gives birth to the inspired idea of a pageant for Armistice Day – a pageant depicting the Progress of Mankind, in which the two little "armies" would have a competitive drill in front of various dignitaries representing the Spirit of Christianity, the Spirit of Big Business, of Finance etc.

The only opposition comes from little Samuel, the son of Aunt Polly's sister Susan, who stubbornly refuses to be a Christian soldier. He gets together with a Jewish boy and a Negro boy who had not been invited to join the Scouts and they print a newspaper which isn't exactly complimentary to the patriotic project. As the day of the competition draws closer, the two "outsiders" are subjected to increasing pressures to force them to desert Samuel. The Jewish boy is offered a bribe, the Negro is threatened with warning notes signed by "Patriotic Citizens." Samuel unwisely prints all these facts in his paper, with the result that a gang of patriotic Christian soldiers in white sheets raids the newspaper office, beats Samuel up, and smashes his printing press to bits. Armistice Day begins properly enough with a church service attended by all Scouts, and an impressive sermon by Aunt Polly's clergyman, who proves that the sword of Christ had been wielded exclusively on the side of the victorious Allies. Aunt Polly follows this up at home with the last chapter of her story, which proves that the American Revolution was the only right kind of revolution because Americans are now living under the only right kind of government. "And so," she concludes, "the world was getting better and better, and the Christian nations found themselves occupying more and more territory in the interests of their religion and people were becoming happier and happier, until for no reason at all Germany brought on the Great War. But we have won that and the Treaty of Versailles has been drawn up by statesmen who were broad-minded enough to forget their country's ambitions and so they made a peace which guarantees that there will never again be any war. And we who live nice happy comfortable lives in these nice happy comfortable surroundings should be very grateful at that happy ending to my story." Then it is time for Aunt Polly's pageant, which takes place on the grounds of the Country Club. Aunt Polly, as the "Spirit of History," is dressed in a beautiful long white robe and carries a torch which she passes on to various "Ages" until "The Glorious Present" and "Mankind," aided by "Peace" and "Christianity," are to take up the torch and hold it high while Aunt Polly asks the audience to sing the "Star Spangled Banner." But unfortunately, just before this occurs, a fight breaks out among the Christian scouts at the rear of the stage, and soon all the boys are kicking and punching and scratching each other and Aunt Polly's pageant ends in disaster for all the little soldiers – except David. David had slipped away when the fight started, and that night when Aunt Polly and Uncle Frederick see a light in his room they tiptoe softly to his door and there they see their little son, sitting up in his bed, counting one by one the shiny fifty-cent pieces which he had got by selling guns to his classmates, "and as he counted, the little boy was smiling happily to himself and humming softly 'Onward Christian Soldiers.' "

The completion of this satire was, to my mind, a fulfillment of my obligation as a humorist to be a gadfly rather than a comforter. There was a great bitterness in my generation about the war and I felt it my duty to reflect that as fiercely and as deeply as possible. I awaited publication of the book in the certainty that it would explode like a bombshell and incidentally elevate me to a leading position among American writers, perhaps even among world writers. I remember asking Gene Saxton, at my publisher's offices, if it would not be a good idea to notify the Nobel Committee of the book as a competition for the Peace Prize. Gene advised, patiently and without sarcasm, that we wait until publication, and I somewhat reluctantly consented. What he didn't tell me was that George Doran had not wanted to publish the book at all, as it was almost certain to offend those who were looking for more *Perfect Behavior* pleasant humor, but had been persuaded that they more or less owed it to me since my first two books had done so well.

The period of waiting for my bomb to burst was an exciting one. Bob Benchley, Marc Connelly and I spent a weekend with Bob's family on the island of Siasconset off Cape Cod where we put on a show for some local benefit. Bob did the "Treasurers Report," Marc had a very funny burlesque of Ruth Draper, and I devised a lecture on birds called "Our Feathered Friends" in which I imitated and interpreted the call of "The American pippit, or titlark" and others. Bob, incidentally, had an interesting complex about birds. He was certain that they disliked him, so, being no fool, he disliked them. He was full of examples of their deliberately going out of their way to fly close to his head in order to frighten him. He got back at them whenever he could. Once while shaving (that is, while Bob was shaving) a bird landed on the bathroom window without being aware that he was within. Bob carefully crawled on the floor up to the window and suddenly yelled "Boo!" at the bird. He also developed the theory that, since we know nothing about the working of a bird's brain, it was highly possible that the song of a meadowlark might be a cry of pain, perhaps from a severe headache. This idea delighted him.

In the fall the Swedish Ballet, about which I had been so enthusiastic in Paris, came to New York, and I found that my enthusiasm for modern ballet was shared by practically nobody with the exception of Edmund Wilson, Gilbert Seldes and a few others of us "avant garde." The show was a terrible flop. Broadway was not Paris, and the ballet company was discouragedly facing even greater failure in their engagements in Philadelphia and other American cities. Wilson got the idea that it might help if I were to come in front of the curtain and explain (with humor) what the various ballets were supposed to be about. One excuse for this was the tremendous success which Bob Benchley was having every night with his "Treasurers Report" in front of the curtain of the Music Box Revue, and as the management were desperate they agreed to let me try it out in Philadelphia. Over the years a great many large eggs have been laid on Philadelphia stages, but mine must be reckoned as an achievement worthy of its heritage. Having seen Bob get screams of laughter by impersonating a nervous Treasurer, I figured that if I was twice as nervous I would get even more laughs. On the opening night I gave a beautiful performance. I completely lost myself in the part of a nervous man. I also completely lost the audience, who were not able to perceive that I was merely acting my nervousness, which, by that time, I wasn't. To the relief of all concerned I abandoned my attempt to explain Swedish ballet to the backward Philadelphians and returned to New York with increased respect for Benchley, and with the firm decision that I was a serious writer, not a comedian. The next step in my profession, therefore, was to finish the novel which I had begun in Capri. Deems and Mary Taylor had just acquired a small, very rundown farmhouse near Stamford, which they were eventually going to equip with proper heating and lighting facilities so that they would have a livable place for the summer. "Just what I'm looking for!" I exclaimed. "A place where I can work – where I will *have* to work because there won't be anything else to do." Their reply was very forthright. "You're crazy," they said. "There is no electricity, no heat, no telephone. It's ten miles from the Stamford station, and we have no automobile." "Exactly right!" I cried confidently. "When can I go out there?" I was possessed with the conviction that I needed absolute solitude in order to fulfill my destiny as a writer. It was for this that I had gone to Budapest, Capri and the MacDowell Colony. The next stop was obviously a lonely farmhouse where I would be driven into creation. So in the middle of October I had my wish. A friend of Deems named Antoinette Perry had lent me an old Ford station wagon, and Deems had given me driving lessons so that I could at least start and stop it. I bought wood, kerosene lamps, oatmeal, condensed milk, coffee and cans of everything. I even got a mouse trap. I unpacked my edition of *Ulysses*, my Picasso prints, a box of pencils and reams of blank paper. I had all that a serious writer could ask for.

And nothing happened. The novel didn't go ahead, and I didn't know what to do about it. Perhaps the original impulse, my despair at the tragic loss of the glorious reckless defiance of the world, was beginning to die down. It didn't occur to me that I might not be a novelist and, strangest of all, it didn't occur to me to study the craft of a writer or to ask questions of others. Perhaps because of the easy success of my first two books I thought that all I had to do was to get alone by myself and wait for God to fill those blank pages.

In every writer's life there are, of course, those happy moments when what I call the ouija-board begins to move and he finds his characters beginning to say and do things which he had not anticipated. That had happened at Capri – at least when writing my play – but it didn't in Deems' farmhouse, and I began to find excuses for driving the Ford around the countryside. I discovered to my delight that Peggy Wood was living on a nearby farm with her husband, the vigorous young Chicago poet John V.A. Weaver, one of my Coffee House companions. An even more profitable discovery in nearby Mt. Kisco was Philip Barry, whom I had not seen since he had competed for the Yale *News*. Since that time he had studied drama under Professor George Baker (at Harvard), his first play, *The Youngest*, had been a success in the preceding season on Broadway and he had married a wonderful Mt. Kisco girl named Ellen Semple. Phil gave me much needed encouragement about the play I had written in Capri but my wavering enthusiasm for the possibility of enticing a novel out of the solitude of an isolated farmhouse came to a merciful end one night when I awoke with a yell of pain to discover that I had been bitten on the nose by a rat. He (or she) must have been very hungry, but whatever loss of dignity I felt was somewhat assuaged by the fact that I now had an excuse to postpone my noble experiment for a while. I fled eagerly to the un-Thoreaulike atmosphere of the Yale Club, Jimmy and Eddie's, and a couple of pink ones with Bob Benchley.

But the indignity inflicted by a rat was as nothing compared to what I suffered when *Aunt Polly* was published. My bombshell exploded with a faint "pop" which was not heard even in the offices of the literary critics, let alone 'round the world. I had expected the loud denunciation of outraged patriotic and religious societies. I was firmly prepared for social ostracism and certainly expected to be put on the Index by an indignant Pope. Remembering Tom Paine, I was ready for the mobs with their tar and feathers. What the bewildered satirist of 1923 received was a resounding silence. The few reviews which the book did get were what might be termed "mild," and, to my astonishment, the publications which I had counted on most for enthusiastic cheers, such as the *New Republic* and the *Nation*, disregarded my satire completely. The only indignation I aroused seemed to be among the booksellers who had been let down by a best-selling humorist. I later learned that they had been cautioned not to recommend the book, possibly so as not to offend my fans with my unexpected vitriol, but whatever the reason, the publication was a dismal flop.

Although I wasn't conscious of it at the time, this was a rather crucial disaster. It is fruitless, of course, to speculate on what might have been my subsequent career if *Aunt Polly* had been a great success, or at least had been acclaimed by one or two important critics as a distinguished contribution to American satire. I felt that it deserved it. I still do. But even if it had been enthusiastically welcomed, the role of Chief American Gadfly was one for which I was singularly unfitted both by nature and education. I was a rather timid middle-class conformist who hated fights and wanted desperately to be well-liked. It might still have been possible for a man of that nature to write bitter satire out of the unconscious conflicts within himself, for, as I have said, who can tell what really directs that ouija-board when it starts moving the pen across the blank page? One trouble with *Aunt Polly*, however – and with me – was that because of the Russian Revolution the real problems of the Capitalist world had profoundly changed and in 1923 I did not understand or reflect that change. My mockery of the illusions and hypocrisies of religious belief, although no doubt shocking to many Americans, was slightly off the target. I thought that I was being daringly iconoclastic, and I was merely being in the wrong century. I was closer to the target in my derision of the holy "patriotism" of Big Business and Finance, and I was dead-on in my cry against profiteering from the Crucifixion of Youth in war. But that was as far as I could go. I was a Humanist and a Liberal, with no clue as to any possible next step, either evolutionary or revolutionary. *Aunt Polly* was a good try, but as a satirist I had a great deal to learn. And nothing in my past or present life gave me any key. It was a crisis in my growth toward maturity – a crisis which was resolved by the diversions of my gifts into "crazy humor" and a retreat in my life toward the happy irresponsible playtime of childhood.

The failure, actually, wasn't particularly depressing. My friends liked it. Bob Benchley and Deems Taylor thought it was very good. Dorothy Parker was particularly encouraging. That, incidentally, was one of Dorothy's great gifts. She always made you feel that she was on your side, especially against critics. And if you had a hangover, Dotty always pretended to have a worse one. Somebody in New York gave a lecture on "Donald Ogden Stewart and Aristophanes" and I carried the newspaper clipping of that announcement in my purse for years. I almost got around to reading Aristophanes.

The impulse toward "crazy humor" was encouraged by the success of a skit which Bob Benchley, Marc Connelly and I did for the annual dinner of the Authors' League, which had been written for us by Ring Lardner, and was called "I, Gaspiri (The Upholsters)." Act I was "A public street in a bathroom" and among the directions were "A man named Newburn comes out of the faucet which has been left running. He exits through the exhaust. Three outsiders named Klein go across the stage three times. They think they are in a public library." Bob played a mandolin while we conversed deadpan in sentences which had no relation to each other or to anything else. The only bit I remember was:

Me: I know a girl who was born out of wedlock.

Bob: That's a might pretty country around there.

Once or twice a week I would drop into the Music Box to hear Bob do his "Treasurers Report." Once, after the performance, Irving Berlin came with us up to Dorothy's apartment where we celebrated my twenty-ninth birthday and with the aid of champagne helped Irving write the last two lines of a new song called "What'll I Do?"

Then at Christmas I went back to Columbus, and after a happy family reunion I decided to stay there and make one more attempt to get on with my novel. Clara was living at a rooming house on Town Street and I rented a bed-sitter in an alley near the Carnegie Library. Columbus somehow seemed much smaller than I remembered it, and there's something upsetting about returning to one's home town as more or less of a celebrity. I had the unpleasant feeling of being constantly under suspicion of having a swelled head, which meant I had to play the false role of being the "same old Don." Columbus wasn't in the least interested in the artistic ferment of Greenwich Village and Paris and I had one horrible evening as guest of honor of a Literary Club where I discovered that the average age was sixty-five and the favorite author Dickens. Edna St. Vincent Millay gave a much more successful lecture at the Deshler Hotel and we had a wonderful get-together afterwards. I was beginning to get pretty homesick for the Algonquin and for the Murphys in Paris. One of Irving Berlin's Music Box Revues came to the Hartmann, and I happily discovered that in spite of speaking French and having met Cocteau and Picasso I *was* still pretty much the "old Don." Al Jolson was the star, and there was the "A Pretty Girl Is Like A Melody" number, and I went to every performance. "Let's face it," I whispered to myself. "This is your dish." And I began to suspect as a corollary that I was being quite phony about modern art and modern music which I didn't really understand at all, any more than I understood the Swedish Ballet, the expressionistic theater or surrealist poetry. The interesting thing about this is that I still felt no obligation to find out what the new modern techniques were trying to do. I suppose I must have had a belief in myself as a sort of Delphic oracle who would only be inspired to give voice to the divine answers if the processes of intoxication, hallucination and divination were not investigated or interfered with. As "interference" covered practically all of the techniques by which I might eventually have learned the craft of writing, it seems now to have been a particularly unintelligent way for an ambitious oracle to act. Anyway, the solitudes of Columbus didn't seem to be any more inspiring to the oracle than had been the lonely farm in Connecticut. So, in early April of 1924, I gave up the fight temporarily and fled to Paris with Phil and Ellen Barry.

13

My God, it was good to be back in Paris. The Barrys went down to their villa in Cannes, but the Murphys welcomed me with their matchlessly open arms. Ernest and Hadley Hemingway's open arms weren't so bad either, and Madame the proprietor of the Hotel Venetia gave me a big kiss and my old room. The only cloud on my horizon was a financial one, since *Aunt Polly* had sold very few copies and I had got out of the habit (and desire) of writing short humorous pieces for magazines. I rather hesitantly showed Ernest my attempts at a novel and to my delight he said that he wanted to publish some of it in a magazine called the *trans-atlantic* which he was publishing with Ford Madox Ford. I was really happy that Ernest approved of it, but *trans-atlantic* didn't pay any money to its contributors – or at least they didn't offer any to me. Ernest and Ford did, however, set me up to a gay wine-filled luncheon, after which we saw Ford off on his train for London and embarrassed him unspeakably with our boisterous American farewell at the station.

Perhaps it was Paris, or possibly it was Ernest's encouragement, but shortly after that there came to me, seemingly from nowhere, an idea, a concept, an I-don't-know-what. I had promised to give Gene Saxton a new humorous book for the Doran fall list, and one morning at the Venetia I began to experiment with the sort of crazy humor which seemed, for whatever reason, natural to me. I had first begun to get laughs with nonsensical non sequitur shortly after college, usually with the help of alcohol. When I got to New York I found several other practitioners of the art who, in short humorous pieces and on the musical comedy stage, could be said to be carrying on the crazy torch. And there had been Ring Lardner's "I, Gaspiri." But as far as I knew, no one – at least recently – had written a whole book in the nonsense idiom. Without having any idea of where it would lead me, I started out with a Columbus Ohio family on their way to Europe, and decided on a tentative title: *Mr. and Mrs. Haddock Abroad.* Mr. Haddock was a business man and this was the first trip to Europe for him, his common-sense wife Hattie, and their little daughter Mildred. They looked like what might be called an ordinary representative American family. The world about them, however, turned out to be far from ordinary, nor was it representative of anything except their lively imaginations.

The trip with the Haddocks became, in a way, a journey into the American Middle-West subconscious, or at least into the daydream region where one hopes that life is more romantically surprising than it is in the lumber business in Columbus. For example, when the Haddocks get to New York, and Mr. Haddock wishes to inquire about hotel accommodations, he finds himself speaking to a white-clad street cleaner who is plying his trade on Vanderbilt Avenue outside the Yale Club.

"Excuse me, sir," began Mr. Haddock. "My name is Haddock; and this is Mrs. Haddock and my daughter Mildred."

"How do you do?" said the Street Cleaner, removing his white hat and one white glove and bowing politely. "Not the Boston Haddocks?"

"No," said Mr. Haddock. "We're from the Middle West."

"Ah yes," said the Street Cleaner. "I see." And the tone of his voice became somewhat more reserved.

"My grandfather came from Boston, though," asserted Mrs. Haddock proudly.

"Of course," said Mr. Perkins, for that was the Street Cleaner's name. "Of course. And this is your first visit to our city, Mr. Haddock?"

"No indeed" said Mr. Haddock quickly. "I have been here twice before – once for three days and once for two."

"Charming place, don't you think?" said Mr. Perkins. "But probably you don't like it – most strangers don't at first. Mrs. Perkins and I are very fond of New York – and it's really the best summer resort in America, too. Are you here for long, Mr. Haddock?"

"We sail for Europe tomorrow" said Mr. Haddock.

"Ah yes," said Mr. Perkins. "On the Aquitania?"

"No" said Mr. Haddock, after an embarrassing pause.

"We couldn't get passage on the Aquitania," added Mrs. Haddock quickly.

"I see," said Mr. Perkins, stroking his mustache with a slight smile. "Well, well – I certainly envy you the trip. Paris, I suppose?"

"Yes" said Mr. Haddock.

"Ah – Paris, Paris" said Mr. Perkins, and leaning on his broom handle he smiled reflectively. "I suppose Berry Wall and the Princesse de Lorme are still holding forth at Longchamps. You *must* go to Longchamps for the races."

"Are you fond of horses?" asked Mrs. Haddock sympathetically.

"I detest horses" said Mr. Perkins with a sudden convulsive grasp of his broom handle.

"Oh" said Mrs. Haddock, biting her lip. "I'm so sorry. I forgot."

I think it took me slightly under a month to write *The Haddocks.* From the very first page the story raced happily along. I didn't have any idea at the beginning of a day what the Haddocks were going to do next, and I enjoyed myself immensely. Every evening I would take the day's pages over to the Murphys' apartment and after dinner would read to them. I can still hear Sara's marvelously raucous laughter. Sometimes my audience would include the Hemingways, or John Dos Passos, or Gilbert Seldes, or Archibald MacLeish who, after graduating with top honors at the Harvard Law School, had abandoned a potentially brilliant law career in order to write poetry. *The Haddocks* required a rather special audience who could follow Will, Hattie and Mildred into cloud-cuckoo land, and when I proudly submitted the finished book to Doran there was not the universal shout of joy which my evenings with the select circle at the Murphys had led me to expect. But Gene Saxton once more came to my rescue, as he had with *Aunt Polly,* and I looked eagerly forward to my fourth published book in four years.

The oracle had recovered its tongue, and I felt that in crazy humor I had found my individual medium of expression. No need for me to study the craft of novel or play writing. This was my particular genius, and I would await further developments. In *The Haddocks* I had abandoned any pretense of despair, of anger, of political criticism; there was no longer a young man searching for an answer. *The Haddocks* was a gentle frolic aimed at promoting laughter, and the friendly satire was directed only at certain lovable American traits and laughable customs. It was as though in *Aunt Polly* I had fired all my guns and exhausted my ammunition. The dedicated battleship had been dismantled and made ready for a series of pleasure cruises.

Paris in June of 1924 was a very good embarkation point. There was continuous pleasure, starting with the exciting ballets promoted by Comte Etienne de Beaumont, with extraordinary decors painted by Picasso, Leger, et al. Music was by Stravinsky and the *Group des Six*, with new Cocteau creations like *Les Biches* and *Le Train Bleu*. Gerald Murphy and Cole Porter contributed one ballet on an American theme. Gilbert Seldes contributed an off-stage wedding and we drove *a la Française* in a horse-drawn bus through the streets of Paris to celebrate his marriage to Alice Hall. There were dancing nights at Zelli's in Montmartre where being a guest of the Murphys entitled on to "the royal box." Joe Zelli's night club was by far the most exciting in those days and had the best jazz band and the prettiest girls.

In July Dos Passos and I went down to Pamplona for the fiesta of San Firmin. Ernest and Hadley Hemingway had gone the year before, come back full of enthusiasm and arranged for the party. This, incidentally, wasn't the one that Ernest wrote about in *The Sun Also Rises;* that was to come the next year. Besides Dos and myself on this first occasion there were his Paris friends William and Sally Bird, Robert McAlmon and Bill Smith. We all stayed at a hotel on the main square. Pamplona had not yet become popular for tourists, and we were, as far as I can remember, the only foreigners in town.

Ernest was terribly concerned about bullfighting and I was equally concerned about not letting Ernest down in his opinion of me. I liked him tremendously and after I had heard him sound off on people who didn't care for bullfighting I wouldn't have wanted to criticize the sport. Ernest was somebody you went along with, or else. In this around-the-clock wine-drinking, street dancing gaiety I discovered that I liked bullfighting almost as much as Ernest did. I didn't care for the cruelty to the horses, but when Ernest explained to me the technical necessity for this second stage in the ritual I accepted it as part of the dramatic ballet of courage and grace, which came to engross and fascinate me. I also acquired two other bits of more or less useful information, one being that on entering the ring the bull instinctively seeks a "corner" which he can call his own and from which he can be tempted to his death only with great difficulty, a tactic of self-preservation which I have found exceedingly effective at literary and other cocktail parties. The other helpful morsel of tauromachy was that a *cow* cannot be used as the victim, for the simple reason that she can only be fooled into charging the cape once; the next time it is waved at her, she charges at the man.

So I went happily through the fiesta, excited, drunk, hot, hungover, enjoying the warm friendship, worshipping Ernest's bullfighter hero Maera, dancing enthusiastic solos in the square, drinking even more enthusiastically from the hospitable native wineskin.

The only time I was uncomfortable was in the early morning when Spanish ideals of courage required that the young men run through the streets ahead of the bulls. I still associate the hot smell of the Spanish wood used in the street barriers with a feeling of panic in my stomach. Until the very last day I avoided facing Ernest's challenge to go down into the ring in the morning when the Pamplonian youth perform as amateur *toreros* against three or four non-lethal small bulls whose horns are padded so as to prevent any serious accidents. They didn't look small or non-lethal to me and I wandered miserably around the edge of the arena hoping that Ernest would be too triumphantly occupied with his own fearlessness to notice my abstention. Dos had the excuse of his extreme nearsightedness, but even he ventured into the ring and there was one tense moment when he leaped back into what he thought was the safety of the barriers without being aware that the bull had also made the same leap. Two Pamplonians rescued him just in time, but in avoiding the bull I had jumped into the arena and was quietly tiptoeing along the sand minding my own business when two Spaniards spied me and noisily extended to me the warm hand of Pamplonian friendship. To my horror I realized that these hospitable hands contained a large red cloak, and that they were trying to assure me that a visiting Americano was permitted to give proof of his own country's bravery. I started modestly to decline the honor, but a crowd of happy Spaniards quickly gathered, all apparently determined to show me that they had no hard feelings against the country which had taken Cuba and the Philippines away from them in the 1898 war. I found myself standing alone in the midst of an audience of thousands with the bull glaring at me from a distance of six feet. I gulped, grinned, and raised the red cape in front of my body in what I thought to be the proper gesture. The movement attracted the bull's attention, and he started toward me. I quickly moved the cape into position number two – outside my right leg. Unfortunately that should have been position number one. The bull did not swerve as I had expected, and I was hit full force. My glasses flew in one direction, the cape in another, and I was tossed into the air amid a great gleeful shout from the spectators. When I hit the ground, however, an amazing thing happened. I lost my fear completely. And not only that – I got mad. I grabbed the cape and started to chase my enemy. When I got to him I held the cape, once more in front of me, yelling "Come on, you stupid son-of-a-bitch!" The bull may have been a S.O.B., but he wasn't as stupid as I was; when he started toward me and I persisted in moving the cape to the right, he again tossed me triumphantly in the air and galloped away. I picked myself up, beaming with delight. I was triumphant too. I had been hit by a bull, and it was nothing. I was right back on the football field at Exeter. I had shown that I could take it. Ernest clapped me on the back, and I felt as though I had scored a winning touchdown. After we left the arena I discovered that a couple of my ribs had been fractured, but that couldn't spoil the last frenzied night of drinking and dancing. It had been a memorable week, a male festival, a glorified college reunion.

Then came the quiet and peace of the French Riviera. The Murphys were at Cap d'Antibes where they had persuaded the proprietor of the Hotel du Cap that this winter resort might possibly be attractive to summer visitors. None of the other communities along the Riviera had considered this revolutionary possibility, and when Dos and I arrived we found Gerald, Sara and Co. installed at the hotel in solitary grandeur. In a way, there was a reason for this tradition that the Riviera was suitable only for winter vacationists. The summer climate was treacherous for the unsuspecting new-comer, and the first week or so was apt to be spent in getting over a disagreeable diarrhoetic complaint known as the *mal du midi.* But once that had been conquered, life was sheer paradise. There was as yet no elegant Eden Roc restaurant or swimming pool but the Murphys had discovered a small private beach in the vicinity, and I settled down to the engrossing occupation of acquiring a bronzed body and an appetite for superb meals on the hotel porch. This was varied with visits to Phil and Ellen Barry at their Cannes villa, where my typescript of the *Haddocks* was welcomed with cheering laughter. Sun, blue sea and not a cloud in the sky. There were even copies of Ernest's *trans-atlantic* on sale in a Nice bookshop with "Work in Progress by Donald Ogden Stewart" advertised on the cover. Other "works in progress or to appear" were by Joseph Conrad, Ford M. Ford and Jean Cocteau. It was very encouraging.

But when I got back to New York my work in progress didn't progress. Bob Benchley had decided not to go out to Scarsdale during the week, so he and I, after buying our customary fall derbies at Brooks Bros., took a small two-room-with-bath at the newly opened Shelton Hotel on Lexington Avenue. *The Haddocks Abroad* was published, and well received, especially by my Algonquin and Coffee House friends. One of my happiest recollections of this period is of listening to Deems Taylor's laughter as he read it, seated in my Shelton room. There are many other happy memories. Bob was the theater critic for *Life* and I usually went with him on the nights when Gertrude didn't come in from Scarsdale. Bob and I also went over to see the Music Box show in Philadelphia; it was the revue of the preceding season in which Bob had starred with his "Treasurers Report." The entire company loved Bob, and for the first time in my life I sat late at night in a small hotel room drinking wine with chorus girls. The speakeasy situation had improved considerably since I had first come to New York and in spite of occasional raids by the hated dry-agents the only difficulty was in selecting the nearest. One of our favorites was run by a not-yet-famous Jack and Charlie at 42 West 49th. There was talk at the Algonquin of a project for a new magazine to be called *The New Yorker,* but I wasn't interested in writing for magazines. Eugene Saxton, my guardian angel at Doran's, had transferred to Harper's, and Dos and I agreed to follow him there for our future books. Albert Boni, of Boni and Liveright, had set up his own publishing firm with his brother Charles, and I signed a contract for one book with them before my first at Harper's. All this meant advance money in the bank, and I also accepted an offer to go on a lecture tour, with engagements as far West as San Francisco and Los Angeles.

The first of these lectures, at the annual dinner of some men's club in Connecticut, was a dismal flop, partly because the toastmaster's introduction was "I don't know anything about Donald Ogden Stewart, but I understand that he's supposed to be funny," and partly because my inexperience had left me completely unable to cope with drunks who shout "louder and funnier!" Hostile and unreceptive audiences always cause me to lose all my confidence, and my despairing lecture bureau was about ready to call it quits after my initial disaster. But luckily my next engagement was more successful, and the tour was on again. The awful thing about a humorous lecture is the obligation to prove to the audience that you can make them laugh, and if you are comparatively unknown you can feel their spines stiffening as the beaming chairman announces that "today they are going to listen to one of America's funniest young men." And always in the front row is a grim old lady who gets older and grimmer as you struggle on. But after one or two more fairly successful bookings in the East I began to acquire a little technique in sizing up what an audience wanted, and by Christmas I was ready to set forth across America, accompanied by my portable Victrola and a collection of my favorite jazz records.

First stop was Columbus where, although they didn't blow any whistles or declare any half holidays in the schools, I was interviewed by James Thurber who was then a reporter on the *Columbus Despatch.* Jim and I, with the aid of some bootleg whisky, devised a "crazy humor" interview which seemed screamingly funny to us at the time. He listened very appreciatively to my stories about Benchley and Dorothy Parker, and I'm sure I must have given him much fatherly advice about how to succeed as a humorist (he was born six days after I was). At any rate, the next time I heard of him was two or three years later when Benchley and Dorothy began telling me about the wonderful stuff he was writing for *The New Yorker.*

In Detroit I took time off to have lunch with Ernest Hemingway's married sister whom I tried to encourage about her brother's literary future. Ernest had sent me his *In Our Time* short stories which I had unsuccessfully urged George Doran to publish. Actually, I didn't have any idea that Ernest was a very good writer. I liked him, and I wanted to help a friend; however, when he had sent me a "funny" piece about myself to submit to *Vanity Fair,* I had decided that written humor was not his dish and had done nothing about it. On the jacket of the first edition of *In Our Time,* which Boni and Liveright published later that year, there are fulsome tributes to Hemingway as a short story writer by Edward J. O'Brien, Sherwood Anderson, Waldo Frank, Gilbert Seldes, Ford Madox Ford and me. I am quoted as saying, "After trying to make a meal out of the literary lettuce sandwiches which are being fed to this country, it is rather nice to discover that one of your own countrymen has opened a shop where you can really get something to eat." I admired him tremendously as an honest unsentimental man who was trying to write the truth about life.

I thought that I was doing the same by way of my humor, which was still fairly correct as far as my books went. But on this lecture tour I was beginning to compromise in a way Ernest never did. I was learning the dangerous technique of how to satisfy an audience. Readings of my more disconcerting bits of satire were gradually replaced by sure-fire laughs and a patriotic eulogy to the great artistic possibilities in the newly discovered coming-of-age of America – our over-powering skyscrapers, our rhapsodies in blue, our "seven lively arts." This technique of crowd-pleasing was by no means dishonest: I did like making audiences laugh, and I certainly believed in what I was saying about America. The sight of the Bush Terminal building in New York filled me with reverence, and when I heard in Paris the first performance of "Pacific-231," Honegger's salute to the locomotive, I muttered: "We can build more beautiful musical locomotives than that." Still, such crowd-pleasing represented for the author of *Aunt Polly* a retreat in the face of the enemy.

It had been, aside from that, a very worthwhile trip. I had written the first chapter or two of my book for Boni which was to be called *The Crazy Fool.* The idea for it had come to me in Columbus when my brother-in-law had told me of a French novel in which a young man had inherited a brothel. I devised a different version: A young American would inherit a run-down insane asylum, with the obligation to build it into a successful profit-making institution before he could marry the banker's daughter and, presumably, live happily ever after. Within the framework of a "crazy humor" book I envisaged a satire on the whole American success dream, with the constant parallel between the U.S.A. as reflected in daily newspaper headlines and life in an institution. Since this was to be a book of good-natured laughter, there was no attempt to introduce any really mentally unsound characters, which was just as well, as I was completely ignorant of psychology, psychiatry and psychoanalysis. My hero, named Charlie Hatch, was to be myself, partly because of the opportunity which that presented for having fun with my earlier ambitions to "make good" in the business world. Another character, a kindly and wise older gentleman who accompanied me to the asylum I had inherited, was sort of a mixture of Bob Benchley and Gerald Murphy. Then there was a bright-eyed, witty, unhappily married woman who was Dorothy Parker.

That was as far as I had progressed when I arrived at Los Angeles, where I was scheduled for four lectures at four different women's clubs. This bothered me a bit because I only had one lecture, although it had four different titles, (the only one of which I can remember was "Life, Liberty and the Pursuit of Happiness"). But the ladies of the Friday Morning Club didn't attend lectures at the Ebell Club, and the members of the Hollywood Women's Club didn't go out to the Pasadena Women's Club, so all went fairly well. Mrs. William De Mille came to my first lecture with her daughters Agnes and Margaret and they gave me a sort of passport into the film industry.

California absolutely fascinated me, especially Hollywood. I was a pushover for a movie name, especially those of the stars whom Clara and I had faithfully followed in our Columbus days. Many of them were still around and could actually be seen dining at the Biltmore or in the Coconut Grove backroom at the Ambassador. I took a Sunday streetcar ride and was thrilled as we passed my first outdoor movie set, a replica of the "Mayflower" which had been used by Charles Ray in his last picture. The name of my buddy of Yale and Chicago Navy days, Harry Crocker, unexpectedly appeared as an actor in the cast of a play at the Biltmore Theatre, and when I went to see him he disclosed to my delight that he was actually acquainted with several movie stars. He took me out to the home of King Vidor, which perched precariously on the side of a canyon, where Harry and I played tennis with King and a beautiful young star named Eleanor Boardman. Harry also introduced me to Patsy Ruth Miller, whose first big success had been the year before with Lon Chaney and Norman Kerry in *The Hunchback of Notre Dame*. She was crazy about *Perfect Behavior* so I took her dancing at the Coconut Grove where the orchestra played "I'll See You In My Dreams" and I decided that Hollywood was jut the right place to write *The Crazy Fool*. And I discovered the right hotel in which to write it – a small three-story wooden building, very cheap, with an electric sign in front reading "The Mark Twain."

In those days, Hollywood itself was still the place where the studios were located – at least Paramount, Warners, Fox, Chaplin, Columbia and the "quickies" along Poverty Row. The stars had only begun to emigrate to Beverly Hills; Patsy Ruth and her family moved there before I left in March. But that time I had become completely captivated by the place, and pretty well captivated Patsy Ruth (known as "Pat") and her circle of young starlets who were celebrated as the Wampas girls, a name derived from the Western Association of Motion Picture Advertisers who picked a certain number each year as star prospects. In addition to the glamor of being a star, Pat was a lot of fun, and not only that but her father was a great friend of one of my boyhood baseball heroes, Mike Donlin of the Giants. I spent as much time as possible at the Miller home.

Hero worshipping is an interesting subject. Why should I, at the age of thirty, have been so absolutely bowled over by meeting an old baseball player whom my brother Bert had once seen play in 1906? Why, for that matter, was I now so completely thrilled in the presence of the movie stars of my twenties? I had met actresses in New York, I knew prominent writers and critics rather intimately, but the movie world exercised for me a romantic enchantment which far exceeded anything else. Most writers pretended to despise Hollywood. I found that I adored it, and part of the reason, I suppose, had to do with childhood idols. The Hollywood silent film characters were still something out of this world, and I felt incredibly flattered to be in their company; conversely, they seemed to have a certain exaggerated respect for me as an author of published books. Rudolph Valentino was photographed on his set with me or, shall we say, I was photographed with him. I took the famous vamp Nita Naldi to dinner and told her about Montparnasse and Picasso. Eleanor Boardman invited me to watch her do some scenes under the direction of Paul Bern, and once more photographs were taken which I hastened to send home to Clara in Columbus. Rupert Hughes organized a dinner in my honor at the Writers Club, at which I met Lew Cody and Jack Pickford and felt more thrilled than if they had been Dreiser or Arnold Bennett. Rupert Hughes himself was the Grand Old Man, the symbol of Belles Lettres among the Hollywood barbarians. It was still the wild untamed territory of Before-Sound, and before the cultural pretentiousness and social snobbery which were to come. There were still living vestiges of the days of Mabel Normand and the Keystone cops, of Francis X. Bushman and Pearl White, of John Bunny and Theda Bara. I was in Wonderland, as I had been in Chicago Society and Dayton Big Business. But this time I felt that I belonged.

This was, of course, not a very intelligent feeling for a dedicated writer to have. But I didn't any longer have a standard for myself and my work by which I could judge and reject Hollywood. Ernest Hemingway knew what he wanted to do. So did John Dos Passos and Scott Fitzgerald. I was depending on the Oracle to speak at the right time and, up until now, it had. But without being aware of it, I was beginning to drift, and the Oracle was getting conflicting reactions. One of them, revealed on my lecture tour, was a tendency to pay too much attention to pleasing an audience. Another, also nourished on my tour, was a growing desire for fame – a desire to which Hollywood is not entirely alien or unhelpful. And in the golden climate of California I began to feel the first faint stirrings of certain financial ambitions which I thought I had forever buried four years ago in Dayton. Fame had come, but evidently not fast enough or wide-spread enough. And fortune? Well, money was still unimportant to a writer, of course, compared to his obligation to tell the truth. But if they really needed good writers in Hollywood as badly as they told me they did, I would be foolish not to think this over carefully – especially as I would be able to tell my truth to so much larger an audience. That was it: I could cleverly – but with integrity, of course – use the movie technique to reach millions! It looked like a God-given opportunity. And since my publishers were daily importuning me for the *Crazy Fool,* why not write it in a form which would also recommend it – and me – to these eager movie producers? Why not, indeed? So with one eye now to the screen, I gave the oracle the signal to spout forth another masterpiece. My hopes of selling it for a movie seemed bright. James Cruze, who had won fame as director of *The Covered Wagon,* was interested in the possibilities of screen fantasy, and I spent a realistically fantastic Sunday at his palatial home trying to find the time and the place to read my book to him. He had invited me out for that purpose, but unfortunately he kept what might be described as "open house" every Sunday. In the front hall you were greeted by a hospitable array of empty glasses and full gin bottles, and the rest was up to you and the fifty to one hundred other guests. Jim really wanted to listen to my story and I finally succeeded but it was a tough fight. An even tougher audience a few nights later was King Vidor. This time there was no "open house," and after a Mexican dinner cooked by Eleanor Boardman she and King took comfortable seats and I began to read. There was a great deal of appreciative laughter at first, and neither of them went to sleep until the third or perhaps fourth chapter. I tiptoed out to the garage and got the chauffeur to drive me back to the Mark Twain, resisting the temptation to read *The Crazy Fool* to him on the way. Next morning King and Eleanor with apologies told me that they were sure that what they had heard would make a good movie. Jim Cruze had been complimentary, too, so I left Hollywood with a hopeful heart and autographed photos of Patsy Ruth and Mike Donlin. On the way to New York I stopped for a lecture engagement at Ohio State University in Columbus, then to Syracuse University and Dartmouth College. Colleges had always been my best audiences, and I landed at the Algonquin full of pride and joyful anticipation of another educational summer in France.

14

My anticipations were at first not disappointed – at least as far as the education was concerned. On the boat a New York Society woman whom I had never met made violent love to me. This would have been quite flattering if she had been a bit nearer my age, but this poor woman was going through a bad attack of what the French call *retour d'age* and I felt terribly sorry for her. I had another declaration of love from a certain rather distinguished New York judge whom I had met at the Coffee House. He began joining me on my walks around the deck and then, on the last day, he casually asked me if I would like to continue my voyage and go around the world with him – all expenses paid. It took a minute or two for me to get the picture, after which I declined – but with embarrassment and pity, rather than anger. I had never been propositioned before by either sex – and here on one voyage I was getting the full treatment. I was relieved when the boat train reached Paris and I could plunge into the normal healthy sex life of the girls at Zelli's.

As a matter of fact, I had become especially interested in one particular girl named Paulette, who remembered me from the year before and greeted me enthusiastically. She was a hearty peasant girl from Brittany and I had liked her for her gaiety. I also thought that she would make a nice person to help me with my efforts to master the French language, so I proposed that she and I take a permanent room instead of the customary one-night stand at one of the sympathetic hotels on the rue des Martyrs near Zelli's. Paulette, being extremely interested in my improvement in the language, agreed and we found a hotel on the rue Lepic. It was, for me at least, a Bohemian dream come true. I was living in Montmartre, in the shadow of Sacre Coeur, with a mistress! I was unbelievably happy at playing married, especially at having a woman in my bed every night; after an evening at a prize fight or a bicycle motorcycle-paced races with Ernest, it was thrilling to find her waiting for me when I returned.

The only cloud was that she began to worry about her future. What was she going to do when I left? And then one night in bed she murmured something which I didn't understand. She sighed deeply and repeated the sentence, which was "Oh! Que j'adore le commerce!" Gradually it became clear that the fondest dream of her life had always been to own a little grocery store, an *èpicerie* all her own. And not only that, but she knew of one in the neighborhood which was for sale at an unbelievable bargain. Well, I wasn't exactly crazy about the idea at first. A grocery somehow didn't fit in with the *La Bohème* libretto which I was currently scribbling in the blank pages of my life. "You mean" I asked (in French) "things like vegetables?" "Oh oui," she replied ecstatically, "j'adore les legumes." She not only adored legumes, it seemed, but canned sardines and soups and kerosene oil – and if she could just get started selling them .... So the next morning I had a look at the place. It was really very small, and so was Paulette's budget. Besides, it seemed like an opportunity to give this splendid Brittany girl a start in life other than returning to Zelli's. I forget how much her original request for a "loan" amounted to, but it wasn't a shattering amount, and I had received word that *The Crazy Fool* was on one bestseller list after its first few days of publication. So, within a week or two, the Epicerie Paulette opened its doors – or, rather, its door. The Murphys were now living out at St. Cloud, so I couldn't really ask them to become steady patrons, but Ernest and Hadley came all the way from Montparnasse and bought a lot of things they didn't need, and promised to send Gertrude Stein and James Joyce, which didn't impress Paulette as much as it should have. After a week it looked as though the venture had a fair chance of success, and I benignly left with Bob Benchley for a tour of Vienna and Budapest.

This trip might be described as one of almost continuous delight. To be with Benchley was to live in a companionship of complete understanding. There was in him no competitiveness. His world was rare and wise and often marvelously mad. It was a world which I had been seeking and the value of sharing it with him outweighed everything else. Our joyful progress through the museums and vineyards of Austria and Hungary was interrupted only once or twice by touches of reality. At Vienna I received a telegram from Paulette stating that if I didn't send ten thousand francs immediately she would be dispossessed of our *épicerie* by a mysterious figure called a *huissier,* which Bob's small dictionary defined as "an usher." However, another dictionary informed me that a *huissier* was also a sheriff's officer, so I sent the ten thousand and told her not to worry. Then to Budapest came the second message from Paulette thanking me for the money but telling me that she was quite worried on account of discovering that she was pregnant. I had had evidently gone into more than the grocery business.

The Benchley-Stewart tour ended in Switzerland. He went down to Antibes to join *his* family and I moved somewhat breathlessly toward Paris to join what I hoped was not mine. I need not have worried. Paulette was reasonably reasonable and I suppose I was fortunate to have escaped from being tagged with the fatherhood of anything beyond a small grocery. Paulette and I parted as friends. It had been for me a romantic interlude, and I wasn't going to let the fact that she had deceived me slightly about her pregnancy spoil my Bohemian memories. I did feel, however, that she had reached the limit of her usefulness as a teacher of French, and I pinned her diploma to my green-papered wall in the Hotel Venetia and prepared for post-graduate work.

But it was time to join Ernest and Hadley in Pamplona for the Feast of Saint Firmin, so I prepared for another rowdy reunion with the gang. But when I got there I found that someone had left the door open and Eve had walked into my male Garden of Eden. Eve's name was Lady Duff Twisden and she was right out of the gay brave hell of Michael Arlen. She was distant and rare and beautiful in a black broadbrimmed Spanish hat. I was scared as hell of her until I discovered that she had a terrible hangover, which always endears people to me. With her was someone whom I took to be her lover, another "Green Hat" character from the overdrafts of Mayfair named Pat Guthrie whose charming worthlessness immediately won my heart. The third new member of our club was Harold Loeb, editor of *Broom,* whose presence, as I discovered later, was not entirely in the interests of literature. Somehow or other sex rivalries didn't seem to belong in the celebration of the martyrdom of Saint Firmin, and I wondered in my innocence why Ernest and Hadley had brought in these strangers. Anyway, good old Bill Smith was there and so were the bulls and the bands and the wineskins. I determinedly set about showing myself and the newcomers the glories of the fiesta as I remembered them from the last year.

But little by little the glory began to slip away. It wasn't the same, no matter how much I drank. At first I figured that maybe it was because we were no longer the exclusive foreign participants in the show. Rolls-Royces from Madrid and France stood outside the hotel, and the presence of the American Ambassador didn't add anything to the spirit of peasant gaiety. Pamplona seemed to be getting ready for the hand of Elsa Maxwell. But that wasn't what was spoiling things for me. Ernest had changed. Hadley wasn't the same. One night there was almost a fight between Ernest and Harold Loeb. The fun was going out of everybody. But the dancing and singing kept going on all around us and gradually it looked as though the spirit of the fiesta had swung them up out of their triangles or quadrangles or whatever the hell it was. On the last night we danced and toasted each other and made plans for next year's fiesta and good-time Donald fell into bed very happy.

But next day the hotel bills came in and all the camaraderie fell to pieces. It seemed that our English companions had come down without any means of paying for anything, and it also seemed that this came as a surprise to Ernest who barely had enough to settle his own bills. His bitter fury was justified. He had trustfully introduced us all to his great friend the hotel keeper, and this was a betrayal of that trust. But for me the terrible thing was the revelation of the tenuousness of human relations when confronted with financial conflict. It was an intrusion of that same sickness which had crept into my heart at Yale when I had tried too zealously to collect dues from my fraternity brothers. Here in Pamplona a joyful if temporary comradeship was being destroyed because of an unpaid debt. Money wasn't worth that much, I decided, and as I was luckily able to transform my decision into financial action the spirit of fiesta, if not some of the friendship, survived the crisis. On the way from Pamplona to the Murphys in Antibes it occurred to me that the events of the past week might make interesting material for a novel. The same idea had apparently occurred to Ernest, who started working on *The Sun Also Rises*. I bought a bottle of sun-tan lotion and relaxed on the beach.

In Antibes, as at Pamplona, I experienced a growing sense that "things ain't what they used to be." It hadn't been discovered yet, but there were ominous signs. The Hotel du Cap was now more than half full of wealthy vacationers and the small exclusive beach on which the Murphy children and Dos and I had run wild was now shared with a Mr. and Mrs. Pierpont Morgan Hamilton and assorted guests. On our side of the beach were the Benchleys and the Barrys, the Scott Fitzgeralds and the Archie MacLeishes, all of whom had by now become close friends of the Murphys. There was no communication between the two camps. After devoting two weeks to the intensive sun-tanning of my body, I began to think about beginning to think about a subject for my first book under the Harpers contract. The success of *The Haddocks Abroad* seemed to call for a sequel to be known as "Mr. and Mrs. Haddock in Paris France." After a week or so of false starts, however, I decided that the climate of the Riviera wasn't right for the project, so I went to Paris in order to get into the proper atmosphere.

As an atmospheric beginning, I met the beautiful girl who, a year later, was to become my wife. Her name was Beatrice Ames, she was living in Paris with her father, mother and younger sister Jerry, and I went to see her on the recommendation of my old Yale friend Harry Crocker who was engaged to her. Her father was a retired manufacturer from Oswego, New York and after he had made up a horrible cocktail with cream called an Alexander, I took Beatrice out on the Yale blue-plate special tour of Paris, including the royal box at Zelli's, and ending up in the early morning at Les Halles for a spot of onion soup chez "Le Pere Tranquille." I concluded that Harry was a very lucky boy, but as she and her family left Paris almost immediately I didn't see her there again.

Curiously enough I then met a girl whom I think I might have married, or at least have proposed to, if I had fallen a little more in love with her. Raymonde was attractive, French, the best educated girl I had ever known – and the most serious. She had been recommended to me as someone who might help me with my French pronunciation, but my education soon embraced a much wider range of subjects. It was my first contact with a highly educated French mind and she soon had the Yale Bachelor of Arts groggily reaching for the ropes. Luckily she liked to dance, and more fortunately still she was tremendously impressed with *Aunt Polly's Story of Mankind.*

The brief, pleasant and "intellectual" interlude with Raymonde terminated with a cable from my publisher announcing that *The*

Crazy Fool had been bought by Metro-Goldwyn-Mayer and that I was urgently invited to come out to Hollywood to write the script. I didn't hesitate very long about accepting the invitation. I knew that Hollywood was regarded with contempt by most of my writer friends, but I argued myself into believing that it would offer me a new and much wider audience. The fact that I didn't really have anything to say was not apparent at the time. I only knew that I hadn't been able to get ahead with either a novel or a play. Besides, I would only go out there for a few months, and what harm could that do?

It was exciting to be treated as an important "catch" in the New York offices of M-G-M, to be photographed for the front page of the *Mirror,* and to have a drawing room reserved for me on the California Limited. It was thrilling to inform people on the train that I was going out to Hollywood "to write a picture." Did I actually know Rudolph Valentino? "Oh sure – and Patsy Ruth Miller and Nita Naldi; you'd be surprised how unspoiled they are. And intelligent, too!" I had all the answers.

It was a little disappointing that there were no photographers awaiting me at the Los Angeles station, but I made haste to telephone M-G-M of my arrival and my immediate readiness for work. No one at Metro seemed to have the faintest idea who I was, and there was certainly no one particularly agitated about my arrival. It was my first disillusionment about the true position of the writer in the Hollywood hierarchy. And hardly had I settled into my little room at the Mark Twain hotel when there came another illuminating discovery about the customs and habits of the strange Wonderland in which I was now living. Ever since I had signed a contract to do the screenplay for *The Crazy Fool* I had been enthusastically making notes and writing possible new scenes. I now eagerly laid these before King Vidor, whose recommendation had been responsible for the purchase of the book. King seemed curiously reluctant to investigate my suggestions and then, with his characteristic grin of embarrassment, he explained. "Well, you see, Don, I did get Irving [Thalberg] enthusiastic about your book by reading bits of it to him one Sunday out at Catalina. Oh, he was crazy about it." My heart began to sink "And he isn't *now*?" I asked. King grinned again. "Oh sure" he said. "But the only catch is that I had taken the wrong book with me. What I read was some of your *Perfect Behavior.*" "But," I protested, "he bought *The Crazy Fool!*" "That's right," said King, "I just didn't want to upset him. He had a lot of other things on his mind. It's a good joke on him, but I wouldn't say anything about it for awhile."

It was also a good joke on me, as I had had great hopes for the Alice-in-Wonderland possibilities of the *Crazy Fool* screenplay. But I bravely swallowed my disappointment and the payment for the wrong book and reported for work. M-G-M had only been in production in Culver City for a year or so and there were comparatively few stages, with the administration building adjoining a long wooden line of dressing rooms along Washington Boulevard. A small office was found for me in the administration building, but for the first few weeks (@ $250 per week) there didn't seem to be much need for my valuable services. King Vidor was busily engaged in shooting *The Big Parade* which Laurence Stallings had come out to write after the great success on Broadway of *What Price Glory*. Harry Crocker had a big part in the picture, and at first most of my weekends were spent on King's tennis court with Harry, Eleanor Cohn, and a bright young Harvard graduate, Harry Behn, who had helped Stallings write the *Big Parade* script. Patsy Ruth Miller had become interested in another beau and I didn't see as much of her as I had expected. I bought my first automobile, a very second-hand Buick roadster, and sent for Clara to come out from Columbus into the California sunshine. Clara loved Hollywood and the Mark Twain and soon became the favorite of all the twenty-eight roomers.

But my own enthusiasm was beginning to droop, and it didn't get any particular boost when M-G-M decided that as a Yale graduate I was just the right boy to write the script for an old time play called *Brown of Harvard*. I should have recognized the crucial dividing line between independent creative work and the occupation of an employed screen writer. There are many reasons why I didn't, chief among them being a mixture of self-confidence and trust in Fate. I had fortuitously and unexpectedly become successful; perhaps I should also achieve fame and fortune as a screenwriter. Besides, I had only signed up for six months and it would be another interesting experiment. Why not give it a try? What could I lose?

So I dutifully appeared each morning at my office and filled sheets of paper with what seemed to me a rather brilliant scenario. I conferred at decent intervals with my producer, Harry Rapf, with whom I found myself anxious to "make good." The key to all this, of which I was not conscious, was that I had again become an employee, and having a clock to punch brought back a feeling of security which had been missing since I had launched out as a freelance writer. There was now that good old weekly pay check, and it was wonderful to watch the bank balance grow. I had returned from Paris without much money laid aside for the future. Now, for a while at least, I needn't worry, even though *Brown of Harvard* was not exactly up to my high opinion of myself.

My day-to-day self-esteem wasn't doing too badly, however. Michael Arlen paid a visit to Hollywood, and the Writers' Club decided to give him a banquet at which most of the crowned heads of filmdom were present. Rupert Hughes, an extremely witty toastmaster, set the tone as one of rather boisterous ribbing of the distinguished visitor and when it came to my turn to speak I had one of my lucky evenings, especially in the reception of my gag of the Green Hat heroine who wants to take her part in the Hollywood epic by "laying the Atlantic cable." It can't quite be said that I awoke next morning to find myself famous, but word got around in the small village which was Hollywood and I began to be asked to make speeches at everything from Hearst Milk Fund benefits to the openings of new movie theaters and grocery stores. It was great fun and it made me a lot of acquaintances among the stars, but it didn't have anything to do with my ambition to become a successful screen writer. My *Brown* was plodding his way around Harvard without attracting much interest from Irving Thalberg or anyone else at M-G-M. However, no one seemed particularly in a hurry and I settled into the rather enervating semi-tropical rhythm of the California climate.

In those first weeks, nothing seemed to be quite the way it should be. Football in the Coliseum was played before spectators in their short sleeves. High-stepping drum majorettes cavorted between the halves. No coonskin coats. The Pacific Ocean didn't seem at all like what a proper ocean should be. There were no wild storms, no raging waves on a stern and rock-bound coast. Just sand and beaches and all that smooth water. When Bob Benchley came out later, he was able to explain my feeling of strangeness about the Pacific. "I don't trust that ocean," he said. "It's just pretending to be peaceful. It's waiting for the right time to sweep up and in and over everything." But Clara loved the ocean and the climate and I took her for drives along the coast, especially after my second-hand car was happily replaced by a new make of roadster called a Chrysler. Clara had heard that bootleggers were buying Chryslers because they could quickly outspeed police cars. The bootleg problem, incidentally, was much more serious in Los Angeles than in New York; there were no speakeasies, and liquor was very scarce and expensive. Fortunately, there was a man named Rudy at M-G-M. who took care of the more demanding thirsts.

Actually, there wasn't much drinking in Hollywood in those days or wild dissipation – perhaps partly because of the fairly recent Fatty Arbuckle scandal. My usual companions on the few evenings I went out "on the town" were either Jack Gilbert, or Lew Cody and Jack Pickford, and the "orgies" consisted in telephoning a certain Lee Frances and waiting an hour or so until she could assemble and send out the required number of girls. Occasionally Jack and I would ourselves call at Lee's apartment, since Jack was living at the Athletic Club which was not exactly the best place in which to receive midnight visitors. Once I was included in an official visit to Lee's by M-G-M. executives who were entertaining a celebrity from New York, my memory of which records Eddie Mannix and Irving Thalberg, among others, reading the early morning *Examiner* while the celebrity was being entertained in another room by the girls.

For the most part Hollywood worked very hard and minded its own business. The afternoon before Christmas was the big common festival of "anything goes" at all the studios. There was an unwritten law that everyone got drunk without penalty, so that Thalberg and Rapf and even the great Louis B. Mayer would find their office filled with bit players and "juicers" and prop boys with loud uninhibited suggestions as to what they could do with the studio. On some of the stages there would be attempts at working, but any star who had a reputation for being over-impressed with his or her own importance acted that afternoon in great danger from nuts and bolts and monkey wrenches dropping from the scaffolding above. Jack Gilbert got drunk very early after lunch and wandered around the studio, his pocket full of five-dollar gold pieces. Whenever any of the drunk employees would start to speak to him he would smile and hand him some money, as though to say "Please – don't take a sock at me!" I never went with him to a public restaurant that some man didn't leave the woman he was with and come up to our table and try to pick a fight with him. Jack was a flaming radiant person in those days, a bright and shining star. *The Big Parade* had just shot him into the sky; Garbo had not yet risen on his horizon.

With Jack, on Marion Davies' invitation, I went up to the famous

Hearst ranch for one of these fabulous weekends at which thirty or more assorted guests would depart from the Pasadena Station in private cars attached to the regular train. They would descend at midnight on San Simeon, to be driven for hours through the Hearst domain – amid wandering zebra, antelope and other fellow guests – until deposited in one's room. The room would very likely contain a bed which had probably belonged to Cardinal Richelieu and a ceiling from the chamber of Marie de Medici, and one would hope that one of the Louis XIII doors opened into a bathroom. Then for lunch one assembled with the other whispering guests under the roof of a thirteenth-century cathedral and waited for the arrival of our host, who was referred to by those close to the throne as "W.R." or "The Chief." I had been warned that everything depended on what sort of mood The Chief was in, and that any guest who gave any evidence of enjoying himself until the right signals had been hoisted on the castle tower was usually in danger of being later found hanging from a tree in the forest with giraffes nibbling at his lifeless toes. Among the guests for this first lunch were several Hearst executives, as well as our "Friends of Marion" group which included Charlie Chaplin, King and Eleanor Vidor, Jack, and Harry Crocker. Eventually the Chief arrived, accompanied by Marion, and it was immediately evident that this was not going to be one of his happier meals. We dutifully and quietly sat down at a long table. W.R. was surrounded by his executives and nervous sobriety descended over the board. Finally, after dessert, Marion tried to liven things up a bit by calling for speeches and as someone had told her about my Writers Club effort she waved her wand in my direction. By this time I had had some wine and, being rather fed-up with the ridiculous atmosphere of feudal subservience to the Lord and Master, I decided that if I was going to be a Court Jester I might as well be thrown out for a sheep as a lamb. So I proceeded to launch into a pseudo-scholarly exposé of the falseness of the Hearstian importations with which we were surrounded. The exposé began with two early Spanish wooden saints which I pronounced to be palpable fakes, and continued with a piece-by-piece revelation of the forgeries which poor Mr. Hearst had mistakenly purchased. For the first minute or so of my "rib" there was absolute silence. I plunged along recklessly. I didn't dare look at Marion or anybody. And then, thank God, W.R. chuckled. I was in. I got a big hand when I sat down, and a kiss from Marion.

This unfortunate self-satisfaction was clearly reflected in my second *Haddock* book, which I completed shortly after this. My efforts at M-G-M to bring truth and light to the problems of Brown at Harvard had been received with pronounced apathy by Harry Rapf, who called in two title writers to apply their expertness in what was called "continuity." I suggested that I be relieved temporarily of further obligations to bring the advantages of a Yale degree to the improvement of M-G-M films.

My offer was happily accepted, and I quickly settled down at the Mark Twain, once more a self-propelling creative artist. This time my message to the world was concerned almost exclusively with the problem of "play." Mr. Haddock was on his vacation from the lumber business. In Paris he found a city in which the inhabitants seemed to know how to enjoy life – or at least to take it at a more leisurely and less competitive pace than in his home town. He found a companionable American called "The Bottin" who sympathized with his problem. This American, like Mr. King in *The Crazy Fool,* was meant to embody the wisdom and understanding of Bob Benchley and Gerald Murphy. (I had dedicated the first book to Bob; this one I dedicated to Gerald and Sara.) The Bottin, having lived in France for many years, explains that "the soul of Europe" is sick and is looking for guidance.

"And that guidance," he said "may come from you – or it may come from the East – I mean India. Or perhaps Russia. But it won't come from America until America finds itself – until everything alive in that country – skyscrapers, subways, farms, grain elevators, Ford factories, steel – reaches up simultaneously – higher – and finds its soul. And if that happens – if America flowers – powerfully, overwhelmingly, beautifully – there will come a new religion – or a great rebirth of the old religion – and people will once more build churches which will be great beautiful churches because in them will be the expression of the great beautiful soul of this commercial industrial scientific age which is our own – and which is now groping so blindly in the dark – in America.

"And that," concluded the Bottin, "has somehow got something to do with you and Mrs. Haddock and the Americans, because you're all over here looking for something – something you're not getting in America. You don't know what it is but you think maybe it's over here in Europe, and then you get sore when you don't find it.

Mr. Haddock puffed his cigar thoughtfully.

"Is Mrs. Haddock unhappy?" he asked at length.

"Well," said the Bottin, "no. Not actively unhappy. But she's not happy either. She knew she wasn't having a good time – but she had never learned how. That's the trouble. So many Americans are just like Mrs. Haddock – they don't know how to play. They work and work and work and they think that some day when they've accumulated enough money they'll go somewhere – Paris, Palm Beach, anywhere but where they are – and enjoy life. And the terrible thing is that it is *always too late.*"

That was the essence of the book which Harpers later published – and it was pretty much the essence and limit of my own thinking at that time. The "flowering of the soul of America" and the "coming of a new religion" were wonderful abstractions about which I had talked on my lecture tour and about which I could still talk excitedly, especially after the third or fourth cocktail.

My own ideals and realities were now becoming concentrated on the problem of getting married. Beatrice Ames had returned from Paris and was living with her parents in Montecita, just outside Santa Barbara. She had broken her engagement to Harry Crocker; we were both looking for marriage and the inevitable came to a boil in March in front of a Los Angeles jeweler's window when it suddenly occurred to me to ask her if she would like a ring. She laughed heartily and moved on to her hairdresser, but a week or so later as we were sitting in my Chrysler in a grove of blossoming orange trees (no kidding!) the chase ended.

Bea was young and beautiful, and I was very happy. She was a gay "fun" girl, loved parties and dancing, understood my kind of humor and had plenty of her own. Clara and she got on together beautifully and I could hardly wait to introduce her to Bobby and Dotty, the Barrys and the Murphys. We postponed the wedding, however, until her younger sister Marjorie had been "finished" at Miss Porter's School in Connecticut and I had been ditto by M-G-M in Culver City.

My failure as a writer for the silent screen didn't bother me very much, partly because I naturally considered the failure to be M-G-M's, and partly because *Mr. and Mrs. Haddock In Paris France* had been sold for serialization to a new magazine called *College*

Humor. I had also contracted with the *Chicago Tribune* syndicate to write a weekly humorous series during my honeymoon, so that the financial problem of married life seemed adequately solved – at least for the first year. My cup of joy flowed over when Bobby, having accepted a movie job, came out to be my Best Man.

With him, also on first film assignments, came Marc Connelly and Herman Mankiewicz, both charter members of the Algonquin circle. We all lived at the Mark Twain. Another occupant was a young Scot named John Grierson who had been sent by his Edinburgh paper to do a series on Hollywood, and after I had introduced him to Chaplin I shared several interesting discussions between the two and also with Charlie's circle of young assistants and ex-assistants. These included Jim Tully, the hobo-novelist; Harry d'Arrast, who had directed *A Woman of Paris:* Harry Crocker, who was acting in Charlie's current production *The Circus;* and Joe von Sternberg, who showed me *The Salvation Hunters,* an experiment which Charlie had encouraged him to produce and direct. Most of our discussions took place in a delicatessen restaurant on Hollywood Boulevard which Charlie had financed for old Henry Bergman, his beloved "heavy" from Mack Sennett days.

The conversation was always on one subject: movies. Perhaps Charlie discussed other topics when world-famous writers and philosophers came to lay their tribute at his feet. But Hollywood itself was in its own orbit. "Reality" was whatever was recorded on film at the end of each day's shooting, and events of political or economic significance were left to the newsreels. It was no wonder that I was later to fit so successfully into this dream world, for I myself was living happily in a personal Paradise in which no essential realities were allowed to disturb my determined play and pleasant dreams. I was indeed a lucky fool – on an extended leave of absence from infelicity.

15

Having officiated as an usher at so many of my friends' nuptials, it was thrilling to play the leading male role. My sister Anne came out from Columbus, and it was great fun introducing her to my group of silent-film celebrities. My Yale roommate Don Shepard arrived from Wisconsin in time to be one of my ushers; others who donned cutaways and silk hats in my behalf were Marc Connelly, Harry d'Arrast, and two friends of Bea's in Santa Barbara, Chris Holmes and "Dutch" Hoeffling. Chris had an interesting hobby which Bob Benchley hadn't been warned about. When he called at the Holmes residence for the first time and the butler showed him into Chris's study, he found all of the seven chairs occupied by Great Danes who growled ominously each time Bobby moved. Then through the window leaped a small monkey who jumped playfully on to his shoulders and chattered in a language which Bob didn't recognize. After a bit of this the door opened and in came a medium-sized orangutan who proceeded to search eagerly through Bob's pockets. Chris had quite a zoo attached to his estate; Bobby was merely getting the usual guest treatment. He got an even more unexpected treatment at another Santa Barbara home where one of our pre-wedding dances and parties was being celebrated. No one told him where the bathroom was, and in searching for it in the dark he fell into the cellar. So my Best Man performed his remaining functions with one leg in a plaster cast which was appropriately and lewdly autographed by the guests at my bachelor dinner, among whom were Rupert Hughes, Charlie Chaplin, Jack Gilbert, Lew Cody, King Vidor, John Grierson, Joe Cohn, Milt Gross, Herman Mankiewicz, and my ushers. After all possible bachelor dinner toasts had been drunk and all possible Ambassador Hotel glassware smashed, some of us adjourned thirstily to Jack Gilbert's new home on Tower Road. As the first carloads of Lee Frances girls began to arrive I returned chastely to the Mark Twain and my New Life.

The wedding was celebrated two days later in Montecito at the Church of All Angels by the Sea. Everything went well according to most angels' requirements and in a shower of rice and rose leaves Beatrice and Donald left on a honeymoon that lasted – at least in Donald's romantic imagination – for ten and a half years.

Bea fitted into my dream world perfectly. The *Tribune* met us at Chicago with photographers and her picture appeared in rotogravure sections as "a California society girl." My New York literary friends and speakeasy owners liked her, and she liked them. Every meal was a gala.

We sailed for France after two delirious days at the Plaza, in the course of which the Tarzan bridegroom hurled numerous phonograph records from our window into Central Park in showing his bride the technique of midnight discus throwing. After stopping in Paris only long enough to order a pair of riding boots for me (my first) at the shop where her father always had *his* riding boots made, we took off for Antibes. The Murphys and the Hemingways were waiting at the station. Ernest ran along the platform beside our compartment, leaping high in the air with shouts of welcome. Phil and Ellen Barry joined in. So did Archie and Ada MacLeish. Everyone liked Bea, and I was very proud.

But Antibes had certainly changed. It had become The-Place-To-Be-Seen-At. Grace Moore had a villa, as did many other Big Names of stage and society. The Murphys wanted none of it and politely withdrew outside the rather gaudy spotlights which now shone on their little private domain. Gerald bemusedly came home from a luncheon at Eden Roc where he knew none of the famous guests. He had been seated next to a lady author who seemed much more interested in waving and calling out to various celebrities than in paying any attention to Gerald's attempts at conversation. She asked him something about sailing in the harbor and when Gerald told her that he had a small yacht, she cried, "Oh do tell me all about it. I love boats!" So Gerald obediently began the story of what had happened to Sara the preceding week when she was sailing alone. He wasn't sure that his partner was listening but he went bravely ahead toward the climax. "And then," he continued, as the lady author waved to a new arrival and screamed "Hello there, darling!" "And then," went on Gerald, "there came up one of those sudden dangerous Mediterranean storms and the sky was pitch black and the wind was tossing the boat furiously. Lightning began to crash and suddenly there was a terrific gust of wind and the boat swung over sharply and Sara was thrown into the water. She tried desperately to swim ashore, but a wave hit her and stunned her and carried her dangerously towards those rocks, you know the rocks in front of the Clews' house –" And at that Gerald's partner turned to him and beamed, "Oh tell me – how *are* the Clews?"

There were other changes at Cap d'Antibes that summer besides the transformation of Gerald and Sara's quiet little group into a celebrity circus. Ernest was beginning to become a celebrity himself. His *Torrents of Spring* had been published without much success, but *The Sun Also Rises*, the novel I had sensed waiting to be made out of the fiesta week at Pamplona the year before, was on its way to making his name known in twenty-five countries. When I first read it I couldn't see what everyone was getting so excited about, and exclaimed: "But this is nothing but a report on what happened. This is journalism." I had a feeling that I could have turned out a much better, much truer novel.

Meanwhile one kept one's head above the calm beautiful blue water of matrimony by writing weekly pieces for the *Chicago Tribune* syndicate. I didn't let the problem of supplying laughs to any *Tribune* readers interfere with the joys of honeymooning, and after I had duly conducted Beatrice to Munich, Vienna and Budapest in order to show her the places where Bob and I had had so much fun, we ended up in Paris at the new leftbank *Pont Royal* hotel in a romantic room-with-bath which we shared with Lucy, a newly purchased Schnauzer bitch who somehow seemed a necessary adjunct to married life. A miniature bellboy in uniform took her out early each morning and returned when, as he proudly reported, she had "faite tous les deux." Married life was gradually developing into a pattern of play and laughter which was to be followed with minor variations for the next decade. Every meal began with a discussion of what would be just the right cocktail. Whenever the opportunity was offered there would be more elaborate feasts, with guests. Dotty Parker appeared in Paris with a Scottie bitch, Archie and Ada MacLeish had rented the Pierpont Hamiltons' apartment, Ernest and Hadley and the Murphys returned from Antibes.

On Bea's birthday in October I gave a party at Prunier's where I discovered to my dismay that Ernest's marriage to Hadley was breaking up. I also discovered at around this time a curious bitter streak in Ernest. This first displayed itself in *The Torrents of Spring*, a book I loathed both for its bitterness and for its inept attempts at humor. More serious, for me, was a viciously unfair and unfunny poem about Dorothy Parker which Ernest read at a party in Archie MacLeish's apartment. I told him what I thought of his poem and our friendship, to my lasting sorrow, came to an end.

My honeymoon blissfully went on. Dotty and Bea and I, accompanied by our two bitches (both in heat), sailed in November and were met in New York by Bob Benchley, Marc Connelly and photographers sent by Doran & Co. in the interests of *Mr. and Mrs. Haddock in Paris France*, which was not doing very well either with the critics or in the bookstores. But everything else was perfect. The New Weston was a good hotel, the speakeasies were flourishing, the excitement of night life was increasing, Jack Gilbert was in town. Bobby took us to a marvelous night club where we gloried until dawn in the wonder of a new comic genius named Jimmy Durante with his superb companions Lou Clayton and Eddie Jackson. It was as though my own crazy world had come to life and I had found the environment in which I belonged. Gerald and Sara came to New York and I gave a party on my birthday for them and Dotty and the Barrys where Bobby delivered a talk on wild flowers including his new discovery "drover's wet lace" or "false goatsbeard."

Then in order to have Christmas with Clara and Bea's family we went out to Hollywood where we set up our first "home" in a small rented house on La Pere [sic] Drive. Our first cook was a wiry young Filipino whose name was Namba and who disapproved thoroughly of our way of life, in spite of all my efforts to get him to like me. In his second week he asked for a day off in order to celebrate the Filipino National Independence Day and when I roguishly suggested that he might have a bit of a hangover on the day after, he sternly told me that Independence Day was to be observed with a "literary and musical program."

The determined investigation of the enjoyable possibilities of leisure time continued apace. Jack Gilbert was our most frequent companion: his flaming affair with Garbo had begun to die down – at least on the Swedish side – and poor Jack was often in need of cheering up. One night at our house, after a considerable amount of horrible bootleg "Napoleon brandy" (which came in impressive bottles thick with dust fresh from the M-G-M special effects department), Jack decided to make one more assault on the Scandinavian fortress. He rushed away in his car with that wild look in his eyes which betokened that the internal emotional pressure was approaching the safety-valve point. We didn't quite know what was on his mind, as the conversation he so abruptly abandoned had been on the subject of a painting of the crucifixion by Pieter Breughel, a reproduction of which I had bought in Vienna. About two in the morning the telephone rang. The police had Jack and said that he wanted us to bring him immediately our picture of the crucifixion. It seemed like a rather normal Gilbertian request and when we arrived Jack was in a cell surrounded by an attentive audience of policemen and firemen to whom he was lecturing on the subject of Art. The reason for his presence in the cell was that after leaving our house he had driven directly to Garbo's Santa Monica hotel with the intention of telling her about Breughel. When she had refused to let him interrupt her sleep even for such a high-cultural subject he had become annoyed and tried to climb up the outside wall of the hotel to enter through her balcony window. Unfortunately the police had interrupted Romeo's ascent and as hell hath no fury like a film star scorned, they had been obliged to run him in. The net result was that Garbo got her sleep, the Beverly Hills police got the inside dope on early Flemish painting, and Jack got a lot of unfortunate publicity.

Our first experiment in domesticity wasn't all cognac and skittles by any means. There were my weekly *Tribune* pieces, some of which came off with facility, some with great moil and toil. To write a funny piece a week sounded easy when I first undertook the assignment, but to keep it going for fifty-two weeks was something I would never tackle again. And as I never heard from anyone who ever read my attempts, it was like dropping pebbles into the Grand Canyon. I had also accepted an invitation to write a play about Hollywood with Max Mercin who had had two or three Broadway crime-detective-type hits and who thought that my dialogue plus his experienced dramatic craftsmanship ought to produce another winner. We met every morning and I found myself unhappily trying to interest myself in Max's plots of tricky double crosses and Hollywood sex scandals.

In the spring of 1927 we decided that we wanted to live in New York, and I celebrated our arrival there by catching erysipelas and almost dying. I was saved at the crucial moment by a doctor who came in one Sunday afternoon from his vacation holiday retreat with a new experimental serum. I had no idea how close to death I was, but Bea had been told that there wasn't much hope. Bobby spent an entire afternoon walking all over Manhattan with her, both dreading to telephone the hospital.

After the crisis I improved rapidly and about the time that Lindbergh flew to Paris we moved up to a small cottage in Maine for a summer of recuperation. I divided my time between golf and the hopeful preliminary considerations of a Major Work of Art which was to be called *An American Comedy*. In neither was I particularly successful, especially on the golf course. Just as in boyhood baseball, there was a fatal lack of coordination between my eyes and my muscles. But again I stubbornly refused to accept nature's limitations. In my mind's eye was a vision of a perfect back swing, a sharp click as my beautifully timed rhythmical down-swing hit the ball into a drive which slowly rose, rose, rose until it dropped onto the fairway some 300 yards nearer the hole and my caddy whistled appreciatively and said, "Gosh!" For the next ten years that vision persisted. I read every book on the subject. I got out of bed at night and in early morning to practice new stances, different grips, improved body swings. I dragged poor Beatrice or anyone who would submit out into rain and sleet and tempest to tell me what I was doing wrong. In France, in Monte Carlo, in Haiti, I persisted without success. Many caddies in many languages whistled and said "Gosh!" as I drove – but not in awed appreciation. And then finally, one Sunday afternoon on Long Island in the year of our Lord one thousand nine hundred and thirty-seven, in anger and under circumstances which I shall describe later, I hit my dream drive – and I have never played since.

But in that summer of 1927 that was many bunkers away, and in the autumn I rather discouragedly packed up my clubs and my notes of *An American Comedy* and returned to New York. The discouragement wasn't very deep and it didn't last very long, for Beatrice discovered that a baby was to be born the following May. So we took a two-year lease on an unfurnished apartment in one of the new buildings which were feverishly going up along the East River. Ours was in Sutton Place, and it was great fun to buy our first armchair, to argue about the color scheme of curtains and carpets, to wait for the arrival of pots and pans and soap dishes, to unpack silver wedding gifts. Every day (with the aid of charge accounts) was like Christ-mas. Bobby bought us an antique English oak kitchen table, and promised to use the spare room as his own until the baby came. Dur-ing the summer he and Dorothy Parker and Heywood Broun had become involved in the agitation against the execution of Sacco and Vanzetti, but I hadn't been interested, and in fact hadn't tried to un-derstand. I was getting ready to play the new role of the responsible head of a family, a New York solid citizen with an apartment, a wife and a child.

My sense of responsibility had been somewhat increased by the fact that my father-in-law had recently lost his entire fortune by prematurely anticipating the stock-market crash, and my own finan-cial worries had again begun with my illness and the termination of my *Chicago Tribune* contract. By the time I had furnished the apart-ment I was just about broke, and beginning to experience for the first time in many years the terrifying uneasiness of unpaid bills. The cure for this, as developed by Beatrice and myself, was laughter; the reality of our fears was made to seem all the more nebulous by the fact that all of our friends were every day in every way becoming richer and richer. Phil and Ellen Barry and the Archie MacLeishes had introduced us to some of their friends with whom we soon became quite intimate. One of Bea's earlier boy friends was Alex-ander "Sandy" Hamilton, whose name came from his distinguished ancestor and whose mother was the sister of J. P. Morgan. Sandy's older brother was the Pierpont M. Hamilton I had encountered on the beach at Cap d'Antibes; he and his wife Marise also became our almost daily companions. One of Bobby's intimates was the young John Hay "Jock" Whitney, son of Payne Whitney. All of these were wealthy "socialites" who were eager to enjoy the exciting world of the speakeasies and the night clubs, and it wasn't long before Bobby and Dotty and Bea and I found ourselves exchanging weekends on the north shore of Long Island for dinners at Jack and Charlie's (still 42 West 49) and hilarious evenings at Jimmy Durante's and the Dizzy Club.

The effect on me was slightly disastrous, for I once more came to associate the friendship of Society and the Rich with the security which from childhood had been connected with Big Names. I managed, however, to keep our financial nose still in the clouds chiefly with the aid of short pieces which I did for the *New Yorker* and from an advance which I got from H. N. Swanson, editor of

College Humor, in anticipation of a novel to be called *Father William.* One of the other financial life rats to which I was rather hopefully clinging was the play about Hollywood which I had helped Max Mercin write. I was overjoyed when Max unexpectedly appeared in New York with the breathtaking news that George M. Cohan was "crazy about it" and had scheduled it, with the title of *Los Angeles,* for December production.

The name of Cohan was like Zeus to me. He had been one of father's and Bert's gods, and I didn't believe he could go wrong. My heart sank, however, when Max showed me the tasteless melodrama to which his and my name were attached, and it sank even lower when I went to one or two of the rehearsals. However, I needed the money, "George M. Cohan must know his business," there were promises of big movie offers, and besides – look at *Abie's Irish Rose.* So I allowed my name to remain on something of which I was thoroughly ashamed, and I got what I deserved from the critics when it opened just before Christmas and lasted two weeks. The dismaying truth about this venture on Broadway was that I cared more about money than I did about artistic standards.

Yet the beautiful irony of this period in my life was that although I was nearer financial bankruptcy than at any time before or since, I *felt* secure because I was surrounded by friendly wealth and social position. I loved to come home to find my living room occupied by the Elite who were accepting my wife into their group. I felt that I was providing her and the child-to-be with the best of good neighbors. And it wasn't that these friendly people were exclusively rich or "socialite." They hated the stuffiness of Newport and all that pre-World War pretentiousness. The women were young, gay and beautiful. The men were high in Wall Street. The group also included writers like the Barrys and the MacLeishes, and they appreciatively welcomed Bob Benchley and Dorothy Parker into their group. I was very happy – and felt very secure about the future of my family.

Now began the race to finish my novel for *College Humor* before the bill collectors got ugly. Bobby, who was living off and on in the "nursery," helped by arriving one gloomy afternoon in February with an ecstatic announcement: "Kids, our trouble are all over!" It seems that a thing called "talking movies" had been invented and a producer named Tom Chalmers had persuaded Bob to try his "Treasurer's Report" as an experiment in the new medium. It was such a success that he wanted three more, so we all celebrated at Jack and Charlie's, went to see Fred and Adele Astaire in *Funny Face*, and I borrowed enough from Bob to pay some of the November bills. Incidentally, my idea of complete heaven (aside from paying bills) was to watch Fred Astaire dance; Bob had worked on *Funny Face* with the genial Englishman Fred Thompson who lived next to us on 57th Street, so the equally genial doorman at the Alvin Theater used to let Bea and me stand up once or twice weekly at the back of the theater. Whenever I felt a little low, watching Fred could always reassure me that this was the best of all possible worlds.

Fred, Bobby, Jock Whitney and Jock's great friend Jimmy Altemus of Philadelphia constituted a marvelous four-musketeer outfit, ready at the sound of a midnight boat whistle to take off for anywhere the boat was going. Those midnight sailings don't occur any more, but in 1928, if the wind was right, in Sutton Place we could hear that whistle from the docks on the other side of town. Bobby, Bea and I used to look at each other and long to be on board. Bob did go once that spring with Jock and Jimmy to the Grand National in England; his report of the race on his return was of a misty drizzly fog, a huge crowd, a cry of "They're off!" and a frantic attempt to see the course through his binoculars which were, he believed, concentrated on the final jump. When a great shout announced that the race was over, he discovered that he had been gazing resolutely at the hair on the neck of the man in front of him.

As May approached, the novel, *Father William* was beginning to take final shape. I had abandoned the serious but amorphous *American Comedy* and returned to the only theme which seemed to inspire me, the same theme as the *Crazy Fool* and the second Haddock book: the lament for the loss of youth and the play-spirit in the obsession with the making of dollars.

"You are old, Father William" the young man said
"And your hair has become very white;
And yet you incessantly stand on your head –
Do you think at your age, it is right?"

Indeed, the character from whom the book gets its title goes back to my very first novel, the *John Brown's Body* I started so hopefully in Capri six years before when I was trying to write tragically of the loss of the defiant spirit of Yale undergraduate youth. But now the characters and the values have changed places; the hero is the middle-aged Austin Seabury trying to recapture his youth against the opposition of his Yale undergraduate son, Philip, and his culture-snob daughter Harriet at Vassar. Austin Seabury, age forty-five, widowed, gay, wants life to be fun. His deceased wife was an ambitious serious-minded woman, and has unfortunately left the imprint of those worthy qualities on his children. Austin has come to New York to enjoy the Christmas vacation with them. He falls in love with a beautiful flapper named "Pussie" Woodhouse who embodies for him the spirit of his own youth. Unfortunately his son has also fallen for Pussie, and the novel ends on Christmas morning in Austin's suite at the Plaza hotel. Father, wounded by his children's disapproval of his daring "at his age" to court the youthful Pussie, inveigles Philip into a playful contest with boxing gloves. The play becomes serious: light taps on the nose turn into stiff jabs to the chin and father finally lands a beautiful right uppercut which knocks son off his feet and into the Christmas tree. At that moment arrives a Christmas message from Pussie with the glad tidings that she has become engaged to another man. Father and son look at each other, grin, shake hands and walk out together arm in arm.

Insofar as *Father William* is a projection of myself, the characters make a rather revealing commentary on the change which had come over me since my own undergraduate days. Austin's "philosophy," as he expressed it, was that of a man who didn't see much purpose to life, "so why not enjoy things while the going is good?" He gives himself away emotionally at only one point when he and Pussie have been talking as they are seated in a car in a huge empty garage and he unexpectedly murmurs, "God! God! darling – I *am* lonely." Any elaboration of this cry for help is drowned out by the raucous blast of the car's horn, onto which poor Austin has inadvertently leaned, and the scene ends with a laugh. In keeping with Austin's character, the book ridicules "culture vultures" and financially ambitious people who could not agree with Austin's search for laughter in a purposeless but by no means gloomy world. This was myself in 1928.

But while *Father William* was being finished Bea and I were preparing for the birth of our child. We met frequently with our charming and confidence-inspiring obstetrician, and Bea's dresses became increasingly tent-like. The expected day arrived, and nothing happened. The next day – and the next. Poor Bea's attitude became increasingly apologetic. Everybody was full of advice. Bets were placed at Jack and Charlie's, Tony's and the Colony restaurant. Finally on May 20th hopeful signs appeared. Bea hurried to her rendezvous with life, and I drove all afternoon around Central Park with one of our new group, Adele Lovett, who had had two children and appointed herself a remarkably efficient cheerer-upper. But by seven there was no news, so she turned me over to Pierpont and Marise Hamilton who faithfully stood watch over me until midnight when sleep was advised for the would-be father. At three in the morning the telephone rang and I rushed to the nursing home where I joined three other equally nervous young expectants in the small waiting room. At about six a.m. I emerged into the daylight at 61st and Madison, the dazed and happy father of an eight-pound boy, to be named Ames.

Bobby and Dotty were immediately appointed godparents, with instructions from the Episcopal prayer book to fulfill their functions by renouncing (in Ames's name) the devil and all his works, the pomps and vanities of this wicked world, and all the sinful lusts of the flesh. This they dutifully proceeded to do, starting that afternoon at Jack and Charlie's. Under the mistaken idea that godparents were like ushers at a wedding, I also asked Robert and Adele Lovett, and Pierpont and Marise Hamilton to come in on the act. Although they were officially disqualified from devil-renouncing, they accepted in spirit and remained very helpful pseudo-godparents for many years. Peter Hamilton's mother invited Bea and me to take the baby out to their Tuxedo estate in order to get temporarily away from the daily din of riveting from the several new apartment buildings that were going up around us, and as soon as we had hired a stumpy little Irish nurse named Margaret we took advantage of the offer. Another reason for leaving the city was that our Filipino cook had become so nervous about the delay in the *accouchement* (or so he said) that he had taken to the bottle, or bottles; and as it was my bottle or bottles, we decided to fire him while Bea was still in the nursing home. But as I had never fired anybody, I felt the need of a little bottle treatment myself and it ended with Arthur and me in tears, after which he kindly put me to bed and resigned. I didn't have enough in the bank to pay his last two weeks' salary but the Bankers Trust Company had become very patient with me as I had made a funny speech at one of their annual banquets and had also brought in two distinguished new customers: Robert Benchley and Dorothy Parker (whose net assets at the time were slightly below mine). I remember one of Bobby's overdrafts, cashed at the Dizzy Club, which began "Dear Bankers Trust – wish you were here!"

Anyway, Bea and Ames and Margaret and I journeyed out to Tuxedo to be the guest of J. P. Morgan's sister just as an angry telegram arrived from our landlord threatening to dispossess us if he did not immediately receive a check for the last two months' rent. We laughed at the irony of the circumstances and spent three weeks amid the greatest imaginable luxury. Mrs. Julia Morgan Hamilton was a warm hospitable person, even though her face, with its heavy black eyebrows, looked so exactly like the hostile cartoons of her father which I had seen in Columbus papers in my boyhood that I was constantly terrified of displeasing her. My workroom for my daily writing was the Gunroom, the walls of which were lined with hunting rifles and shotguns, an admirable inspiration for work. The final scene of *Father William* was finished on the last day of our visit, and a lovely check from *College Humor* chased several of the more ungentlemanly wolves away from Sutton Place.

Then for the remainder of the summer we went up to Cape Cod, where we shared a cottage with my old roommate Larry Tighe, his wife Hester and *their* infant son. An amusing comedy might have been written by me on the desperate efforts of fraternity brothers to extend the bonds of brotherhood to include wives, babies, cooks and nurses, but before I had time to consider it, an amazing event caused the Donald Ogden Stewart pinball to veer off in another direction.

I became an actor. I hadn't meant to become one any more than I had ever considered being a writer. In fact, when Phil Barry asked me to play a role in his new play *Holiday* I almost refused. It was all right for a Bones man to be the Life of the Party or to go on a lecture tour as a humorist, but to be paid a salary for being an actor – well, that was different. In spite of having written six books I was still thinking of myself as a sort of Richard Brinsley Sheridan who wrote them when the spirit – or his creditors – moved him, and who was really in a different class from Broadway professionals like George Kaufmann and George Abbot. My happy connection with the elite group of which Bea and I now considered ourselves resident members also tended to confirm this separation; indeed, in the joy of belonging to the group, I was rapidly isolating myself from any members of the human race outside my own rather narrow circle. But when I read *Holiday* I became intrigued with the role Phil had cast me in, and since two of the other members of the cast were likewise amateurs, as well as being "in Society," and since I was once more near the bottom of the financial barrel, I decided to take a chance.

The hero of the play is Johnny, who comes from poor parents. All action centers around Johnny's struggle to remain his own Self in spite of efforts by what he calls the "Vested Interests" to commit him to the ambition of making more and more money. After he has made a few thousands on the stock market he astonishes his Vested Interest prospective father-in-law and his fiancee Julia (the younger sister of Linda, the heroine) by announcing: "I just want to save part of my life for myself. Part of the *young* part. Retire young and work old. I'm quitting as long as these thousands last and try to find out who I am and what I am and what goes on and what about it. I don't want to be identified with any class of people, I want to live every which way, among all kinds – and know them – and understand them – and love them." My role was that of a sort of Gerald Murphy in a "Gerald and Sara" couple whom the heroine calls "the rightest, wisest, happiest people I've ever known!" Johnny agrees, saying that "Life must be swell when you have some idea of what goes on, the way they do. They get more fun out of nothing than anyone I know." It was, of course, the "fun" part that made Phil think of me for the part.

The star of the play was Hope Williams, who had attracted the attention of Arthur Hopkins, the producer, while acting in amateur performances at the Comedy Club. She had made her Broadway debut with great success in Phil's hit of the preceding year, *Paris Bound*. Another amateur was a lovely and lively beauty named "Babs" White who was married to Douglas Burden. She had the role of Susan Potter, my wife. Beatrice was given the part of a maid, and as she had gone to the same finishing school as Hope and Babs there might have been danger of a certain justified resentment from the professonal members of the cast at this Social-Register club of amateurs. That this didn't ever become a serious reality was due largely to the wonderfully down-to-earth unphony character of Arthur Hopkins, aided intelligently and cooperatively by all members of the cast. The part of Hope's super-snobbish sister (in the play) was taken by a beautiful aristocratic-looking girl from Brooklyn named Dorothy Tree. And straight from Bryn Mawr, as understudy to Hope, came a fresh, perky, freckled miss by the name of Katharine Hepburn. The men, aside from myself, were all good experienced actors: Ben Smith played the hero, Monroe Owsley played the brother of the rich Fifth Avenue family, and Walter Walker – old Vested Interest himself.

Rehearsals were great fun, with the exception of occasional thunder-and-lightning outbursts from Arthur Hopkins's well-known temper. Arthur's "method" consisted in telling me through which door to enter, where to stand, when to move, and which door to exit from. I kept waiting to be told how to "act" but that wasn't Arthur's way, at least not with this production.

My hesitation about entering the profession should never have bothered me, and I can truthfully say that after two years with Arthur I could not under any circumstances or on any stage have been taken for an actor. Fortunately Phil had hand-tailored a part which fitted me comfortably and required no knowledge of technique. My first entrance (early in Act Two) was into a small New Year's Eve party which was going on in the heroine's Fifth Avenue mansion, and any un-naturalness I might have felt was covered by the fact that I immediately began opening champagne and being good old Don, the Life of the Party. The lines were good and got a lot of laughs when we opened the play in New Haven in November. Phil and Arthur decided the next morning, however, that the party needed even more life, so Phil wrote me a "crazy fool" speech to the guests on the subject of how I had invented the bottle. It began "I arrived in this country at the age of three months, with nothing in my pockets but five cents and an old hat check. I had no friends, little or no education, and Sex to me was still the Great Mystery." After quite a bit along those lines it ended, "And that, my dears, is how I met your grandmother."

The night of a Broadway opening is sheer hell for professional actors, but I didn't know enough about it to appreciate fully what a fearsome chasm was yawning before me. I spent the first act up in my dressing room going over my lines with Bea, putting on my tuxedo and applying greasepaint to my rather pale face (my type of paint was called "juvenile robust"). Roars of laughter from the audience were also very confidence-inspiring and at the end of the first act Jimmy Hagan, the stage manager, told us that it was going very well. Then came the lowering of the house lights, the hush, and I was standing in the darkness backstage waiting for my entrance cue, feeling neither juvenile nor robust, but with a blessed calm of desperation. The cue came, I pushed open the door, bounded onstage – and got a big laugh with my first line. So far – good, but there was that crazy speech getting closer and closer.

I needn't have worried, for by that time the audience loved the play so much that if I'd broken down entirely it would have made them laugh all the more. I didn't break down, however, and the speech was a great success. So was the play. All the reviews next morning were practically raves. Hope became a star, and I became a comedian whom strangers looked at in restaurants.

DOS by James Montgomery Flagg.

Gerald and Sara Murphy and family.

Zelda and F. Scott Fitzgerald

Photo courtesy of Kevin Brownlow

*DOS in **Not So Dumb**.*

Photo courtesy of John Kobal

Irving Thalberg, Lillian Gish, Louis B. Mayer, 1925.

Hollywood, 1932: Elizabeth Allen and Philip Barry, foreground; DOS, leaning forward, is at the table in the background.

Left to right: DOS, Marc Connelly, Philip Barry, Robert Benchley (back to camera).

Robert Benchley and Marc Connelly.

Left to right: George Cukor, DOS, Beatrice Stewart, Ames Stewart, Stewart maid.

*James Stewart, Katharine Hepburn in **The Philadelphia Story**.*

Joan Crawford in **A Woman's Face.**

George Cukor, Spencer Tracy, Katharine Hepburn on
the set of **Keeper of the Flame.**

16

Personally, I wasn't hitting the money jackpot yet. The wages of *Holiday* were fame but not fortune – and the enjoyment of fame led to a certain carelessness about balancing the budget. In fact, there wasn't any budget; there was only the momentary sickish feeling in my stomach at the end of each month when checkbook stubs were added up, but that always disappeared in the evening on the stage of the Plymouth Theatre when the audience began laughing at my lines. A responsive audience is an unfailing cure for anything, including head-colds and hangovers. It is also, like alcohol, an extremely dangerous substitute for reality-facing. Why worry about bills or about getting down to serious work when there is that lovely audience waiting every night?

Actually, as concerns alcohol, I took the obligations of my new profession very seriously. The only time I appeared on the *Holiday* stage a bit high was on New Year's Eve. I had nourished the belief that "if the audience thought I was funny when I was sober, just wait until I show them the Life of the Party when he's tight." So that night I substituted real champagne for the ginger ale and as I had also had quite a healthy amount of the same at dinner, I gave what I thought was a most magnificent performance. The effect on poor Hope and the others in the scene, however, was quite the opposite: My reaction-time had slowed down to minus-zero and dialogue which seemed to me to be rushing along at an unusually brilliant pace was actually proceeding at half speed astern. Fortunately, most of the audience were also tight on that eve of 1929, so I didn't really do any damage, but I never repeated my interesting experiment – at least, not in *Holiday.*

The new year brought additional joys and an additional feeling of "group security" to Bea and me. After almost every performance there were "fans" in our dressing rooms – old friends from Columbus, Yale, Greenwich Village and way stations on my climb upward, and many new friends from the circle into which Phil and Ellen Barry had introduced us. The Princeton representative in this Yale circle of young tycoons was Jim Forrestal and his beautiful Southern-voiced wife Josephine.

All these were the close friends with whom Bea and I were to become increasingly intimate during the next six years. Our very closest friends of all, however, were to be Jock's sister Jean and her husband Charles Payson, whom Jock and Bob Benchley had brought back to our dressing room one night. After two or three post-theater parties and a visit to their Manhasset, Long Island home where we met Mrs. Whitney, we were delighted to be invited to rent one of the three houses on the Payne Whitney estate if and when we were ready to give up our Sutton Place apartment. We leaped at the chance, especially since Mrs. Whitney very tactfully suggested an extremely low rental for such a perfect home. It was a beautiful old white clapboard farmhouse which had been completely modernized for Joan and Charles to occupy after their marriage while their own home was being built a mile or so away on the huge estate. Now that that building had been completed, the "Mouse Hole" (as Joan and Charlie called it) was empty, and the Stewart mice happily prepared to move in when spring came. It was another unbelievable stroke of good fortune, for in addition to providing us with a dream-come-true house, it also provided Stewart the Serious Writer with a workroom far away from those tempting city parties. And not only that but there was on the estate a private golf course exclusively for my use, with two swimming pools including steam room and massage. All this in case there was any danger of my ruining my health from overwork.

So I postponed beginning any major literary effort until I could take full advantage of the pure country air of the north shore of Long Island. When I had first considered acting in *Holiday,* one of the advantages it seemed to offer was that I would have the daytime (except matinee days) for writing. But somehow or other, it didn't work out that way. At the end of each evening performance Bea and I would be so keyed up that sleep was impossible, and the night club life offered so many possibilities to us as celebrities that we very seldom got to bed before three or four. That, in turn, necessitated sleeping until noon – and there were so many exciting invitations to lunch that we frequently didn't get back to the apartment until four. Then, of course, we had to rest before the night's performance.

But, as I have said, neither artistic conscience nor financial tightrope-walking bothered me, even through *Father William* had received very little notice from either the critics or the buying public. It just wasn't in the air to bother about money that year. Jim Forrestal, a vice-president of Dillon Read, gave a friendly bit of freedom from such sordid worries by opening an account there in my name without telling me anything about it. Jim's thoughtful idea was that although Bea and I didn't have any capital, there was no reason we shouldn't share in the general prosperity of a constantly rising market. The first I knew about it was when I began receiving statements of credits to me from sales of stocks I had never heard of. I went down to Wall Street to protest to Jim and he, pipe in mouth as usual, advised me not to be a horse's ass, so I bowed to his superior financial wisdom. About the same time Jim and Charlie put my name up for the Racquet and Tennis Club, one of my secret dreams since Harold Talbott had given me a visitor's card to it in 1920. Bob Lovett contributed to our welfare by giving us an almost-new Chrysler roadster, his excuse being that he had decided to turn it in on a new Cadillac but preferred to give it to us in view of the small trade-in allowance. Pierre Hamilton registered a number of shares of stock in some project he was financing in the name of his "godson" Ames. Tommy Gamage, one of Babs Burden's friends on Wall Street, offered me a job at a terrific salary in his brokerage office. No, financial cares were always good for a laugh in 1929 and *Holiday* ran merrily along with its encouraging admonition to "find out what life is about – with the aid of several thousand dollars to be easily picked up in Wall Street."

In the interests of finding out about life, therefore, Bea and Ames and I moved out to the Payne Whitney estate early in April. It did not occur to me that such a move might arouse negative reactions among my friends, and cause a gradually increasing alienation from them. My blindness was partially self-induced. No American man likes to admit to himself that he is a social climber. But the step was practically inevitable and there were certain justifications for my "going Whitney." Jock was an un-snobbish person, and his best friend was Bob Benchley whom I loved and admired more than any man. Neither Jock nor Joan nor their mother was "High Society" in the commonly accepted derogatory sense of that term. Mrs. Whitney's girlhood ambition (she was the daughter of John Hay) had been to write poetry. (After our second year at Manhasset she shyly showed me some of her poems and asked if I would let Dorothy Parker read them. Dorothy's report was on the whole very favorable.) I am not arguing that successful social climbing doesn't create jealousies and alienate former affections, or that it is the best possible thing for a creative writer. But the fact is that in 1929 I was concerned with giving Bea and myself the most joyful life possible.

With the help of the rich gay group with which we were now surrounded we certainly succeeded. Every morning one of Mrs. Whitney's gardeners brought flowers and vegetables from the garden and the conservatory. Milk was delivered from the estate herd. We had engaged two wonderful Norwegian girls, Nana and Borghild, as cook and maid. Margaret was a good nurse, and Ames flourished. Bea and I could drive to the theater in about an hour, and we indulged much less in night clubs before driving back. Sunday mornings were spent on the golf course or at the large swimming pool near the Paysons', followed by a family dinner at the main house. Mrs. Whitney presided at dinner, Jock was usually present, and occasionally there were the two other families who lived on the estate. The main house itself was a rambling two-storied affair with no signs of the grandiose hand of an interior decorator. The furnishings were what might be called "disorderly Edwardian" and the atmosphere was as "homey" as you could feel in the presence of butlers and footmen. For Bea and me the key to the comfortable simplicity of the place was the sincerity and friendliness and unpretentiousness of Mrs. Whitney.

Sunday afternoons after lunch meant a continuation of my desperate quest for a decent golf score, followed by a swim either in Mrs. Whitney's beautiful indoor pool or at the open air pool at the Payson's. I passed up the opportunity to learn to play polo, or even to ride with Bea on one of the horses in the Whitney stable, though I had those riding boots from Paris. I did put them on once for a masquerade and once I even got onto a horse in order to be photographed for an article I wrote for *Town and Country*.

Horses and I have never really understood each other, although I hypocritically pretended to be tremendously interested in Mrs.

Whitney's Greentree racing stable and loyally lost money whenever we went with Joan and Charlie to Belmont Park. Not that Greentree horses never won; there was a notable afternoon when a footman hurried out to the golf course to breathlessly tell me that Twenty Grand had just won the Kentucky Derby. Incidentally, the name of the winning horse should have been "Fifty Grand," as Mrs. Whitney had intended to name it after Ernest Hemingway's short story, but a difference of thirty thousand dollars isn't really very serious in the name of a winning horse. Mrs. Whitney was usually extremely painstaking about the correct and felicitous naming of her colts. Bea and I could spend evenings with her trying to suggest what the son of Falstaff's Apple out of St. Agnes Eve should be called. I was never any good at it; in fact, guessing games of any kind produce in me a sort of state of malignant apathy. You have only to suggest "Let's play 'I am not animal, vegetable or mineral' " to turn me rapidly into a combination of the latter two.

Meanwhile, on 44th Street, *Holiday* was drawing toward the close of its run. That experience taught me a great deal about what is called "consumer reaction." I would advise any aspiring play-wright to get the practical knowledge which comes with experience in front of various audiences. The difference between dialogue on the printed page and that same dialogue when spoken in the theater is often tremendous, as is the reception at Saturday matinees of can-dy-eating females as contrasted, say, with Saturday nights when the gin-happy breaths from the first three rows almost knock you over. And most important of all is the revelation of the subtle differences in writing which go into constructing a scene which will "play"; nothing is so wonderful to actors as the approach to that moment when over the audience comes that miraculous hush which tells those on the stage (and in the wings) that the scene is holding the bastards breathless.

In the third week after we had moved out to the Mouse Hole I got an idea for a play. The idea came to me in the course of a visit from a young man who had been in love with Bea before she became my wife. Shortly after we married he had rapidly followed suit, and there was a bit of a suspicion that he had done it on the rebound from his disappointment with Bea. Whether or not that was true, when I met his wife I began to wonder about these "rebound" wives and in a very short time had blocked out the first two acts.

It was exciting and extremely satisfying to be doing a play of my own again instead of the Hollywood, *Chicago Tribune,* and *New Yorker* titbits. In my two acts I had progressed, I think, beyond the somewhat lighthearted lament for lost youth which had been at the basis of *Father William.* I was attempting the transition from the satirical world of *Aunt Polly* and *The Crazy Fool* into the depths of living characters and current human problems with which I had labored in Capri in my first dawn of creative hopefulness.

This was an important step in that it marked the end of my career as a professional "humorist"; I never again wrote short pieces for *The New Yorker* or other magazines. It was important also in another larger sense. At the very time when I seemed to have succumbed most completely to the childhood lure of security through social position, I began to write a play that showed forces working within me which were to bring my inner conflict to another such crisis as had happened in Dayton. The Whitneys had provided me with a sense of security and a quiet workroom, and my first act in that environment was to become creatively active, which forecast the possible reemergence of an independent individual.

The creation of the vital third act of *Rebound,* which was to be the first faint note of this theme, was postponed until the fall by a surprising invitation to go out to Hollywood to act in an M-G-M movie to be directed by King Vidor. But could I, the creative writer, postpone the important completion of *Rebound?* I certainly could – and did, partly because my little heart was doing nip-ups at the thought of being a real movie actor, and partly because I was two months behind in my rent to Mrs. Whitney (who had not, bless her, shown any awareness of the oversight).

In June, as was the annual ritual, the Whitney galaxy joined other assorted yachts in moving up Long Island Sound to New London for the Yale-Harvard boat race. Charlie Payson had rowed on the famous 1921 "gutless crew" which had against all expectations heroically beaten Harvard. Jock had also rowed in a Yale boat, so the races were a family tradition. Some of us went on Mrs. Whitney's large "Captiva"; Jock brought others on his own smaller craft. Our group, which was to be practically unchanged for the next six years, consisted largely of Charlie's Yale friends, including Stuart Symington and his wife Evie Wadsworth (whose mother was Mrs. Whitney's sister).

We joined a large fleet of yachts gaily decorated with Yale and Harvard colors near the finish line, then went ashore for the customary night-before dance at the Griswold Hotel (which I hadn't been able to afford after my own graduation in 1916). The Yale and Harvard world, poised arrogantly on the brink of President Hoover's dream of two cars in every garage, danced happily until dawn, and Bea and I danced with them. This was our world of youth, of fun unending. Not the cultured elite of which I had once dreamed, but yachts are very nice as a means of transportation, and so are private railroad cars.

After the boat races came another traditional event, the wedding anniversary ball of Joan and Charlie. Hundreds of guests, thousands of colored lights in the trees, millions of bottles of champagne – or so it seemed the next morning. Once more we danced all night and talked about it all next week at the swimming pool.

Then it was time for me to pack my "juvenile robust" grease paint and journey out to Hollywood. Clara was by now the undoubted oldest inhabitant and queen of the Mark Twain hotel and I happily settled into my old room, prepared to finish Act Three of *Rebound* between takes at the studio. The movie script was an adaptation of Marc Connelly's and George Kaufman's first Broadway hit *Dulcy*, now renamed *Not So Dumb*, with Marion Davies playing the role which had lifted Lynn Fontanne to stardom. By a rather obvious bit of casting, my part was that of an escaped lunatic. Perhaps it was the studio's tactful method of showing their memory of my having written a book called *The Crazy Fool*, their script for which was (and still is) what they call "not yet quite licked."

This was the first year of Hollywood's complete surrender to talking pictures, which was a lucky break for me in that very few of the stars had ever used their voices on the stage, and my lack of Thespian technique was partially covered by the fact that whenever I spoke into the microphone it sounded amazingly like a normal human voice. It was Marion's first shot at a "talkie" play, and as her only stage appearances had been in the chorus of the "Follies," there was a certain amount of apprehension and much time off for easy steps for little vocal chords.

The whole business was very enjoyable. Although King Vidor had had his own baptism in the new medium of sound with his very fine *Hallelujah*, this was his first shot at stage dialogue, but his wonderful sense of humor and his patience kept everything rolling along. Irving Thalberg, whom I hadn't been able to impress with my scenario writing in the "silent" days, actually praised my depiction of the gay mad character named Van Dyke, and I was allowed to add three or four crazy gags of my own invention. Later I was to get a "Best Supporting Role" award in *Photoplay* magazine. But best of all, in the midst of the shooting there came to me a solution of my third-act troubles for *Rebound,* and by the time I got back to Long Island I was pretty sure I had the makings of the kind of play I had hoped to write.

In a way, my trip alone to Hollywood had worked out as sort of a parallel to the solitary walk along the Mississippi river which I had taken ten years before "pour arranger mes pensees." In *Rebound* I had once more ventured to look inside myself, and instead of writing as a humorist or satirist I had, in creating the character of Sara, opened up a rather important problem in my own life. *Father William* had been Don Stewart trying gaily to preserve the happiness of youth and playtime in a world that wanted him to grow serious and "important." Now, without quite knowing what I had done, I had opened in *Rebound* a much more important can of tomatoes.

At the end of the second act Sara has been faced with the possibility of losing her husband to his old girl. The major new factor is that since her marriage she has come to love him, and is now up against the difficult problem of a choice between her new-found love and her self-respect. It was then, in Hollywood, that the key scene came to me, and it came in a sudden flash of remembrance of Chicago and my love for Diana. I had lost Diana (or so I believed) because I had been so overwhelmed by my love for her that I had surrendered my Self. Whether or not that was an inevitable product of real love and an indisputable evidence of its depth and purity, it had certainly not had the required effect on Diana. And remembering that, I worked out the climax of my play in the following terms: In the third act, while Sara is hesitating, bewildered, crushed, torn by the apparent defection of her husband, her formerly undecided suitor Johnny returns, now genuinely in love with her. When, in the despairing fervor of his desire he throws himself at her feet and cries "Oh Sara, I need you so!", she is overwhelmed by the fact that these are the very words she had used when tearfully pleading with her husband about their marriage. She suddenly realizes that "love has made me into a weak and cowardly person." Her courage returns; she faces herself with the knowledge that "marriage isn't as important as something inside me that's been dying," and in the final scene she faces her husband with "I saw love tonight, Bill. I saw it for the first time and I know now that love is dependent, poignantly dependent. It needs so much from the loved one. It was the need I felt for you tonight when I went begging. I turned beggar. I begged you to love me. The need has gone now. I'm alone again. But I'm not lonely. At this moment, Bill, marriage is of no importance to me. Neither is love. My love doesn't need you any longer." Faced with this, Bill quickly comes to his senses and the curtain falls on two people whose marriage now has hopes of becoming a "real" one.

More important than that, however, is the recapture of her Self by Sara, the symbolic "me" whose threatened loss of self-respect was the unconscious worry which had set the play in motion. Plays are like dreams; they clothe the unconscious in symbolic form. The theme of the play, as expressed by Sara, was "Don't ever kneel before anyone. Don't ever belong to anyone. Belong to yourself – and thus be free." This theme of the sacredness of individual freedom was symbolically expressed in the play in terms of a marriage, but, as in a dream, the real content was concerned with something quite different, something which I was hiding from myself. My marriage wasn't causing me any worry. I was completely happy as far as that was concerned. But somewhere inside me something was beginning to make me feel concern about "individuality" and "freedom."

Anyway, *Rebound* was to be produced if Arthur Hopkins liked it, and that depended somewhat on the availability of Hope Williams for the part of Sara, which I had written with her exclusively in mind. I showed the play to Arthur during our rehearsals for the tour of *Holiday* and the next morning the telephone at the Mouse Hole rang. "This is Arthur Hopkins," said the voice. "Oh yes, Arthur." I gulped, and waited feverishly. There was no sound of life from his end of the line. Finally, after a silence of several minutes, I ventured, "Arthur, are you there?" "Yes," he answered, and there was more silence. Finally came the words "I read your play." "Yes?" I said – and he said nothing for at least another two aeons. Then: "I liked it" – and my breakfast returned happily to my stomach. But "it needs a lot of work" (the play, not my stomach), so we postponed any decisions, since *Holiday* was expected to play Boston, Philadelphia and Chicago until the summer.

The road tour began in the Bronx during Yom Kippur, the Jewish Feast of Atonement. We suspected on opening night that the audience had got the theater mixed up with the Synagogue. It was a most nerve-shattering performance, especially since Hope had been knocked out the day before with a bad cold and there had not been time to rehearse the understudy. Katharine Hepburn had forsaken *Holiday* and taken a part in a new show but she bravely agreed to help us out, which was doubly courageous in that she had never once played Hope's part during the entire Broadway run. Furthermore, it was Bea's first appearance in the stage role of my wife, and the audience's atonement atmosphere was not very responsive to our drinking of champagne and nonchalant nibbling of turkey legs.

However, we got through the evening without disaster, and a week later journeyed up to Boston to spread our cheerful warning about the dangers of becoming too rich too quickly in Wall Street. We opened on October 28th, which also happened by a curious coincidence to be the opening date of the Wall Street Crash and poor Phil's message was received by the Boston mourners with an impressive two and a half hours of silence. The next day brokers in New York began jumping out of windows and by the end of the two week run we felt like joining them. Philadelphia wasn't much better, and Arthur decided to call off the rest of the tour.

Aside from the closing of the show, the Crash meant nothing financially to Bea and me. Ironically enough, from the time of the Crash and all through the Depression years, when unemployment hung heavily the American way of life, my bank balance steadily soared.

The closing of *Holiday* was actually my good fortune, since Arthur Hopkins needed a play for Hope Williams who had built up a substantial audience of enthusiastic devotees. Hope read my play and wanted to play Sara. Phil Barry liked it. So Arthur went to work on the casting and early in January of 1930 started rehearsals. For the part of Sara's husband Bill we had a very attractive and experienced actor Don Cook. Bill's seductive temptress was entrusted to an amateur, Kay Leslie, who was the tempting and seductive sister of Charlie Payson's classmate Warren Leslie. The most difficult role in the play was that of Sara's friend Johnny, and Arthur found an actor named Bobbie Williams who came through beautifully. I played the rather unimportant role of Les, Sara's older brother-in-law, and for Sara's father we were lucky to have nice old Walter Walker from *Holiday*.

The rest of the cast were up to Arthur Hopkins's high standards, and with excellent sets by Robert Edmond Jones we opened at the Plymouth the first week in February. Hope and the company gave brilliant comedy performances, there was almost continuous laughter, and when the curtain came down at the end of the second act everyone backstage felt that we had a hit. It was the third act, however, that Arthur and I were rightly worried about. This was the act in which a comedy was expected to develop, without irritating the audience, into a serious crisis in the soul of the leading comedienne. I was taking an awful chance: A humorist who temporarily lays aside the cap and bells is generally subjected to an outrage only slightly less universal than that accorded to a matricide. When the final curtain came down, however, I think that my attempt had been a success.

The reviews the next morning seemed generally to agree. Heywood Broun called it "the best light comedy written by anybody hereabouts in ten or twenty years." The *Evening Journal's* Jean Anderson said, "Its sly mixture of superb idiocy and compelling drama makes an evening of rare quality." Alex Woollcott wrote that "The finale of that second act is one of the most exciting things I ever saw in a theater." John Mason Brown told the *Post* readers that "it is equally fleet and equally facile in unloosing its nonsense of a joyous, irrational kind." Arthur Pollock called it "One of the funniest plays of the season," and Dorothy Parker wrote "*Rebound* did not stop for me with the last curtain. It came home with me and will stay. Brave and beautiful things don't leave you." *Rebound* was not the smash box office hit that *Holiday* had been, but we ran until May or June, and at least one critic picked it as one of the "Ten Best Plays of 1929-30."

17

So 1930 began for me with a new high in my literary career. I remember my happiness when Clara came from Hollywood and we walked toward a theater above which was my name in lights. I nudged her and pointed and she almost cried as she pressed my arm. Then we turned back to Broadway and I pointed again where, above the Capitol Theater, was another electric sign. *Not So Dumb* it read, then came "Marion Davies," then "Elliot Nugent" – and then "Donald Ogden Stewart." Clara wanted to watch it some more; after the second time I had to get to my dressing room to put on my "juvenile robust"; I left Clara still gazing as Broadway surged around her. *My* Broadway now. I had conquered. My name was in lights on three other theaters before the end of the year. One was for a Paramount comedy short on the subject of the new traffic rules which I madly explained, Benchley-like, with blackboard and pointer; once for a similar short in which I delivered my bird lecture, "Our Feathered Friends"; and then, in the fall, my musical comedy *Fine and Dandy* opened as a new hit for Joe Cook at Erlanger's Theater.

While *Rebound* was still playing, Bea accepted Jock Whitney's invitation to be one of a party he was taking over to England to the Grand National, which he hoped was going to be won by his Irish-bred jumper "Easter Hero." Bobby sailed with them, as did Fred and Adele Astaire, Jimmy Altemus and Jimmy's sister Liz, whom Jock was to marry later in the year. It wasn't fun going out alone to the Mouse Hole every night after the show, and in one lonely moment I decided to cheer myself up by talking to Bea over the newly installed transatlantic telephone. The cost of a call was terrifically high in that first year, but I figured that I could afford at least three minutes, so on a Sunday evening I put an alarm clock in front of me and waited excitedly for the connection to go through. Finally the bell rang, I lifted the receiver, and heard Bea's voice. We exchanged happy greetings. "Tell me, darling," she said, "How is Ames?" A wonderful idea struck me. "Wait," I cried and rushed in to Ames' nursery, grabbed him from his bed (he wasn't asleep), and held him in front of the telephone. "Say 'hello, mummy' " I whispered. There was a long pause. "Say 'hello mummy' " I urged, my voice rising as I glanced at the clock. Ames didn't seem to be aware of the expensive minutes which were ticking away. I shook him, gently at first, then with increasing irritation. "Say 'hello Mummy!' Say, 'hello mummy!!' " Over the Atlantic cable reigned supreme silence as my clock ticked away. I became stubborn. "Goddamnit, kid!" I shouted. "Speak! Say something!" And after seven minutes and forty-five seconds (or $138.20) the little darling looked up at me said said: "Hello, daddy." It was worth another $25 to tell Bea the story and hear her laughter.

There was one other notable event while Bea was in Europe, and this time there was no laughter. One night after I came off from the final curtain with applause still sounding in my ears, there were two strangers in my dressing room. I greeted them with my customary phony modest hit-author smile and asked them how they liked the show.

They hadn't seen the show, it seems, but they had seen my Federal Income Tax returns for 1925 and they had some questions to ask me. 1925 was the year before I married Bea, and I remembered with a sudden sick feeling that on the 15th of March 1926 when I asked her to marry me I had spent the morning at the office of a red-headed female Income Tax "expert" to whom Jack Gilbert had enthusiastically sent me and who had assured me that she would make out a very satisfactory report if I would just leave her all my 1925 canceled checks. In those days income tax was something, like Prohibition, that you resented as a governmental intrusion into an individual's private affairs. Without any investigation I had signed the papers and gone out radiantly to meet my future bride. And now these two Federal detectives were confronting me with those canceled checks, many of which had been falsely listed on the tax return as "business expenses." They also spoke of a possible indictment, trial and prison sentence.

I didn't sleep a wink that night, partly because I have a deep belief that good luck sort of evens up, and that it was now my turn to take the rap. In the morning I guiltily watched Ames innocently eating his breakfast, and drove to see Kenneth Simpson, a Bones man who had married my old friend Helen Porter and was a lawyer with, I had been told, good political connections. Ken was sympathetic but not exactly comforting. He would go to Washington to see what the score was. The score seemed to be vague. I went to Washington and told my true story to some rather cold man in a bow tie and brown suit. More sleepless nights. Bea came back from Europe. I told her of the income tax boys and she was furious at them. It did seem sort of ridiculously unreal; things like this just didn't happen to nice people like us. Finally, after weeks of suspense, they let me off the hook and decided to go after only the "experts." It had been a very sobering nightmare and I resolved never to try to play any jokes on the government again. But the government itself still remained in my mind a vague entity, a "they" down there in Washington who hypocritically passed Prohibition laws and crookedly made deals for oil leases and with whom I, as a writer, fortunately had no connection – except when they needed my services in time of war.

The time when I really began to be guilty of a crime – at least that of becoming a "commodity" on the markets – started with the closing of *Rebound.* Of course, I had been a "commodity" for the American Tel. and Tel., for the Talbotts, even for a brief time to my lecture audiences and to the M-G-M studio in Hollywood. But fortunately I had not been enough of a success at these ventures to have them take complete control. The pinball on its way to the jackpot seemed, in *Rebound,* to be moving again under its own steam. Unfortunately, this was an illusion: The pinball didn't have any idea where it was and could not therefore set up any alternative course in opposition to the strong pull of the jackpot forces.

So, when Walter Wanger of Paramount asked me to write a script for a film to be called *Laughter,* I rushed to accept. Part of my reason was that I could work at my Long Island home and with the director Harry d'Arrast who had been one of the ushers at my wedding. Then, too, I was ambitious to show the movie world that M-G-M had been mistaken when I didn't make good as a writer in the silent days – and, of course, there was that lovely money. Harry Kurnitz once described movie writing as a horrible ordeal in which sadistic producers torture you almost beyond endurance by holding your jaws open while they drop a monotonously maddening succession of gold dollars into your helpless mouth.

I opened wide – and didn't close it for many years, partly because of my ear for dialogue, and partly because this was the beginning of a frantic search by talking-picture producers for just such writers. Harry was a sensitive, well-educated Frenchman with impeccable taste that applied equally to wine, women and art. He had learned about movies under Chaplin, having helped direct *A Woman of Paris,* and this was to be his first shot at the talkies. Assigned to us by Paramount as a recorder of our dialogue was an ambitious young man just graduated from CCNY named Milton Sperling. The working conditions were admirable. We met each day in the beautiful gardens behind the Mouse Hole or at the Payson swimming pool, and the script progressed rapidly. *Laughter* was a comedy of marriage, another version of the "youth vs. age" theme. A young actor named Fredric March who was still working at the Paramount Long Island studio in *The Royal Family,* was destined for the lead as a penniless young composer. Opposite him was to be Nancy Carroll, with Frank Morgan as her wealthy but laughter-less husband.

Before the script was finished I was asked by a Broadway producer named Morrie Green to take another job, a stage musical comedy for the crazy-humor comedian Joe Cook, and as Joe had long been one of my great delights, I gladly accepted. Joe lived on a mad gag-infested estate in New Jersey which bewilderingly expressed his genius. On his three-hole golf course one drove off confidently into what looked like a fairway only to have one's ball rebound sharply over one's head from a huge rock which had been cunningly camouflaged. The last green was a golfer's paradise in that no matter where the ball landed it rolled obediently into the hole. Conditions inside the house were similarly deranged. The "butler" was one of the contortionists, acrobats, midgets or other show-business people whom Joe had picked up his years in Vaudevill. Poor Mrs. Cook lived bravely in this cuckooland and struggled apologetically to bring some degree of common sense into the madhouse.

On my first visit, for the avowed purpose of having a "story conference," Joe finally became serious and told me that he had the whole plot for my script already worked out. This was a great relief for me, as my engagement depended on whether or not Joe approved of my work. If he already had a story he wanted, the rest should be easy. "It's along these lines," said Joe. "I come on the stage driving a big steam roller, with a loud whistle that shoots out firecrackers. Dave [that was Dave Chase, Joe's principal stooge] is sitting in a chair up above a big tank of water, pretending to be fishing but he's asleep. Then a lot of kids in baseball suits come in from Stage Left and a lot of Indians run on from Stage Right and they get into a fight and Dave is knocked out of his chair into the tank and there's a big splash." He stopped and looked at me for approval. "Wonderful," I laughed. Joe was pleased. "It came to me the other night," he said. "Now do you think we can go into rehearsal early in August?" "But Joe –" I asked "– you said something about a plot." "I've told it to you," said Joe. "I thought you said you liked it."

So I went to work along those lines, but more generally along the lines of my *Crazy Fool,* and we actually went into rehearsal in August under the name of *Fine and Dandy.* The music was being written by "Kay Swift" and the lyrics by "Paul James"; their real names happened to be Mr. and Mrs. James Paul Warburg, and they were delightful collaborators.

The process of putting on *Fine and Dandy* was quite unlike that of *Rebound* – in fact, it was quite unlike anything in any sane world, theatrical or otherwise. The routine of casting was fairly normal, although I hate the procedure under any circumstances. To sit like a Lord High Chief Justice in the fifth or sixth row of a theater while some poor actor or actress has to come out on a cold, hard, badly lighted stage and read or dance or sing for you still makes me squirm, especially at the memory of having to sing out to the unsuccessful candidates: "Thank you very much. *We'll* call *you!*" There were, however, some rather thrilling moments; I remember especially the afternoon when an unknown Eleanor Powell came on from the wings and began her tap dance.

Eleanor was chosen for the show. I can't remember the other names, but in a Joe Cook production it didn't make any difference. Neither did the script. If Joe thought of a new gag, in it went; one afternoon I discovered five midgets in a scene which I thought had been about love. The explanation was that they had played once with Joe in Kansas City and were now down on their luck.

Finally we all moved up to Boston and the real thrills began – also my headaches. The thrills came with the dress rehearsal when, for the first time, I heard the music with an orchestra and saw the dances and the costumes and the numbers which had been rehearsing in a different theater. The headaches ensued after the opening-night performance which, although the Boston critics had praised it, didn't satisfy Joe. It was then that I learned about the insatiable hunger of comedians for laughs and more laughs. Little by little, as the New York opening approached, everyone seemed to lose their friendliness and their confidence in my book. Joe wanted to cut out musical numbers, Kay and Jim Warburg wanted to add musical numbers. Our prima donna wanted another song, the midgets wanted to put in a banana-eating routine which had wowed the audience at Keith's in Cincinnati in 1925. Finally, however, the day came when further changes were impossible and I went down to New York resolved never to touch another musical. The truth was that I was still an amateur and becoming, because of my easy successes, an increasingly spoiled one.

When I got off the train at Grand Central I gave my bag to a young Negro porter and asked him to follow me to a taxi. He surprised me by saying, "Yes, Mr. Stewart" and it turned out that he had seen me in *Rebound*. Then, just before we got to the taxi, he surprised me even more by asking if I could do him a favor. I thought he wanted an autograph and reached for my pen. But I put the pen back when he told me that he was at Yale, or rather, that he had finished his Junior year there, but hadn't got high enough grades to get an additional scholarship which would enable him to graduate. He didn't ask for money; he only wanted me to use any influence I might have with the scholarship committee. I didn't have any, but I was suddenly happily engulfed by a wave of benevolence, and when I had checked on his story I arranged to pay the expense of his Senior year. It seemed to me – and still seems to me – a rare bit of luck to stumble on somebody at a crucial moment of need, and I suppose that his being a Negro made me feel even better. It wasn't very much money and it meant no deprivation to myself, so there is no particular credit coming to me for doing something which I am sure almost anybody in my position would have done. And the reward, in relief from an unconscious sense of guilt about my rich, happy life, was tremendous. My luck was marching on.

I missed the successful opening of *Fine and Dandy* because I was getting successfully drunk at Jock Whitney's bachelor dinner the week before his wedding to Liz Altemus. The dinner was held at the Madison Square Garden Club. One of the guests was Gene Tunney and in an inspired moment I thought what a good joke it would be to pick a fight with Gene. So I walked up to him, told him to take off his glasses, and prepared to swing. There was a God-awful moment of suspense when I thought he didn't know it was a joke, but the fact that he didn't have any glasses to take off (plus the look of terror which must have come into my face) saved my life, and I got my laugh. When the bachelor dinner ended, I floated down to Joe Cook's dressing room at Erlanger's Theater where all the horrors of Boston were washed away in the good fellowship of a hit opening.

A week or so later the producer Gilbert Miller asked me to adapt his French hit comedy called *Le Sexe Faible* for Broadway, and as it was still running in Paris he suggested that Bea and I go over to see it. We accepted his suggestion, sailed immediately, and were delighted to find Bob Lovett, "Di" Gates and Jim Warburg on the boat. These three bankers were going abroad on business but we managed to intersperse quite a bit of pleasure.

Of these three, Bob Lovett was the one to whom I felt most closely attached in friendship. He had for Bea and me a real affection, as he did for Bob Benchley and Dorothy Parker. Perhaps it wasn't so much affection as interest. I think that our irresponsible madness somehow fascinated him. He himself was the most solid, sane, reliable of Rocks of Gibraltar. If I had ever been in trouble in those days, I think that Bob would have been one of the people to whom I could and would have gone. With him and with his wife Adele there was one of those friendships which, like that of the Gerald Murphys and the Phil Barrys, I treasure among my memories.

When we got to Paris the banking boys went about their business of checking on the state of European finance (in which Bea and I had not the slightest interest), and we went to the theater to see *Le Sexe Faible.* Then we made a quick visit to Gerald and Sara Murphy upon whom tragedy had suddenly and overwhelmingly descended. Their son Baeoth had been stricken with tuberculosis and died. And now, as though fate had not been cruel enough to this glorious family, the youngest boy Patrick was fighting for his life in one of the Magic Mountain resorts high in the Swiss Alps. The moment Patrick's doctor had told them this was the one hope for saving the child's life, Gerald and Sara had abandoned everything, and were living in this last-resort community of dying men and women.

When Bea and I arrived it was infinitely more grim than we had imagined, even though Patrick was "improving." Gerald and Sara were as gaily charming as ever, and Dotty Parker, who had been visiting them for a month, tried her best to cover the horror with tenderness and laughter. Gerald warned us that the first night of sleep was usually difficult for the newly-arrived, and he was right. Not because one couldn't sleep, but because of the horrible dreams which emerged in the topmost Alpine atmosphere. But even before bedtime, the haunting shudders closed down with the early setting of the sun behind the mountain peaks. For four years Bea and I had spent our evenings in an atmosphere of excitement, either in the theater, in a speakeasy, at a party, or, if at home, with guests who, even if dull, could usually be transformed by mutual application of alcohol into what seemed to be fascinatingly intelligent companions. We had resolutely and successfully shut out sorrow or pain – and were even beginning to be able to avoid inconvenience. And here, trapped on this desolate snow-covered silent mountain, with Death seeming to be waiting mockingly in the cold clear air outside, were the two people who had been our models for the Happy Life.

They themselves gave no sign of any change. Gerald remembered the special cocktails Bea and I had loved on our honeymoon, and Sara had outdone herself with amazing variations of Swiss cookery. Dotty was at her best. After dinner Gerald played new records he had discovered in Germany, including one by an unknown Marlene Dietrich from a film called *Der Blaue Engel.* Sara and he told us of the macabre life-in-death with which they were surrounded, and to which they were attempting to bring some of their own brave gaiety. When one of the patients was given his death warrant by his physician, it was now the custom for him to appear at the club with a small replica of his coffin; those who were also about to die saluted him with champagne. Sara had found some musicians and had actually persuaded them to open a night club, which had become extremely successful. At the end of the evening Gerald went to the piano and Sara, in her lovely alto, sang with him. At the end of the evening Bea and I found ourselves in our bedroom crying our eyes out. Something of Reality had tapped on the windows of our dream house and we hastened to close the shutters.

Next day we fled, taking Dotty with us. The descent from Hell to Earth was almost as nerve-shaking an atmospheric change as had been the sudden elevation to the mountain. On the train to Paris I exploded into my one and only row with Dotty and attacked her bitterly for a profile of Ernest Hemingway which she had written for the *New Yorker,* in the course of which she had praised Ernest as one writer who would never never never be a slave to the society inhabiting the North Shore of Long Island. *Touche* – and it hurt like hell, especially, ironically enough, from Dotty for whose sake four years before I had had a quarrel with Ernest which had helped terminate our friendship. Dotty of course disclaimed that she had been referring specifically to me, and by the time we got to Paris all was love and cognac. And by a curious coincidence Ernest with his new wife Pauline were on the boat which Bea, Dotty and I took for New York.

It was an interesting meeting of two former friends whose dreams had now come true. At the time of the beginning of the friendship there had been a certain similarity in Ernest's and my dreams: we had both wanted to succeed as writers who told the truth about life as we saw it. But in the seven years since then, Ernest's ambition had not been undercut as had mine by other forces. He had held true to *his* course, and had now reached the goal. *A Farewell To Arms,* published the year before, had deservedly achieved his dream of artistic fulfillment. It had also been a best seller; a stage version by Laurence Stallings was playing on Broadway; Hollywood had eagerly paid tribute to his genius.

My own tribute was sincere, with an important reservation. I had said in *Rebound* what I thought about one aspect of *A Farewell To Arms.* Ernest's heroine, it seemed to me, was too exclusively the male idea of the way women *should* act. She was always there when the hero wanted her, and she even obligingly died at the end when her presence was no longer a boon. Partly in reaction to this I had in my play created a heroine who refused to become a male convenience.

At any rate, here we were, two boys who had started out with our bare hands, a pencil and a few sheets of blank paper, and had in a few short years and by different paths hit the American jackpot of fame and wealth. Whose jackpot seemed to be the more important was convincingly indicated, to my dismay, on our arrival in New York harbor when a boatload of newspaper reporters boarded the ship. While I was reminiscently thumbing over in my mind the reviews of *Aunt Polly, The Haddocks* and *Rebound* there was a rush of journalistic feet past my cabin door, all eagerly in search of, for God's sake, Ernest Hemingway. I somewhat sadly tucked my clippings back into my memories and returned with Bea to our study of the profitable use of leisure time amid the Rich.

The schedule of pleasure for the remainder of 1930 began with the regular trip in the Whitney private car to the Yale-Harvard football game, and ended with the Christmas holiday festivities. Joan was a person who took her Christmases very seriously. Early in September, aided by her private secretary, she would begin buying gifts for some two or three hundred people on her annual list. Conversations with Joan on serious subjects were apt to be interrupted by a sudden exclamation of anguish and when you worried, "Did I say something that hurt you?" she would explain "I just remembered I hadn't got a present yet for so-and-so." To take her to the theater was to have the dimming of the lights suggest to her that a bedside lamp would be just the gift for an English cousin.

Charlie took his obligations to the birth of the Savior much less seriously. He and I, in fact, devised the perfect method of painless Yuletide shopping. Neither of us bought any gifts until the 24th of December. Then with good King Wenceslas looking down, we met at Jack and Charlie's (which had by this time moved from 42 West 49th to 21 West 52nd). There we proceeded to drink enough of what he called Scrooge-remover to fill us with the proper appreciation of the occasion and out we would go on our merry way, starting with the first floor of Saks Fifth Avenue.

It's wonderful what four martinis and a charge account can do to promote peace on earth among men of good will. Among women of good will, too, especially the sales girls we encountered during our progress. One of these was Bea's beautiful younger sister Marjorie who was now earning her own living in the sales department of Macy's. When closing time arrived we would bundle her and our pile of gift-wrapped selections into the limousine which had been following Charlie and me on our mad shopping tour, and drive out to the Mouse Hole where all through the houses everybody was helping everybody else decorate the tree. Then at midnight came, at Joan's insistence, our annual bit of church-going – and to all a goodnight.

The "most successful" year in my life drew to its end in a warm glow of friendship and affection. I had become extremely fond of Joan and Charlie. For the next five years they were (except for Bobby Benchley) to be our "very best" friends. It was a relationship based almost exclusively on a mutual search for pleasure. I knew absolutely nothing of Charlie's life in the financial and business world; when he was once written up in *Time* as a "tycoon" it was a great subject for kidding. Charlie fascinated me much as had Harold Talbott and

Jack Gilbert, partly because of the comparative superabundance in him of certain "male" qualities such as arrogance, self-assurance and competitiveness. Fortunately I managed never to be in serious competition with Charlie for anything. I had one ambition, however, which I pursued for years with increasing lack of success. I wanted desperately to outdrink him – and I always failed. I would try to trap him with strange innocent-looking mixtures, especially when he seemed a little tired, but I never won a battle and I certainly lost the war. Bea and Joan would see a certain grim competitive look come into my jaw and would plead "Oh no, Don – *not* tonight!" I haven't seen Charlie now for thirty years, but there come times when I'd like to have just one more go at him. Joan, although condemned since childhood to a struggle against plumpness, was by no means the little brown hen to this red-headed rooster. She had a sense of values and a strong will of her own which would have made her a considerable person even without the Whitney millions. She was also sensitive, although a curtain of defense against the revelation of any weakness had been developed since she was a little girl.

But Joan and Charlie's most important quality was their healthy and insatiable appetite for the enjoyment of life. To this Bea and I could make our own contribution, participating on an equal basis. In our resolute quest for pleasure we four made a formidable team.

In 1931, the year of the steady decline in the national employment figures, the stock of Donald Ogden Stewart opened strong in the literary commodity market, and I acquired an agent as a token of my recognition as a Valuable Asset. A friendly young man named Leland Hayward, stepbrother of a friend of Bea's teenage days, offered to "handle" me with his newly formed American Play Company, and I saw no reason that he shouldn't. He then proceeded briskly to sell *Rebound* to Columbia Pictures and me to Paramount. Actually these first two sales were not too difficult, as both Columbia and M-G-M were strenuously competing for my play, and the great success of *Laughter* made me a pretty hot property. Furthermore, the commodity aspect of the Paramount deal was considerably lightened by the contract Walter Wanger offered, which gave me more-or-less completely free hand in the creation of an original story. I was even so sure of myself after *Rebound* and *Laughter* that I had gone to him and said: "Look, Walter – you tell me what stars you want pictures for, and I'll supply the stories and scripts for all." He had seemed a little doubtful about such a generous offer, but as he was importing a great star of the London stage he suggested that I have first go at a "vehicle" for her.

The star's name was Tallulah Bankhead, whom I had last seen in the chorus of the *No Sirree* romp which the Vicious Algonquin Circle had put on for one performance in 1922. Since then, of course, she had become the Toast of London in plays like *The Green Hat* and I welcomed the opportunity to give her first American vehicle a good push in a much more important direction than that provided by Michael Arlen. Paramount installed me in an office at their Long Island studio and, with the very capable secretary-and-critic Milton Sperling once more waiting to transcribe my dialogue, I settled down to the agreeable task of creation at a nice weekly salary.

I soon found that my over-confidence had led me into rather treacherous waters, especially as I was still obligated to satisfy Broadway's Gilbert Miller with my too-long-delayed adaptation of *Le Sexe Faible*, and Tallulah was arriving (and going on salary) on a certain not-too-distant date. Eventually I had to abandon the French adaptation – or, rather, Miller had to abandon me – but I finished my script for *Tarnished Lady* to the apparent satisfaction of Wanger, George Cukor who was to direct, Tallulah, and Clive Brook who was cast to play the lead opposite her.

My story, as I dimly remember it, was about a poor but beautiful New York society girl who is kicked out by a wealthy husband when he catches her doing a bit of cheating. The poor dear then had to go to work at Macy's (or maybe it was Bloomingdale's basement), but although her husband was now willing for her to come back, she proudly refused. Then came the Crash, his fortune vanished, and since he now needed her – and they had both learned about Life – she returned to his bed and his considerably reduced board.

It was essentially the same story I had written in *Rebound* and *Laughter* – at least it was about the same class of people, with a change only in the problem of the leading character who, incidentally, was always a woman. Sara, in *Rebound*, discovered the importance of her individuality in a marriage relationship. In *Laughter* is revealed the importance to the heroine of marrying the man she loves, even though he is a penniless artist. And in *Tarnished Lady* Tallulah learns the exact opposite: that a penniless artist can be a heel and a wealthy Charlie Payson-Jim Forrestal type can, in the crisis of a financial crash, disclose himself as a fine human being. I felt quite proud of my latest important probing of the joys and sorrows of the American upper classes, and I handed in my script to Wanger with a satisfied smile and the rather arrogant request for "Next!" My satisfaction with life in general and myself in particular was perhaps due to the news that we were going to have another baby around the following January.

In June the shooting of *Tarnished Lady* started, and shortly after that Charlie and I drove in his limousine up to New Haven for his tenth and my fifteenth Class Reunions. It was my first meeting with my class in ten years and I had the uncomfortable feeling (which I tried to drown in alcohol) that something had happened to the old Don of 1916. I tried to play the role, but it was no good, and I dragged my hungover tail back to Long Island wondering a bit miserably if I had become such a snob, or at least why I felt so uninterested in these good old friends. One thing which had cheered me up was the sight of my Negro ex-porter in his graduation cap and gown, but I was awfully glad to get back to my wife and onto Charlie's new yacht, the "Saga," for the trip up to the boat races.

Next on the program after that came the annual Payson wedding anniversary party and immediately following that event Bea and I were on the "Europa" bound for a summer in France. It all happened very curiously. We had been in Bobby's room at the Royalton for our customary drink whenever we were in town. While Bobby was hunting for a corkscrew amid the Stilton cheese, crackers, galoshes and imported German dance-records which served as his bar, the door opened and a rather large man appeared with the following announcement, in a strong British accent: "Robert, I'm *def*initely pissed."

This turned out to be an English actor named Bobbie Newton, and he was so wonderfully amusing that Bea and I immediately invited him to come down to Manhasset with us for the weekend. After he had accepted we remembered that it was the occasion of Joan and Charlie's anniversary party, but he was such fun that we were sure they wouldn't mind one more guest. They didn't, of course – that is, they didn't until one in the morning, when their party was at its most glorious height. The orchestra was throbbing, the outdoor pavilion was filled with dancers, and butlers were passing trays of champagne to one and all. Suddenly the head butler came hurrying up to me with the urgent request that Mrs. Payson would like to speak to me immediately. I followed him toward the outdoor swimming pool where many of the guests were sitting the dance out, but before we arrived Joan ran up to me and cried "Don – your guest – look!" and as she pointed I saw our guest, stark naked, gleefully tripping along the high trellis at one end of the pool. Three footmen were trying desperately to catch him but with an Ariel-like gesture he thumbed his nose at them and all the guests, leaped down into some twinkling colored-lighted bushes, and disappeared.

Joan and Charlie assured us that they thought it a wonderful joke, but we didn't feel so happy about it, especially as Ariel didn't come home all night. When he did show up at our kitchen door around nine the next morning in his evening clothes which he had retrieved from the dressing room at the pool, he told us that he had had a jolly good sleep in one of the bunkers on the golf course and wondered if he might have a spot of breakfast. He apologized for his conduct by explaining that he always did something like that whenever he became angry at finding himself surrounded by perfectly awful people. He added, "Don't let it bother you. It's just my way of kicking against the pricks – the rich stuffy ones, I mean. They close down on me every once in a while. No offence to any of your friends, old boy. Let's get out of here, eh? Let's go in and see the old Benchley."

So we drove in to bathe our somewhat hungover spirits in the ever-refreshing stream of the old Benchley, who prescribed a mixture of champagne and stout known as Black Velvet. While he was putting on the green German houseboy's apron which he always reserved for special drinking occasions, my eye was caught by a headline in a morning newspaper spread out under the Victorian student lamp on the table. "Europa Sails at Noon on Maiden Voyage." I glanced at Bea and pointed to the item. At certain critical moments, small, comparatively unimportant happenings can sometimes influence important decisions – a dog barks or one's hat blows off or a light appears in a window. This time it was the popping of the cork in the bottle of Bobby's champagne. "We'd come right back on the return trip," I said as I hurried to the telephone. Bea happily had no argument. "Joan will take care of Ames," she said, "and Borghild will bring our bags to the dock."

So – instead of taking off my clothes and running naked around the top of somebody's swimming pool, I kicked gently against the pricks by embarking in a first-class cabin. On the "Europa" was Max Schmeling, then the heavyweight champion, and a playful countess named Dorothy di Frasso, who was on her way to shoot lions or elephants or something with a young movie actor named Gary

Cooper, whom she was to meet in Paris.

When our boat landed there was a wire from Gerald and Sara Murphy offering us one of the buildings on their Antibes estate for the summer. I cabled Leland Hayward to put Ames, his nurse and my secretary Milton Sperling on the next boat.

The Murphy dwelling, called "The Bastide," seemed to be ideally situated for creative effort. I resolutely retired every morning with Milton to the large barn-like room which Gerald had fitted up as his studio when he had been a pupil of Leger. A taxi came each morning to take Ames and a very fine Norwegian woman whom we called Nana to the nearest Antibes beach. Ames was now a study three and his first spoken French was "Bijou plage s'il vous plait," addressed to the taxi driver. Bea usually went with them, either to bathe or to call on whatever friends of ours were summer residents.

As for me, I paced despairingly up and down the room, trying to keep Milton from going to sleep or reading other books, and my efforts were not eased by the knowledge that Milton knew that what I was writing wasn't getting anywhere. And then, unfortunately, I discovered that there was a golf course near Antibes. The drive for creation trickled down into a putt and not a very good one at that, although I did win a doubtful ebony cigarette holder as runner-up in the annual tournament. It was the first and only prize I've ever won at any sport, but it didn't quite make up for the fact that I returned to New York with a rather unsatisfactory first act.

But there was always my agent to cheer me up. Hollywood wanted me. Hollywood wanted me very much. Would I please come out just for six months? Perhaps – but first there was a small domestic matter that had to be arranged. And on the fifth of January, 1932, I once more hurried over to Miss Lippincott's Nursing Home to gaze with pride, gratitude, and affection on Bea and our second son who was to be christened Donald Ogden, Junior under the god-parentship of Joan and Charlie Payson. The Stewart menage had returned for the winter to Sutton Place, a furnished apartment at 455 East 57th, and as soon as baby Donald was safely established there, his father went a'hunting – but not to get a rabbit skin. Daddy's eye was on mink, and it wasn't long before he found a lot of it in a place called Metro-Goldwyn-Mayer, Culver City, California.

18

It wasn't actually as easy as all that. When I first reported for duty to Irving Thalberg, I was still full of the happy illusion that I, as a more or less proven humorist, would be asked to create original comedies. But Irving had other ideas, and Irving, as I soon discovered, was the Undoubted Boss. And not only that, but he was in a hurry. A picture called *Smilin' Through*, with Norma Shearer, Leslie Howard and Fredric March, was already in its second week of shooting and Irving was not at all pleased with what he was seeing in the daily rushes. Now if I were to have asked myself at the time what sort of picture I would be least fitted for in all the world, it would undoubtedly have been a solemn bit of unreal schmaltz like *Smilin' Through*. But Irving was not the arguable-with type, and I somewhat condescendingly agreed to help him out, especially as he needed a new scene for the next day's shooting. When I confidently handed it in to him, pleased that I had made the deadline, I got the shock of my life. I had never heard such contempt for anything I had written. Me, the author of one of the Ten Best Plays of the 1929-30, etc. He, a little Hollywood movie producer, etc. We battled it out, and little by little I began to see that Irving knew quite a lot about pictures. It was the beginning of a great deal of wisdom about screen writing which I was to absorb gratefully from him during the next few years. When I rewrote the scene, he read it, frowned, shook his head. Once more my anger rose, but this time I didn't argue. On my third attempt he nodded and mumbled, "not bad." "Not bad, you son-of-a-bitch!" I wanted to yell – but I was to learn that "not bad" from Irving was the equivalent of an Academy Award. I worked feverishly on *Smilin'*

Through and toward the end began to get back my confidence. It was, at the time, the best thing that could have happened to my over-estimation of my writing abilities, at least as far as Hollywood was concerned. I became slowly, under Irving's severe, uncompromising surveillance, a devoted and loyal member of The Team. I also became, for a while, Irving's white-haired boy. *Smilin' Through* was a terrific success, largely because of the excellent performances of the stars and the sensitive direction of Sidney Franklin. But I had contributed and Irving appreciated how much.

It was the most fortunate experience that a writer could have in the film world, for Irving was the unrivaled Top. The effect on me, however, was not quite so fortunate. I now became a commodity, a fairly valuable one, and I enjoyed the position tremendously. I had "made good" with a Boss I respected. Irving became a sort of father, as he did for everyone who worked closely with him. And in trying to satisfy "father" I became absorbed in the technique of screen-writing. Each picture presented a fascinating problem. In a way, it was what Ira Wolfert, after a Pulitzer Prize-winning spell as a war correspondent, described as what happens to any squad of G.I.s when they are given the assignment of handling a machine gun. It becomes their collective responsibility, and the concentration of each individual in taking care of his particular duties removes any thoughts of fear or death or what the war is about. I became involved in the responsibility for making the best use of the material bought for me by the studio. I had little time to consider what that material was, or what its connection with truth might be. I did try, in *Smilin' Through* and others, to insert as much truth as possible into the script. But that wasn't primarily what I was being paid for. Little by little, as my salary rose, my image of the world became blurred by Hollywood until truth came to resemble the celluloid interpretation. I was getting to be a better and better manipulator of my material, but I had long lost sight of my own aims.

Any financial worries were now suspended for what seemed an indefinite period. The demand for the commodity soared. My agent was very happy. I was very happy. I had at last really hit the money jackpot and the eight-room "bungalow" lighted up as the band played Sousa's "Stars and Stripes Forever!" But then a curious thing happened. The pinball (if I may mix a few more metaphors) hit the jackpot and proceeded to go into a tailspin. It wasn't a very sudden or very noticeable tailspin and it certainly wasn't apparent to me. Life went on pretty much as usual, except, of course, that I now had a Boss, an office, regular working hours, and a weekly pay check which kept getting larger and larger. I worked very hard to earn that pay. I also, as is my custom, played very hard when office hours were over. The warning signals of the tailspin should have appeared with the realization that both work and play had reached a level upon which no further development toward my maturity was possible. I had entered a Dead End street.

They weren't entirely wasted years, at least in enjoyment both of work and play. Each new picture presented a problem, even though it was one which had been created by the original work of another writer and I was only the carpenter who more or less followed the designer's blueprints. I think that the "more" would apply in my own case, as I always tried to respect the book or play which they had purchased. This conscientious attempt, incidentally, was somewhat relaxed in later post-Thalberg years after I had been rebuked by Louis B. Mayer for "not scripting for him the novel he had bought." Bewildered, I started to argue and then discovered that his knowledge of a book or play never came from reading it, but from the lips of a bright young girl who had read it and spent one morning a week with the executives telling them her version of the various literary properties they had purchased. I saw the light, and after that, whenever assigned to a script, made a deal with the girl to let me know the gospel according to her before attempting any of my own interpretations.

After *Smilin' Through* came *The White Sister*, another rather curious assignment for a humorist, but one which I went to work on with enthusiasm and hope. The subject was a conflict in Italy between sacred and profane love; for the profane lover they had cast an up-and-coming young actor named Clark Gable, and for the young girl who becomes a nun when she believes that her beloved Gable has been killed in the war they chose Helen Hayes. The producer was a dynamic young man (old to pictures) named Hunt Stromberg whose assistant was Sam Zimbalist; the director was Victor Fleming.

These three were a daily delight to work with, and a revelation to me of the Hollywood psyche. Hunt had been in pictures so long that nothing was what he called "real" unless he had seen it in a film. He had one further touchstone by which he tested all values. I would bring to his office a tender love scene. He would read it, then pick up a riding crop and stride back and forth, spitting fiercely as he moved and more fiercely as he talked. "Son," he would say, "I like it [spit]. I think it's a fine scene [spit]. But how about that dumb Scranton miner? Would *he* understand it?" Hunt had never been in Scranton and I don't think he had ever seen a miner, but every bit I wrote had to get the commendation of that mythic creature sitting in a Scranton movie house. Charlie MacArthur and I once tried to get a friend in Scranton to send us out a real miner, but he claimed he couldn't find one dumb enough. Every producer, incidentally, seemed to have some similar signature-tune for use in conferences with writers. Irving would constantly toss and catch a coin. Others would have their nails manicured, their shoes shined, or their hair trimmed. It was very impressive. I added my own identifying symbol during the shooting of the carnival scene in *The White Sister* when Vic Fleming let me play the rear end of a trick horse.

This symbol, to my sorrow, proved very shortly to be far more apt than I had intended. Owing to a crowded production schedule, *The White Sister* had started shooting before I could finish more than half of the script. This was a dangerous procedure but often had to be adopted because of various commitments both for the release of the picture and the schedule of the stars for their next vehicle. While the cameras were turning on the early love scenes of the flaming lieutenant Gable and the innocent pure Miss Hayes, I was working day and night to satisfy Hunt and his dumb Scranton miner as to the most satisfactory conclusion to their tragic affair. I was also trying to satisfy my own rather high standards of truth, for I had by this time become deeply involved in the characters and their fate and had lost myself in this tragic tender tale as though I had created it myself. In a way, actually, that was partly true, for in bringing the old F. Marion Crawford novel into the period of the First World War I had put into it all I could of my own self-knowledge while trying to do justice to the original creation. Everything seemed to be going well. Hunt was delighted with the daily rushes; so, apparently, was everyone else. When Phil Barry came out to the studio to work with Irving Thalberg on *Annie Laurie*, Hunt proudly showed him the two thirds of our picture which had been cut and assembled. Phil praised it highly and I was very pleased and deeply satisfied. A writer *could* work for a studio and still express himself profoundly and honestly, I told myself.

I was right, too. A writer could work for a studio. He could express himself profoundly and honestly. But he had not the slightest control over whether what he wrote ever reached the screen. That, I learned, was in the hands of the producer. Or the director. Or any star actor or actress. In this case it happened to be Helen Hayes. She didn't like the ending. She refused to play a scene I had written. Before I was aware of what was happinging, the scene was being written by her husband, Charlie McArthur, who also proceeded to write the ending of the picture, an ending which I could not and would not have written.

In a way, it was a fair give-and-take. I had done something similar to the script writers who had worked on *Smilin' Through*. I had also done it, at Hunt's urgent request, to the ending of a picture for Gable and Jean Harlow called *Red Dust*, a film scripted by a young man just out of Harvard named John Lee Mahin. I had not asked for credit for either of these pictures, nor did Charlie request credit for *The White Sister*. But it wasn't a question of that. This picture had been my baby. I loved it – and someone else had been called in at the last moment to put on a false face. From that moment on I resolved never to care what they did to my work. I was now, I told myself, a professional, highly paid for giving my employers what they wanted. And that was the moment when the fun went out of Hollywood. In part, it was also when the tailspin began – in spite of my rapidly rising balance in the Bank of America, Beverly Hills Branch.

The childhood playtime part of my life, however, seemed to remain at a steady level. Bea came out with Ames, Don Junior, Nana, Borghild and Maria, and there was a joyous reunion with Clara, who was still happy in the California sunshine. Bobby arrived on a writing and acting job. Since Bea and I had last been in Hollywood, six years before, the social structure had considerably hardened – one might better say "frozen" – into a rigid pattern of status-grading. The crazy gaiety of the Keystone silent days was now nowhere to be discovered, except occasionally at Marion Davies', where some of the old devil-may-care-ishness of Pre-Sound and Pre-Depression was still retained. Otherwise one dined formally, and was seated according to importance at the box office. Writers, if invited at all, sat at the bottom of the table, below the Heads of Publicity but above the Hairdressers.

A writer's status also varied considerably with the success or failure of his latest picture. During the day, his standing could be most quickly determined by his reception at luncheon by the headwaiters of the various restaurants. News traveled quickly in Hollywood and no ears were closer to the ground than those who apportioned the favored tables at the Vendome or the Brown Derby. In our first year Bea and I were not included among the socially elite. Later on, when Joan and Jock Whitney entered the arena with an investment of several millions in Selznick International, we were graciously accepted into the David Oliver Selznick circle. And eventually we reached the Top, the table of Sam and Frances Goldwyn. Our low preliminary status, however, didn't bother us overmuch. We had old friends like King Vidor, Joe and Bessie Cohn, Lewis Milestone and Jack Gilbert.

Poor Jack had been sunk with Sound, but his wild spirit was still struggling. We had last seen him in New York in the summer of 1929 when he was en route to France on his honeymoon with Ina Claire, who was desperately trying to salve his wounded ego. They had come out to the Mouse Hole to spend the night before sailing; we had taken them to a gay party of our banking friends at the Creek Club; they had gone home after dinner, and when Bea and I arrived about three in the morning, Ina was grimly contemplating an empty bed and the apparent end of her honeymoon. They had had another of their furious quarrels. Jack had left her "forever" and gone back to New York. Leaving Bea to deal with the angry Ina I drove into town and around half past four located Jack at the Ritz. Their boat was to sail, I think, at ten that morning, and I didn't get Jack to make sense until seven or eight. Anyway, the honeymooners sailed on time in a happy nuptial mist of flowers and photographers.

Ina later told me that after a similar quarrel on somebody's yacht in the harbor of Cannes, Jack, quite drunk, had flung himself into a boat and insisted on being taken to the nearest taxi. His order was obeyed, Jack got into the cab, and in reply to the driver's question pointed dramatically forwards and commanded "Paris!" The bewildered driver tried to remonstrate but Jack, in his most forceful Gilbertian manner, shouted: "Stop talking French. I'm John Gilbert. Here's some money. Take me to Paris." The fact that Jack had no idea of the geography of France, combined with the fact that the driver had always wanted to go to Paris, was decisive and off they drove. Jack immediately passed out and didn't come to until they were entering a large city. He knocked on the driver's window and asked where they were. When he was told that it was Lyons, he yawned, gave the driver some more money and said "Take me to

Cannes." "Mais monsieur!" remonstrated the heartbroken driver but Jack only shoveled out some more large franc notes and went back to sleep and Cannes. The marriage with Ina was a little bit like that; it never got where it started out for, and lasted only a couple of years.

But now Jack was showing signs of being his old self. Garbo had asked that he play opposite her in *Queen Christina,* which was exactly what his sinking ego needed. Furthermore, he had a new love, a young actress named Virginia Bruce. She took a liking to Bea and when it came time for the marriage she asked her to be the Matron of Honor. Irving was Jack's best man and all hoped that the Great Lover would at last find peace. He did – but not until four years later. His was the last Hollywood funeral I ever attended. It fully lived up to the local standard; many of the performances were excellent, although Marlene Dietrich stole the show by fainting in the aisle.

Funerals were a bit like first-nights; one never knew what might happen. Sometimes a local rabbi would seize the opportunity to build up his part into a fervent denunciation of sin in the movie colony. On another earlier occasion, at the obsequies for Paul Bern, it was the undertaker who was seized with the improvising spirit of commedia dell'arte. The service at Forest Lawn had come to its conclusion, to the relief of the mourners, without any of the usual sickening divertisements. Then, before anyone had time to leave, the "funeral consultant" bounded to the front of the chapel, took his stance beside the coffin and with modest pride offered Paul's friends the novel opportunity of saying a last fond farewell. At that the coffin mechanically moved into an upright position, the top of the lid gradually slid down, and there was Paul's face staring out at the audience. The curtain slowly fell to the offstage sound of Jack Gilbert throwing up.

Another distasteful event of that social season occurred during the Olympic games. With the huge Coliseum packed with spectators full of patriotic hopes for another series of American triumphs, there appeared four young men in athlete's shorts who started running around the cinder track with placards reading "Free Tom Mooney." I wasn't sure who Mooney was and I had never heard of the Young Communist League, but I was certain about the shocking bad taste of those kids and yelled angrily until the police grabbed them.

That was the year in which Franklin Roosevelt was first elected President, and on the following fourth of March Bea and I were seated with Joan and Charlie in the living room of their house on East 61st Street (later, by an ironic coincidence, the consulate of the U.S.S.R.), listening to his inauguration message on the radio. "We have nothing to fear but fear itself," he said, and encouraged by these words, we descended to the waiting limousine and drove through the wintry slush past several closed banks to the pier where we embarked without fear on a sunny pleasure cruise to Haiti and Santo Domingo. With us were Joe Bryan III, late of Richmond, Va. and Princeton, and his wife whom I had first met as a teenage "Sister" Barnes on the Whitney private golf course.

Haiti, although still under control of the U.S. Marines, was strange and a bit terrifying, especially on the first night when a weird procession of seemingly hostile natives shuffled until early morning past our hotel window on their weekly journey from the mountain forests down to the Port au Prince market. In the daylight our apprehensions gradually subsided, partly with the aid of a drink called Planter's Punch which even enabled us to enjoy a round of golf on a course where large signs warned that it was reserved for bombing practice by American planes and where the "greens" were composed of hard baked sand. The markets themselves were curiously indicative of the extreme native poverty; two of the specialties for sale were empty milk-of-magnesia bottles and exploded cartridge shells. The bathing was superb, and after we had deepened our tans enough to make them conspicuous in New York we took a plane for Santo Domingo, where Charlie owned a large sugar plantation. The Santo Domingo rum is not bad, either, and I dimly remember a small dance given for us in the city by an extremely courteous native whose name I later learned was Trujillo.

When I got back to Hollywood on the second leg of my three-year contract, I found that there had been a rather disturbing palace revolution at M-G-M and that the new king was Louis B. Mayer's son-in-law David Selznick. Before Bea and I had left for our Haitian vacation, Irving Thalberg had had a physical breakdown and had been advised to go abroad for a few months of complete rest. He confided to me that after he returned he might leave M-G-M and form his own company, and invited me to come with him if and when. I gladly and rather proudly accepted. Irving then sailed with Norma Shearer, Helen Hayes and Charlie MacArthur, and as soon as he was gone, Mayer reorganized the studio with Selznick at the top. "L.B." also instituted another innovation called a "voluntary salary cut" for writers, actors and directors (but not, as we learned afterwards, for himself and other top executives). Soon after I got back I was invited to his office, and after he had explained to me – calling me "Don" for the first time – about the distressing financial condition of the industry, his eyes suddenly filled with tears. I accepted, voluntarily of course, his suggestion that I take a 50 per cent reduction and offered him my handkerchief. I'm no monster – especially when a nice fellow like "L.B." needs my help. It was about this time that the first Screen Writers Guild was formed for protection against any further unselfish volunteering, but as I was by now one of the top-paid writers I didn't feel that I needed any protection.

I needed protection of some sort, though, for my first assignment under the new revised M-G-M made me feel that my throat had been cut along with my salary. The W. R. Hearst-Marion Davies unit had moved on to the M-G-M lot, and Walter Wanger had been tapped to produce a musical starring Marion and a young singer with a huge radio following whose name was Bing Crosby. Walter asked me to help him and I found myself contemplating (on half pay) a story about a poor but impulsive teacher at a Girls' Finishing School who falls in love with Bing's voice on her radio and follows him to Hollywood. I had sworn after *Fine and Dandy* that I would never mix in with another musical, but Walter was a very persuasive fellow and he flattered me into believing that it was something which I could do with my left hand. I didn't know that if you kid yourself in Hollywood into that assumption you usually end up not only without your left hand but also without your right arm and most of your brains.

The first problem was that "W.R." wouldn't permit Marion to be a schoolteacher; he "just couldn't see her as one." I gladly offered to throw up (the job) but persuasive Walter finally sold him on the idea and the script advanced from Finishing School to Grand Central Station where came the first big musical number "Going Hollywood," from which the picture got its name. The music was turned over to the team of songwriters, Nacio Herb Brown and Arthur Freed, who had made such a success out of *Broadway Melody*. One of my more embarrassingly painful moments, almost as bad as having to judge actors who are reading for parts in a play, was to listen to two songwriters in a small room "putting over" their latest number. But little by little we collectively managed to appease some of Mr. Hearst's doubts, and the good songs from Brown and

Freed were a large factor. Another was Bing himself who proved to be a marvelously calm patient passenger in a rocking boat. Everyone seemed satisfied with the script including David Selznick, into whose favor I had also found time to creep with a scene for Marie Dressler and Jean Harlow in *Dinner at Eight* which ended that picture on a much appreciated laugh. So once more I felt that I was a good craftsman who was pleasing his employers, and as by this time the pay cuts had been restored, I more or less succeeded in concealing from myself the fact that I was now thirty-nine and getting nowhere.

Good old alcohol helped, of course, and pleasant new avenues of escape from the deadliness of well-paid unfulfillment began to open up along the Sunset strip. The Trocadero had a very good dance band and the Purple Gang from Detroit opened up exciting new ways of losing one's dress shirt in luxurious gambling surroundings. Our names began to trickle occasionally into the gossip columns. I pretended not to feel pleased, and the mists of the unreal descended lower over our Bel Air mansion.

When Irving Thalberg returned from abroad, I felt a heartening rise in my hopes for engaging in some decent writing. His trip had apparently cured him both of his heart trouble and his desire to break away from Metro. My hopes for myself were not deceived. Irving was in need of an immediate script for *The Barretts of Wimpole Street* as a film for Norma Shearer and Fredric March, with Sidney Franklin directing. It was the old *Smilin' Through* setup, with the addition of Charles Laughton, an unknown (to America) actor from England. Sidney's favorite writer was an extremely intelligent English woman named Claudine West, and as it was a hurry-up job a third writer was called in, the Hungarian playwright Ernst Vadja. We happened to hit it off very well together and managed to get Irving's approval for our script in almost record time. Irving then wanted us to start on an even more exciting project for Norma to do after *The Barretts* – a life of Marie Antoinette.

But Bea had had enough of Hollywood for the moment, and so had I. She and I, Nana, the kids, and Clara journeyed back on the train, leaving our chauffeur Thulin to drive Borghild and Marie across scenic America. We dropped Clara in Columbus and went on to Long Island where we found a large barn of a house not too far from the Paysons, the Forrestals, the Bill Lords and the Lovetts. Ames started at his first school, and with moderate adequacy portrayed an Indian in the Thanskgiving play. It was a family Thanksgiving, the first we had all had together. Clara came on from Columbus with my sister Anne, her husband Charles, and their tall Princeton undergraduate son Ogden. Their daughter Anne had married Charles Gray, the son of their best friends; they were living in Los Angeles. Bea's father was also now living out there but her mother and sister Jerry sat down with us to give thanks.

In the midst of a Depression-sunk world there was much for me to be truly thankful for. I had no financial worries. I had a marriage which was considered to be a happy one and which was truly so, at least from my point of view, with a wife whose appetite for parties and fun had kept up with mine. The Murphys had been slowed down by tragedy, the Scott Fitzgeralds had cracked up, but Bea and Don went on dancing.

Don, it is true, was beginning at thirty-nine not to hold his liquor quite as well as he should, and there had been an increasing number of "blackouts" about which, when I was told of them the next morning, I felt momentarily remorseful. But there was nothing serious, nothing that flowers and apologies couldn't coax over into laughter. I was still giving fairly adequate performances in the role of a somewhat ageing Life of the Party and in the more doubtful moments of dreadful hangover there was always Bea and Dotty and Bobby to assure me that I had "really been perfectly all right." Further reassurance came with my election to the Racquet and Tennis Club (the Depression had greatly reduced the length of the waiting list), to a new club called the "Hangar" (of which Bobby was also a member) and another new one on the East River which provided me with tennis courts and the additional exclusive privilege of arriving in a yacht should I ever feel an uncontrollable need to own one.

This is not to imply, of course, that my secure and now well-recognized eliteness made me entirely unaware of the miseries and despairs of those less fortunate than I. On two occasions I exercised my gifts in organizing parties for the benefit of the unemployed. The first was in collaboration with a young Irishman named Jim Moriarity who ran an elegant speakeasy on 61st Street between Fifth Avenue and Madison, and a considerable sum of money was raised. Encouraged by this I undertook an even more ambitious affair, to which Mrs. Whitney contributed the lower two floors, including the ballroom, of her Fifth Avenue mansion. I sent out invitations for "a small but determined dance" to a rather restricted list, but so great was the eagerness to see what the inside of Mrs. Whitney's home looked like that more than double the number of invitees crashed the gate and reduced my dance to a hot crowded shambles. My frustration was completed by the early drunkenness of the people in charge of selling the tickets for refreshments, so that although a good time was had by all, the unemployed didn't get nearly as much benefit as intended.

My growing reputation as an Elsa Maxwell, however, suffered a slight relapse shortly after the beginning of the New Year when Bea and I staged a birthday party for our youngest son, then aged two and known as "Dee-dee." Ten or fifteen children came, accompanied by fifteen or twenty governesses and nurses, and Bea and I have never worked harder as entertainers to such a continuously dead-pan audience. I finally succeeded in making four of the well-behaved darlings burst into tears, after which I gave up. They do those things better in Hollywood films. When Ames and Dee-dee later in the year went to Shirley Temple's birthday party, they had a feature-length picture, four clowns, two magicians, and unlimited framed autographed photos of their hostess.

Otherwise, the year 1934 began pleasantly. Before returning to M-G-M for the final term under my contract, Bea and I accepted Joan and Charlie's invitation to spend a week at their house in Palm Beach.

The Palm Beach week was delightful, including warm sandy beaches and tall gin fizzes, daily golf and nightly visits to the gambling tables at Bradley's, and a large party at a night club which Stuart Symington and I, for some now-forgotten reason, gave in honor of a multimillionaire investment tycoon named Harrison Williams. The only unfortunate incident on the whole trip occurred just as we were leaving. We were all gaily gathered in the private car standing in the yards awaiting the arrival of the train which was to carry us back to snow and sleet. Gathered around the car in the sunshine was a small crowd of Negroes, including a poor little three-piece "orchestra" whom we tossed money to when they played *Happy Days Are Here Again.* Being in a private car had originally been for me a romantic experience, but the romance had long since died and something like shame and guilt stirred when I saw the Negroes unsmilingly contemplating the Happy Rich in their conspicuous exclusiveness. Some voice from grandfather John Ogden seemed to be whispering, "What are *you* doing in there?" – and I couldn't answer that one.

Shortly after our return to New York a wire came from a doctor in Los Angeles and I flew out to find Clara in the Catholic hospital. She had been stricken with pneumonia. We had three or four old-time heart-to-hearts before she died three days later. After the services at St. Patrick's in Columbus Anne, Bea and I buried Clara in Green Lawn cemetery beside Gilbert, Bert, and the two older brothers I had never known.

Then rather sadly back to M-G-M, where Irving was anxious to get on with *Marie Antoinette*. We found a Spanish-type house with tennis court on Beverly Drive. Ames entered a Beverly Hills school, and I resumed daily conferences with Sidney Franklin, Claudine West and Ernst Vadja, with hopes that in six months at the most I would at last be back at work on a play of my own.

This hope was on the optimistic side. Fourteen months later the head of Queen Marie was still firmly on her shoulders and I was still consulting with my colleagues as to the best way of explaining the French Revolution in terms that would not lose audience sympathy for Norma Shearer. But at the beginning the prospect for doing some really first-class writing seemed to be absorbingly exciting. The gradual disenchantment came partly because writing cannot, in its essence, be done by a committee, but mainly because I was being paid to satisfy Irving, not myself.

Little by little the creative impulse went into low gear. Every evening after working hours, I slid into my dinner jacket like a fireman at the sound of an alarm. We became at one time absorbed into a group centering around Countess Dorothy di Frasso and her house guest Elsa Maxwell. Dorothy in action was something to watch. She had built an iron nerve and a lot of money into an old Italian title, a Roman family villa with a ceiling by Raphael, and a piano lid covered with autographed photographs of nobility and Mussolini. I don't think she had Hitler but she would have got it if anyone could. She once hired a Los Angeles voodoo doctor to stick pins in the wax image of the wife of a movie star she fancied.

When Joan Payson came out to visit Bea and me we rented the Vendome restaurant and gave a masquerade in which guests came as "their favorite or un-favorite movie star." We gave a big party for my sister Anne which began in the afternoon and ended at seven the next morning, with four of the remaining guests playing tennis in white ties and tails. When Bea cracked a bit under the strain of so many parties we even organized a "Nervous Breakdown" party in her honor; guests arrived at noon in full evening dress; Louella Parsons came in an ambulance with Elsa Maxwell dressed as a psychiatrist. Our tennis court was occupied almost every afternoon, and our bar every evening. Our dinner guests usually included Clark and Rhea Gable, Sam and Frances Goldwyn, Richard and Jessica Barthelmess, Lewis Milestone, Kay Francis, Grace Moore, and Whitney de Rham, a refugee from New York society. Another wild and amusing refugee named David Niven wandered onto our tennis court one afternoon and won our hearts. Elizabeth Allen ditto. We fell in love with Fred Astaire's wife Phillis.

Time passed, Marie Antoinette continued. While we were working on the Revolution sequence Irving and all other executives became worried about the horrible possibility that Upton Sinclair might be elected governor of California, so I loyally subscribed to their request for a day's pay in order to fight the demon of socialistic End Poverty In California. Sinclair was defeated and Thanksgiving ensued, followed by Christmas.

The festival of the birth of gentle Jesus had by this time in Hollywood assumed the financial proportions of a National Disaster Fund. We sent out fifty-three gifts, seventeen potted poinsettias, seven orchids (for seven gossip columnists) and three hundred and eleven Christmas cards. The effect on our children was disastrous. The ceremony of opening so many and such expensive presents under the tree became a greedy succession of "What's next?" or "That's mine!" The movie colony, incidentally, is not recommended as a place in which to bring up kids. The chief topic of conversation and controversy among the small fry and their nurses and governesses was the income of the various parents, or else the comparative cost of the family psychiatrists. I once had to break up a fist fight between Ames and young Sammy Goldwyn caused by Sammy's doubts about my weekly salary. Sammy was wrong, but he won the fight.

The social season stepped into a new high with the grand premier, on Washington's Birthday, of Santa Anita racetrack and the Whitney and Vanderbilt racing colors began flashing glamorously under the California sun. So did the owners of the above-mentioned racing stables. Long Island discovered Hollywood – and vice-versa. I felt a bit let down. I had devoted my life to climbing into the invitation lists of the top ranks of exclusivity and here were movie producers – who hadn't even gone to Yale, let alone made Skull and Bones – achieving it in a year. Marie Antoinette wouldn't have understood it, at least until after she had lost her head. And that was still many pages of Revolution away.

19

Meanwhile, a revolution of a slightly different sort was beginning to mutter faint rumblings in the blue Hollywood skies. Since the birth of the Screen Writers Guild at the time of the 1933 wage cuts, the producers had consistently refused to pay any attention to it, dismissing its claims with the argument that writers were adequately taken care of by their agents or the Academy of Motion Picture Arts and Sciences. Since that organization had been founded by Louis B. Mayer and included producers in its membership, there was a fairly reasonable ground for suspicion as to its "representative" qualifications, especially in matters of wage disputes. By 1934 the Guild felt itself strong enough to force the issue, and when the producers still thumbed their noses, the writers decided to reply by boycotting the much-publicized annual Academy banquet at which the Oscars were to be awarded.

A week before the banquet Irving invited Bea and me to be his guests there. I accepted without a thought. Irving was my friend. I had not the slightest understanding of unions, and certainly none as to their connection with such a free individual as a writer. The only time that the question of labor organization had ever entered my consciousness had been when Bea and I were living on Long Island. My old Dayton boss Harold Talbott was by then also a resident of the North Shore, and we frequently met at various dances. On one of these he asked me if I would mind doing him a favor, and as I still felt grateful for the generous way he had treated me, I was really pleased at the chance. But the "favor" was a surprising one, and involved a glimpse into an unknown area of life so bewildering that I actually couldn't believe it. The story was that in one of the large Detroit automobile manufacturing plants there was a nice fellow whom Harold had liked in Dayton, and who was now unfortunately mixed up with the drive to organize the automobile workers into a union. In Harold's words, "he didn't like to see this nice guy get hurt." So I was to write to the nice guy and tell him I had become very enthusiastic about a musical comedy he had written for one of the auto workers' theatrical clubs. I was to ask him if he would like to come to Hollywood, all expenses paid, and work as a writer for a studio, for which I was to offer him a six-month contract, with an option. Harold explained that the automobile manufacturers would gladly pay all these expenses, including his wages for six months "– just to get him away from the dangerous possibilities connected with labor organizing." I didn't have a clue as to what Harold was hinting at, and I certainly had no pro-union sympathies. But somehow or other I didn't like to get involved and declined to assist in his act of Christian benevolence towards a fellow human being, and washed my hands, so I thought, of such faraway subjects as the labor movement.

But now, here on my Beverly Drive doorstep, was this baby of the Academy banquet. No other screenwriters were going, or at least very few. Two M-G-M writers, Tess Slesinger and Virginia Faulkner, came to my office and ended by calling me names like "fink" that I had never heard before. I got angry and stubborn. Bea and I went to the banquet, crossed the picket line, and sat at Irving's table. But I didn't sit there happily in my white tie and tails. It was too much like being "teacher's pet" and I took it out on teacher by getting drunk and making loud derogatory wisecracks during the solemn awarding of the Oscars. Some of the cracks were pretty good. At least, they got big laughs from the surrounding tables, if not from Louis B. Mayer. It was my first real assertion of my self against father Irving, but I had to get drunk to make it.

My second attempt to break the golden cord came a month or so later. My contract had expired the preceding July but I had stayed on month after month because Irving and Marie Antoinette needed me and I just couldn't walk out on my friends. But by mid-April Bea was getting ready to scream, and rightly so. "You need a vacation. Are you married to Irving or me?" Luckily we got Marie to the guillotine before I had to answer that question, and all was set for a May sailing to England in order to help George V celebrate his jubilee. And not only that, but I told Irving that I didn't want to be a screen writer any more. I wanted to write plays, my own plays. Father looked at me sadly, and made me feel that he hadn't heard what I'd said but that he'd forgive me if I'd sign for just one more year. I shook my head firmly, and went home to pack. Irving telephoned. I was still firm. Leland Hayward rang up at midnight to tell excitedly of a marvelous new offer from M-G-M. I declined, and went to bed. Our train left from Pasadena at nine next morning. I was awakened at seven by the doorbell. Bea peeked out the window. "It's Irving," she whispered. "If you don't want me to sign that contract," I warned, "don't let him in." But Borghild had already opened the door. I heard Irving's voice as he called, "Don, are you upstairs?" I signed the contract – but I got permission to write my play first.

George V had a most successful jubilee, and we didn't do badly ourselves. We stayed in London a month – at Claridges. It was perfect. We had letters of introduction from David Niven to a playfellow named Michael Trubshawe; from Elizabeth Allen to her husband Bill O'Brien who got us everything from dressmakers to membership in after-hours bottle clubs. We had a letter from Dorothy di Frasso to Millicent, Duchess of Devonshire. Nightingales sang in Berkeley Square. Barrel organs played "In Your Easter Bonnet" in the street below our room. From our windows we could see the wonderful Jubilee decorations on Selfridge's.

Roland Young was staying on the floor below; we took a quick weekend trip to Paris with him, after which Michael Trubshawe sent me to a miraculous chemist with a secret cure for hangover which he had been dispensing since 1739. Josephine Forrestal and Jane Sanford rented a house, and gave large parties. "Laddie" Sanford played winning polo against England, and was spat upon by a drunken Lord Castleross at a party where Bea and I were at his table. Laddie behaved like a gentleman, and the incident was unobserved by other guests including the future George VI and his queen.

In the last week before sailing, packages of purchases began piling up in our Claridge's suite, including, from Hawes and Curtis for me, eighteen stiff dress shirts, eighteen soft dress shirts, eight white dress waistcoats, twelve white dress ties. I expected them to last a reasonable length of time.

What I didn't expect was that they would lie for the next twenty-five years in bureau drawers and gradually turn yellow from lack of invitations calling for their use. What I didn't realize was that the dancing honeymoon was at last over, and that the perfect month at Claridge's was the climax to the pleasure curise. Nor did I realize that it was also the end of the tailspin, and that ahead lay either an inevitable crash – or else a miraculous leveling out to sanity and maturity. None of this did I know or foresee as Bea and Kay and I were transported in the midnight darkness of Southampton Harbor toward the huge vessel distinguishable in the distance by a brilliant electric sign reading "Normandie." It was the maiden voyage of that ship, and on it I began my own maiden venture into the strange new world of left-wing politics.

I hadn't meant to do any such thing. Since leaving Hollywood I had been probing the possibilities for a theme for my new play. Deep within me had been growing the disquieting realization that my childhood gods had played me false, that my quest for security through social and financial success had let me up the garden path – a very pleasant path but one which seemed to have come to a dead end. The jackpot had brought security but no inner satisfaction.

Something had gone wrong, something was missing – and I decided that that was a worthy theme for my play. It was the theme I had been groping for in my abortive effort four years before, the play I had abandoned in France after completing a first act and some three or four hundred holes of golf. Since then I had been experiencing my "security" more completely, and now I felt that I might truly build toward a climax in which my protagonist could discover that there is nothing in wealth or position which can insure moral security. I wanted to say that the Whitneys and the Morgans and the Vanderbilts – those idols of my boyhood dreams – have no insurance, either, and I gave my play the title of *Insurance.* The protagonist, of course, was again to be myself, just as the play was to be the struggle of various aspects of myself to which I gave the names of the characters both male and female. By the time I set out for England I had blocked out a Payne Whitney-type family headed by an intelligent father and a sensitive poetic mother, in which there was a rebellious son who was questioning all of the family values. I imagine that I had in mind also the Morgan partner Thomas Lamont, who was supposed to be having a somewhat similar problem with his son Corliss. One of the minor characters was to be a Communist, and as I had not the slightest idea of what the dialogue would be for such a character, I asked in a London bookshop for "the latest book on Communism."

They gave me two which I tossed into my suitcase and forgot about. I didn't get around to looking at them closely until the second day, when my appetite for literature and sea air had revived.

The books were both by John Strachey. One was *The Coming Struggle for Power* and the other *The Nature of the Capitalist Crisis.* I found myself reading with bewilderment. It was the same reaction I had had shortly before in Hollywood when I stumbled upon *Man's Fate* by Malraux. I just couldn't believe that such things were happening in the world, and I certainly couldn't understand why a man would be willing to give up so much of his life for a political belief. It seemed terribly remote from Beverly Hills. I wanted to talk about it on the boat but there was no one who seemed in the least interested, so I postponed further study.

Actually, I postponed it for three weeks. When we arrived at the Paysons, we happened to land in the midst of the usual Boat Race-Wedding Anniversary festivities. The atmosphere there was conducive to discussion of little except a place at the bar.

Jim Forrestal might have been an exception; I drove alone with him down to his twentieth reunion at Princeton and thought of asking him some questions. In view of what happened to both of us later in life, it was a curious "last ride together." I was unwittingly and ignorantly poised on the edge of joining the anti-Nazi movement; Jim's banking house (I heard later) was heavily involved in booking the Third Reich of Adolph Hitler. But Jim hadn't read the book, and the subject never came up. I doubt if it would have got anywhere. I was terribly fond of him, but he was the most secretive friend I have ever had. I never saw his betray his own feelings about anything to anyone, including his wife Josephine. Jim was his own boss. He recognized no restraints and obeyed no rules, especially the little ones such as keeping social engagements or not smoking a pipe at a formal dinner. No one ever knew what he was thinking, either – at least I never did, and I learned never to ask. At the time of the Wall Street Crash Bea and I went to see him in a hospital; he had just had his nose badly broken while boxing and he had the flu. There was a rumor also that his own fortune had been completely smashed to bits, and we thought he might need a lot of cheering up. But he merely laughed about his nose, his flu, and the Crash, and about how miserably some of our friends were reacting to disaster. Jim liked to laugh. He liked to have a good time, and he couldn't endure boredom. I had been brought along because he wanted company, and our ride to Princeton that June morning was full of laughter.

The Payson anniversary party was given in honor of Bea and me, as sort of a repayment for the masquerade we had thrown for Joan in Hollywood, and the guests were invited to come as "their favorite character in fiction." Bea dipped gracefully into Thackeray for the part of Becky Sharp, and I dressed up as Rawden Crawley, her husband who died of yellow fever. I managed to survive the night, but the next noon, after the second alka-seltzer, I came to the profound if somewhat overdue conviction that if I didn't get away alone somewhere right away I would never get out of my desperation about myself and my work.

So we got onto Charlie's yacht and started out to find for me an Ivory Tower where there wasn't a golf course but where the meals were good. Charlie thought he knew of a Marion Yacht Club near New Bedford on the coast of Massachusetts where I would be absolutely undisturbed, and he was right. I was put ashore with my typewriter and my creative urge, but without my dinner jacket. As I stood on the pier watching the "Saga" disappearing with Joan, Charlie and Bea in the direction of New York I felt like yelling frantically "Come back!" It was the first time I had been really isolated in a strange land since Capri and Deems Taylor's farm. I didn't know a soul and I wasn't supposed to want to. I pinned up the newspaper photographs of Bea in her "Vanity Fair" masquerade costume and opened my typewriter. Alone at last – and to hell with it!

Gradually my first act began to move – and so did my mind. It was a mind which was badly in need of solitude, and not for the purpose of rest. On the contrary. My mind was dying from disuse. It had been years since I had read a serious book or had a conversation on any level above that of dinner table chatter, for which all one needed was to have read the latest issue of *Time* or *The New Yorker*.

Now I found myself unable to escape thinking. It was, for the first few days, a horrifying experience; I longed for companionship, for a movie, for anything to relieve me of the responsibility of facing myself. And then, slowly, into this vacuum began to slip the ideas which I had found so bewildering in *Man's Fate* and *The Coming Struggle for Power*. I started again, after ten or more years, to read the *New Republic* and the *Nation* and, for the first time, the *New Masses*.

That did it. There was a piece by a writer named Robert Forsythe, as good as most of the *New Yorker* stuff but it was different. This

Robert Forsythe seemed to care terribly about something. He was angry, not just amusing. I began to realize that I had once cared about the same things that he did and that these were the things I had been angry about when I wrote my *Aunt Polly.*

I began to want to write again the way I had then; I had hated Mussolini once, and now there was Hitler. It suddenly came over me that I was on the wrong side. If there was this "class war" as they claimed, I had somehow got into the enemy's army. I suddenly remembered the Negro in Palm Beach looking at me through the window of the private car. "What are you doing in there?" I now knew the answer, and I wanted to rush out and shake hands with the Negro and let him know that I was on his side. I felt a tremendous sense of relief, of exultation. It was the same joyous feeling that had come to me in Dayton when I renounced the climb to business success. I could go and see those friends of my early literary days – John Dos Passos and Bunny Wilson and Doc Walker and Heywood Broun – and say, "Look! I'm back again!" and they would be terribly pleased. Clarence Day had died, but I felt I could have told him that his "battleship" had ended its pleasure cruise and was ready to go into action in the coming struggle against the Nazis and the Fascists. If this meant being called a Socialist or a Communist (I didn't know there was a difference) I was ready for that, too. I even began romantically to think of myself as a Communist.

I had no idea yet of what that involved. The Soviet Union was the country where the underdog had taken power into his own hands, and I wanted to be on the side of the underdog. I especially liked the idea that he must do the job himself by uniting with all other underdogs and without waiting for God or the Rich to take care of him. I felt that I had the answer I had been so long searching for. I now had a Cause to which I could devote all my gifts for the rest of my life. I was once more beside grandfather Ogden who had helped to free the slaves. I felt clean and happy and exalted. I had won all the money and status that America had to offer – and it just hadn't been good enough. The next step was Socialism.

Of course, my "Socialism" was a bit on the romantic side. It was not particularly concerned with any of the details of the administration of my dream when it was achieved. The essence, to me, was the freedom of the individual, and I somehow associated it with the freedom I had surrendered when I went to work for the Talbotts, had regained when I became a free-lance creative writer, and then lost again to Louis B. Mayer. Going back still further, it was the freedom I had had at Exeter and Yale, as well as the team work and the brotherhood of the football field.

Gradually in my mind began to form the image of a "worker" whom I wanted to have the same sense of freedom and brotherhood that I had had at college. Unconsciously, I suppose, I wanted to tap these "workers" for Skull and Bones. And over in the corner of my imagination, behind the worker, there crouched an image of a little man who needed my help – the oppressed, the unemployed, the hungry, the sharecropper, the Jew under Hitler, the Negro. In a way, it was a strange process of delayed action; many become Socialists at seventeen and "get over it" in the competition for success in the American way of life. Here was I, at forty-one, with all the prizes in my pocket, starting out to "get over" my success.

All this, of course, didn't come to me in a single blinding flash. I read everything I could get my hands on, I walked the roads around the clubhouse. I lay awake nights. There was no struggle, however, no anguish, no inner conflict. It never occurred to me that it would make any difference in my relation to Bea or to any of our friends or to my Hollywood contracts. This was something which would, I thought, make them admire me all the more. I could once more become the writer of my own plays, only with an immensely greater understanding of my world and a much more important message to impart. That was what I wanted to do: to spread this great truth of Socialism so that the upper and middle classes would understand the point of view of the working class. And even if they could not yet accept it, they would at least realize the evils of Fascism and Nazism. I had unwittingly become a teacher more than an artist – or perhaps I had always been one. But now I had something to teach.

20

Let it be understood, however, that the romantic "communist" did not beat his Hawes and Curtis stiff dress shirt into a hairy one and set out with a begging bowl to Do Good. Nor did I shred my new dinner jacket and distribute the pieces among the deserving poor. I saw no reason to stop dancing or enjoying the fun and play in life. I wanted to do something about the problem of seeing to it that a great many more people were allowed into the amusement park. My new-- found philosophy was an affirmation of the good life, not a rejection of it.

Nor did Communism mean to me surrendering the position I had won in order to share with the unemployed the horrors of the Depression. I had seen clearly within myself the compromises a man will make with his integrity in order to get or keep a job. Whoever controlled the power of employment also had his hand too close to the controls over the independent spirit of Man, and it was this control which I wanted the workers themselves to share. I most fervently didn't want anyone to be seduced – as I had been – by the siren call to a race for "Success" in which a man became more and more separated from the rest of humanity. My deepest desire was to get out of the pursuit of the Elite and back into the human race. That was the essence of my "conversion."

How much of this I got into *Insurance* would be difficult to say. My guess would be that I wasn't very successful in this first attempt to translate my new vision into the language of Broadway. It was too new and, what is more important, too undigested. The process of writing a play which "says something" is an extremely tricky one.

The playwright's truth must be projected, especially if it is unpalatable to the Broadway audience, in a manner that seems to come so naturally from the characters themselves that suspicion of "propaganda" is overcome by the truth of the situation itself. For a playwright this demands, among other things, that this truth be so assimilated into his bloodstream that when inner motives begin to cause his characters to speak, their words come from his deepest consciousness and not from the latest book he has studied. In the fall of 1935 the truths that had opened for me so many doors of understanding of the world were still largely in my head. So it is quite likely that *Insurance* wasn't a very good play. It certainly turned out to be quite a disappointment to those who had been looking forward to what I would offer after *Rebound*.

This disapproval, curiously enough, came as quite a shock to me. I had finished an act and a half at my yacht club retreat, then enthusiastically rushed out to my Beverly Hills fireside where I feverishly completed the first draft. When Bea read it she tried very loyally to be encouraging. My new faith must have been completely bewildering to her. Serious subjects had long ago been dropped from the agenda of our pleasure-filled married life. We were known as a happy couple, which was a fairly justifiable designation except that beneath it lurked the dangerous fact that our happiness had been buoyed up by an increasing avoidance of anything which might lead to discomfort or disagreeableness. It was one of the ironies of our married life that when I was finally beginning to emerge from my tailspin of successful immaturity, when I was at last showing some evidence that I was growing up, Bea was unable to understand the tokens I was holding out to her.

It wasn't her fault. Nothing had prepared her for the radical leap which I was asking her to take with me. So when I joyfully brought *Insurance* to her, she and our successful friends saw the "message" as just "another of Don's enthusiasms" which, presumably, the crazy fellow would get over in time. Like golf. Or the Hay diet. (A year or so before this I had become enthused by the theory of a Dr. Hay, who later died of stomach trouble, that starches and proteins should never be served at the same meal. So, for two or three months poor Bea and our cook and our guests had struggled with Dr. Hay's menus.) And now it was Communism. Well, let's hope this craze won't last too long or turn a faithful Life of the Party into a Serious Bore. But it wasn't quite the same joke for poor Leland Hayward when he tried to sell *Insurance* on the show-business market. His golden goose had laid a very strange egg indeed – and the commodity price of Stewart Ltd. took a sudden sharp drop on Broadway.

This didn't worry Stewart too much. I believed that my play was a great advance over *Rebound* although it was quite possible that it needed much rewriting. But I had promised Thalberg to fulfill my contract after a certain December date, so I reluctantly postponed my initial contribution to an understanding of the class struggle and went to work, along somewhat different lines, on a Joan Crawford vehicle called *No More Ladies.*

Before I could get completely enthralled by this subject, however, my father-in-law died, and Irving very generously allowed me to postpone Joan Crawford's dialogue until the New Year so that Bea and I could journey to Oswego N.Y. for the funeral. I had become a very fond of Bea's father. The stock market had ruined his fortune and his stomach, but he had bravely endured the last unhappy years of his lonely defeated life. He died in the guest house of our Beverly Hills home, and I shall never forget the horror of his final cries, one of which was "Bring out the dead man!" The nurses assured me that in his state of coma he was without pain or consciousness and didn't know what he was saying, but I have never been able to believe that. It was like the prisoner condemned to execution who, when reassured by the guard that it wouldn't hurt, asked "How do *you* know?"

After the funeral Bea and I had two or three weeks in New York, during which I practiced the first easy steps in reconciling my established social life with my new revolutionary philosophy. The bridge from Right to Left seemed to be quite smooth, mainly because the change in me was not at all noticeable on the ballroom floor or at the bar of 21. I went with Phil Barry to Odets's new play *Paradise Lost*; we both appreciated his dramatic talent, but Phil couldn't quite go along with me in my enthusiasm for what the play said politically. On the way home we argued warmly about Socialism. Phil, a Catholic, was almost the only one of my close friends who listened sympathetically and understandingly to my new ideas. This was mainly, I think, because of his belief in me as a playwright; he didn't much care what inspired me to write plays so long as I got the hell out of Hollywood and started writing them. He didn't like *Insurance* but that, he explained, was because of its faults as a play.

The only other person I showed it to was Joan Payson; she quite understandably thought it was dreadful. We laughed quite a bit about it while dancing at Birdie Vanderbilt's Christmas ball. My "Communism" didn't bother Joan or Charlie at all. Like most, they were amused and sure that I would soon snap out of it. After New Year's they took Bea with them down to the sunshine of Hobe Sound in Florida while I went back to Beverly Hills and *No More Ladies*.

An important feature of my changed outlook – and one which troubled me considerably – was the evident necessity for the convert to take part in some form of political activity. Evidently it wasn't enough to have found a philosophy that made one understand the historical reasons for war and other crimes against humanity. One must translate thought into action. One must *do* something about changing the world.

So when I got out to Hollywood I was all set to "do something." This involved, as you may well imagine, a considerable leap in the dark for someone who had been living comfortably in a dream world. Furthermore, my entire conditioning had confirmed in me a contempt for and distrust of politics and politicians. I wanted to be on the side of "the workers" but I didn't know any to be on the side of. I remember walking past some carpenters on a Metro stage and experiencing a happy warm feeling of satisfaction that I was now their brother, but I wasn't sure that they knew it. I smiled at them, but that was certainly not all that was required.

Then quite by chance I ran into a girl whom I remembered faintly as having been a friend of John Dos Passos. She must have been considerably surprised at the warmth with which I greeted her and asked about "good old Dos" and Jack Lawson and one or two others who were vaguely connected in my mind with the "radical" theater of the twenties. She was a little suspicious of me at first (not surprising in view of my Hollywood reputation as a party-giver and producers' pet), but when I began to praise the *New Masses* and the writings of Robert Forsythe she took a chance and asked me, almost challengingly, if I would mind contributing something to the aid of some migrant workers who were on strike in the Salinas Valley. "Would I mind?" I cried, as I enthusiastically wrote out a check, "My God! Tell me more. Is there anything else I can do?" Well, it seemed that there were several things, and I parted from her with a feeling that I had at last begun, in a small way, to change the world.

A week or two later I actually met my *New Masses* hero, Robert Forsythe. He turned out, to my surprise, to be a feature writer for Colliers named Kyle Crichton who had come out to Hollywood to interview movie stars. Kyle had to use his left-wing *nom de plume* in order to keep his right-wing job, and his first visit to my home for a drink was slightly embarrassing to me. While I was telling him how much his *New Masses* articles had meant to me I was surprised by two other visitors, one of whom was an English peer and the other Alfred Vanderbilt. They had come to see Bea, not knowing that she was in Florida. When I introduced them to Kyle, he thought at first that I was kidding about their names, and when he found that I wasn't he leaped to the conclusion that my alleged conversion to radicalism through his articles was all part of a not-very-funny Upper Class joke. But Alfred and the Lord were good drinking companions and they so obviously enjoyed Kyle's humor that all ended in a happy suspension of class warfare. Kyle's warm friendship and his courageous use of humor as a political weapon were a great help to me in those early days.

Another help came, shortly after, in the person of Herb Kline, a young left-winger who had started a Broadway magazine called *New Theater,* and who had hitch-hiked out to Hollywood in the hope of helping to start what he called the "Movement" amid the dreamy towers of Never-never-land. Herb was my first real honest-to-Marx Red. His father had been a miner, and Herb's conversion to Communism had come as a young boy when he had seen the police ride down and club a street full of strikers. This was the reality which was missing in my own conversion, and I took him into my heart. My admiration for him increased when I discovered that he was actually living on the ten dollars a week which the Communist Party paid its active functionaries. I wanted to give him more. I wanted to buy him expensive meals, clothes, anything he needed. I remember once offering him fifty dollars if he would just spend it on something useless, something he had never had – champagne, caviar, a silk hat. He took the fifty as a contribution to the *New Theater.* I wasn't trying to corrupt him. I was, I suppose, trying partly to appease my guilt about the difference in our weekly salaries. But it was not all guilt. Nor was I completely a romantic fool who was being used. In the first place, I wanted to be used. There was a Hitler and there was a danger to my belief in human rights. And as far as being "used" went, I knew about that. I had been used by the Elite – principally as a Life of the Party – and I now chose to let the using be done by the other side. I had found in Herb Kline a devoted and selfless fighter in the struggle for Socialism. I have since found many, but he was the first.

That is why I treasure the memory of him as he was in that spring of 1936. And that is why, no matter what has happened to him since, I shall always be grateful to him. It was he who showed me the glory of the Marxist ideal of bringing to the underprivileged of the world an insight into their true position in that world, an historical under-standing of the reasons for that position, and an assurance of its betterment through a realization of their united power. The only danger, as I said to Herb, was that of arrogant pride in the rightness of their cause and in the inevitability of their victory. By this time I was saying "our" cause and "our" victory.

I soon had an opportunity to say it more publicly. Another of my new heroes, Clifford Odets, had come out to Hollywood to aid the Movement – at least, it was assumed at the time that he had come for that purpose and not merely to pick up some of the lovely Hollywood gold. Odets started the ball rolling by making an un-heard-of and extremely exciting pro-left-wing speech at a fund--raising meeting for Herb's magazine. The sleeping Hollywood Dragon-in-Wonderland stirred for a moment uneasily in his comfor-table cork-lined castle, then concluded that it was only something he had eaten at Romanoff's and went back in search of the slumbering contentment of his habitual happy dreams. The Movement, he mumbled to himself, was a crackpot irrelevance which belonged in New York, and Hitler was a European nightmare which could be dis-solved by sensibly retreating into one's personal ghetto and pulling down all the blinds. Odets returned to Broadway, and the all-clear sounded.

But then came the announcement that there would be another meeting of those interested in the anti-Nazi struggle. This one was to be held at the Hollywood Womans' Club. A play *Bury the Dead,* by an unknown young writer named Irwin Shaw, was to be read by no less than Fredric March and his wife Florence Eldridge, and the meeting was to be chaired by Donald Ogden Stewart. The friendly Dragon opened both eyes and wondered what the hell was going on. Fredric March was a valuable property. Politics – especially foreign politics – was not the business of an actor. Besides, Germany was an important market for American films. Writers, of course, were drunken, irresponsible people but they were employees, weren't they? They were hired to write scripts and nothing else. What's got into that crazy fool Don Stewart?

The door of my M-G-M office opened and there stood Sam Marx, the Story Editor. "How's the script coming, Don?" he asked with a genial smile, and quickly added: "Don't think anyone's pressing you. Irving's very pleased with what you've done. By the way, he wants to know if you and Mrs. Stewart can come to dinner Thursday." "Mrs. Stewart's in Florida," I replied. "And, damn it, Thursday's no good this week." Sam looked at me a moment, then said "That's the night of that meeting, isn't it?" I nodded, and he came over to my desk. "Look, Don" he said, and he seemed a bit uncomfortable; "Irving's been a very good friend of yours – and he will be very hurt if you make a speech there."

I didn't argue with Sam. There wasn't really anything to argue about – except, perhaps, my job at M-G-M. I was quite willing to give that up, although I didn't for a minute think that Irving would be petty enough to let me go. And I was right. There is a Sam Goldwyn story about a furious quarrel Goldwyn had with a famous actor. He kicked the star out of his office with an explosion of violent curses ending with: "And furthermore, you dirty double-crossing hypocritical son-of-a-bitch, I don't ever want to see you on this lot again!" To which he added, as the actor was hastily exiting, "Unless I need you." My own case wasn't, of course, quite similar to this. I think that Irving was trying to give me some rather deeply-felt fatherly advice, and it probably hurt him considerably to see one of his favorite ducklings starting to swim for himself in some dangerous unknown waters. It certainly wasn't easy for me to break with a "father" to whom I owed so much.

Anyway, the meeting was held and was much more successful than anyone had expected. Freddie March and Florence Eldridge gave a very moving reading of Irwin Shaw's play. It was a bitter diatribe against war, in which simple American soldiers killed in the First World War came out of their graves to look at the world which they had "made safe for democracy" and then to curse their upper-class betrayers and plead for a new world in which the common people would see to it that such a betrayal could never happen again. It was, in a way, the same theme as my *Aunt Polly,* but tremendously deepened by the intervening horrors of the Depression and the Hitlerian Third Reich. The only thing I remember about my own speech – and I remember it because Heywood Broun printed it soon after in his column – was a plea for Hollywood to wake up to what Hitler was doing and to stop making pictures which said absolutely nothing. "Let us," I exhorted at the climax, "let us have no more million-dollar revolving staircases, no more star-filled symposiums of billion-dollar entertainment – but let us have some simple truths, as we have had tonight, some simple truths on a bare stage, against nothing but a plain background." By the time I spoke, mainly because of the wonderfully moving presentation of the play, the audience was ready for anything, and, as Ted Paramore said afterwards, "If somebody had started singing the 'Marseillaise,' we would have marched on the writers' building at Paramount and torn it triumphantly to the ground."

So the Movement began to spread in Hollywood, and some began, at first a bit reluctantly, to listen to the cries for help from the outside world. Shortly after our *Bury The Dead* meeting, there arrived a German Prince Hubertus von und zu Loewenstein, a Catholic who had written a book attacking the Third Reich and had fled to America to help spread the news of what Hitler and his little group were really up to. With him was another German refugee who was traveling under the name of Breda. He had, under another name, written *The Brown Book of the Hitler Terror,* which had contributed greatly to European understanding of the gruesome Nazi techniques. The prince and Breda wanted to raise money for the anti-Nazi campaign in America, and I gave a dinner party to introduce them to some of the film possibilities, including Irving, Mary Pickford, Norma Shearer, David and Irene Selznick, Sam and Frances Goldwyn, and Walter Wanger. The Prince and Herr Breda quickly won sympathy for their cause (the prince was an extremely impressive nobleman, Breda was irresistibly intelligent and sincere, and the champagne was very good, too) and plans were made for a large white-tie-and-tails dinner for which all guests were to pay one hundred dollars a plate.

The affair, when it came off, was a terrific success. Every table was crowded with top-bracket Hollywood names. The Archbishop of Los Angeles sat in his robes beside the Prince at the speakers table. I, as toastmaster, sat beside Herr Breda. It was one of the happiest evenings of my life. It wasn't only that my speech went over very well. That had happened before. But this time my words meant something. The Life of the Party had on his usual costume of white tie and tails, and he was getting his usual laughs, but this time he blended the laughter into something which came from his heart and moved the celebrities to applaud for more than the jokes. I even had the illusion that I was going to be able to continue influencing these powerful people without being asked to surrender the principles which had brought me into the fight against Hitler. When Herr Breda gave his moving description of the Nazi Terror, the details of which he had been able to collect only through repeatedly risking his own life, I was proud to be sitting beside him, proud to be on his side in the fight. I didn't notice that just before he began to speak the Archbishop gathered up his robes and left the room. Someone had tipped His Grace that Breda was a Communist.

I didn't know that, but if I had, I would have been prouder than ever to have been at his side. Here was a man who had devoted his life untiringly and at great risk of death by torture to the principles which I in my dress suit was just beginning to fight for. Herb Kline was my first American Communist, Breda my first European one. I romanticized them both. It is a pitiful comment on political realities that the American later denounced his principles in an attempt to be a Hollywood success, and the courageous devoted Breda, whose real name was Otto Katz, was hanged for "treason" by the Czechs at the height of the Stalin terror.

New opportunities for service to the Movement were opening. Shortly after the Victor Hugo banquet I met my first Negro Communist. I might almost say that I met my first Negro: Prior to this, with the exception of the student I had helped through Yale, my main contact with Negroes had been as waiters or sleeping car porters. Ben was a young inhabitant of the Central Avenue section of Los Angeles, and when I accepted his invitation to meet some of his friends I found myself undergoing one more strange bit of education in dropping off lifelong prejudices. The first time I found myself in a saloon in which I was the only white I just couldn't believe that it was I. My discomfort was increased by the fact that I have always been extremely sensitive to being "different" from everyone else, and I made the usual White's mistake of trying to make my companions feel that I didn't think I was at all superior to them. Luckily one of the group had the humor to say: "Take it easy, man. We know we're as good as you are," and after the laugh on that one I began to relax.

Another mistake I made (as I had with Herb) was to offer Ben some money for his own use. "Save it," he said. "I need it for something else." "Something else" turned out to be a Youth Center which the Communist Party wanted to set up in the district. I hadn't any idea what that might be, but to my Hollywood mind it suggested playing fields, swimming pools, reading rooms and at least one bowling alley. To my relief, Ben took me to a small empty store room and explained that all I was expected to supply was old books and magazines, and money for a punching bag. So I filled our Packard limousine with old novels, cook books, Hay diet menus, annual lists of "Racquet" and "River Club" members, and copies of *Vogue, Harper's Bazaar, Town and Country,* and *The New Yorker,* and delivered them happily at the Youth Center. The class struggle marched on.

Another of my activities, slightly less un-American, was a plunge into the struggle of the Screen Writers Guild against the efforts of the producers to organize a company union known as Screen Playwrights. The original Guild, organized three years previously by John Howard Lawson, Oliver Garrett, Ralph Block, Dudley Nichols and others, had been rather effectively rendered impotent by the steady refusal of the producers to accord the organization any real recognition or bargaining power. This was the Guild which I had thumbed my nose at in the heyday of my "producers'-pet" period. Now, however, I was on the side of "the workers." That meant, in my blissful ignorance, all unions. And so, when the Roosevelt administration gave the green light – or a relatively green light – to new possibilities for labor organizing, the screenwriters, joined now by important "name" writers like Lillian Hellman, Sam Raphaelson, Dashiel Hammett, Dorothy Parker and Charles Brackett, set out to revive the guild into one which would have real power. The producers retaliated in the two conventional ways. They organized a "company" union and threatened to blacklist all writers connected with the revival of the old guild.

When I eagerly rushed into this forbidden activity, I knew that it meant the final break with Thalberg. I had finished my Joan Crawford *No More Ladies* job, and Irving had suggested that I sit in on conferences with Sam Berman and Salka Viertel on the next Garbo script, which was to concern the love affair of Napoleon and Marie Walewska. The first conference, however, concerned nothing but the Guild, and to my delight Salka joined forces with me against Napoleon Thalberg. It was a tough fight, but we held our own. We also held our jobs, and Salka and I even baited Irving about the advantages of Socialism. This was a drawn battle in which Irving disclosed that in his Brooklyn high school days he had been a member of the Young Peoples' Socialist League and had made ardent street-corner speeches. But now he merely regarded us with the sad reproachful eyes of a betrayed parent.

This meeting with Salka Viertel was an exceptionally fortunate one for me. She was – and is – a rare and courageous spirit. She had been a celebrated Polish actress who had married an equally famous Austrian poet and director, Berthold Viertel. She had absorbed her knowledge of political struggle in the German 20's and had fled from Hitler in 1928 to make her house in Santa Monica a home for all refugees and a rallying point for all rebels.

Meanwhile Bea, from Florida, had been writing more and more urgently that I must get out of Hollywood so that I could write plays in the East. I'm not sure whether someone had begun to worry her about my "Movement" activities, but I got a long, serious, well-meant letter from Deems Taylor telling me what a fool I was as an artist to get mixed up in any political activities, especially Communist ones. It was really very decent of Deems, whether or not Bea inspired him to write it, but it was like asking a man who has just recovered his sight to put on blinkers. It surprised me, though, that Deems was so violently anti-Communist; he was the first of my old friends to react that way. Dorothy Parker had "gone left" even before I had, and Bobby Benchley was noncommitally understanding. At my suggestion Bobby started to read the Webbs' *Soviet Russia – A New Civilization* and reported after the first few pages that it seemed like it might be a good idea.

I don't think he got much further in it, but after a few more pages he suggested that I have a physical check-up by a wonderful new doctor whom Lewis Milestone had discovered. I suspected that Bobby might be hoping that the doctor would cure me of my unfortunate attack of political activity, but I agreed that I would let the doctor work on me if Bobby would take the same treatment. The physician's name was Cecil Smith, and after a preliminary examination he sent us both to a hospital for a week of "further checking-up."

It was a marvelous week. Bobby and I were in adjoining rooms; the meals were excellent, and we were allowed wine with some of them. Cecil recommended that Bobby take a certain pill for one or two nights "just to see if we're on the right track." On the third day Cecil came to Bobby's Garden-of-Allah bungalow, and asked him if the pills had had the desired effect. Bobby replied: "Well, I'm not quite sure," and when he pulled off his shirt we saw that a frighteningly realistic growth of silver-fox fur extended from Bobby's neck down to his rectum. "Is this what you meant?" he asked poor Cecil.

Bea arrived shortly after this, and the agreement was definitely made to abandon Hollywood in favor of an Eastern residence, preferably on a fairly secluded farm where I could devote myself exclusively to play-writing. This decision was confirmed by the previously-mentioned harmful results of the Hollywood atmosphere on juvenile education, and I had visions of the curative effects on the boys of a simple country school, preferably an Abe Lincoln type log cabin. I was especially anxious to get Ames away from military school, and remove Dee-dee from the upper-class snobberies of an English governess who had supplanted good old Norwegian Nana.

Our first-and-final-stop was in New York State at Au Sable Forks, where we had been invited by Kendall Lee of Virginia, married at one time to Jules Glaenzer, head of Cartiers, but now the wife of Lewis Milestone. Kendall had a small farmhouse adjoining the much larger estate of Rockwell Kent, who had married her equally beautiful sister Frances in the days when she was in the chorus of the Music Box, the revue which had introduced Bobby's "Treasurer's Report." I found to my delight that Rockwell was an active Socialist, and when he discovered a nearby farm which was for sale Bea and I felt that our search had ended. There was an Italian immigrant tavern-keeper named Louis Monaco who was quite a powerful figure in the district, and at Rockwell's suggestion I engaged Louis to supervise the rebuilding of the place.

The farmhouse, originally constructed around 1800, needed modernization badly, as did two smaller cottages and two barns on the 215-acre property. The place was picturesquely located on a slope above a trout stream, in the midst of the Adirondacks. On part of our estate was a beautiful forest of pine trees, and in another section was a small mountain named Frazzletop covered with superb beeches amid which deer often roamed. Bea and I hugged each other at our good fortune. It was our first real home. I had never owned property before. Louis engaged masons, carpenters, plumbers, roadbuilders, laborers; it was a field day for the local unemployed, of which there seemed to be an ever-increasing number.

After we had gone down to New York (seven hours by train) to observe the annual rites of the Harvard-Yale boat race and the Payson wedding anniversary ball, I settled down in one of our cottages to rewrite my anti-Upper Class *Insurance.* I changed the title to *The New House,* which was a significant indication of my own change of outlook. *Insurance* was a rather despairing search for an answer to the emptiness created by the realization that even amid the rich and powerful there was no insurance of security. The new version aimed to show the struggle involved in personal relations after a young married man had found *his* answer and had started to build his symbolic new house. I centered it, as I had *Rebound,* on the woman's problem, Bea's problem. How was a girl with her Society background, her Farmington finishing-school education, and her deep involvement with the Upper Class going to meet the incomprehensible *volte face* of a husband whom she loves? I had no doubt of Bea's love, or of her eventual understanding of what to me was a recovery of my integrity and my self-respect as a man. As I worked on this fascinating theme there occurred the tenth anniversary of our wedding, and since she was down in the city, I wrote her, out of the fullness of my heart, of my love and gratitude for the joy and glory of these ten years with her. On her return from New York the anniversary was gaily celebrated with the help of Joan and Charlie who came up to nearby Lake Champlain in the "Saga" in order to see our new house.

The house itself was finished before I had completed the play. It was a truly beautiful house in a glorious setting of mountains ablaze with the reds and yellows of autumn. We held one house-warming celebration with Louis and the laborers; another with Rockwell, Frances "Milly" Milestone and Kendall; one with the friendly Rogers family, who were the Feudal Lords of Au Sable Forks, since the Rogers' paper mill was the sole local industry; and another, a most blessed one, with Gerald and Sara Murphy, who had brought their boy Patrick to nearby Saranac Lake in a desperate, and eventually unsuccessful attempt to save his life.

There was only one depressing note to me about all these house warmings, and that was the unfortunate fact that the dream house had cost three or four times as much as I had anticipated. In fact, by the time we finished "improving," it would have been much cheaper to have built three or four completely new buildings. By the time I had finished my triumphant renunciation of Hollywood, I had become so involved in debts and loans that my immediate return was an urgent necessity. Irving had died unexpectedly in September, and his successor was a good friend of mine named Bernie Hyman. When, in early November, I began to get long-distance appeals from him, I hastily finished *The New House* and leaped on to the Chief with hands tremblingly held out to the life-saving golden shackles.

Bea and the boys remained at Frazzletop Farm, under the watchful care of a wonderful old native named John d'Avignon and his two daughters. John, who was about seventy, had served many years as a logger and teamster for the Rogers company. Ames and Dee-dee (who had now justifiably been re-nicknamed "Duck" because of his tendency to sound-off like a Disney Donald) were more or less happily enrolled in the local little red schoolhouse, although my hope that they would turn into little Abe Lincolns was frustrated by the fact that their acquaintance with Clark Gable and Shirley Temple quickly did more to develop their superiority complexes in this rural community than had anything in Hollywood itself.

Upon my return to the studios, I quickly discovered that the happy carefree days of the white-tie-and-tails anti-Nazi movement had gone forever. On my very first day at M-G-M I was unexpectedly and to my utter bewilderment cut dead by two writers, one of whom, John Lee Mahin, had always been most friendly to me since the time I had helped him out (without claiming screen credit) with the script of his first film *Red Dust*. I discovered that I was now considered a Communist, a loathsome person whom some of the members of the company union, the Screen Playwrights, had decided to consider un-American and unworthy of even a morning snarl. The same sort of patriotic righteousness had also arisen in connection with the attempts to enlist Hollywood in the fight against Hitler Germany. After my departure the enthusiasm aroused by our banquet had resulted in the formation of a Hollywood Anti-Nazi League, with me as president and Oscar Hammerstein, Fredric March, and Dorothy Parker among several other well-known names on the executive committee. The League had at first been welcomed by the producers, and had been supported in the film colony with such enthusiasm that offices had been rented, several successful public meetings held, and a weekly paper published. The Warner brothers had offered us the facilities of their radio station KFWB and a series of weekly programs based on my *Mrs. and Mrs. Haddock Abroad* had been broadcast. But gradually the producers had been made suspicious that the League might be a Red Organization. During the summer this had resulted in the withdrawal of all producers' support, with the exception of Warner Bros. Harry Warner in particular had refused to yield to the arguments. Hitler was the enemy and Harry was willing to use any help, even from Reds, to fight him.

By the time I arrived, many of our "name" supporters had also yielded to the fear of being associated with Communism. I remember having long arguments as to why the League didn't also attack that "ism." My answer was: "Because it was organized to fight Nazism. If you want to fight Communism, get up another league." But as I declined to accept the need for our League to be "also anti-Communist" there was also an increase in the number of people who declined to speak to me, and in the amount of the dust on my Hawes and Curtis stiff dress shirts and white dress waistcoats. Our League continued to grow, however, even without the big producers and the "names," and we gradually achieved a membership of some five or six thousand.

But for me it was the beginning of a strange period of adjustment to the realization that people were beginning to regard me as a traitor. My lifelong need to be well liked was finding this rather difficult to take, especially as I was despairing of ever being able to convince Bea and my closest friends of the rightness of my new desire to fight for the principles of Socialism. I was ready to join hands with the workers, but how in hell did you get to meet them? Without admitting it to myself, it was like one of those "When a feller needs a friend" cartoons – and it is just another example of the luck which has blessed me all my life that at the very beginning of my exposure to a sense of isolation and loneliness I found that friend.

21

One Saturday morning, in the middle of November, I was in my office at Metro engaged in doing three rather contradictory things at once. I was trying to think of a scene for a film, the name of which I can no longer remember; I was reading the second volume of a history of the Russian Revolution by Leon Trotsky; and I was listening to the Yale-Princeton game on my radio. Usually a high-salaried screen writer doesn't go within miles of any studio on Saturday, but I was anxious to show Bernie Hyman that my political activities were not interfering with my devotion to good old M-G-M. Suddenly, just as Yale was on the eight yard line, the telephone rang and I cursingly answered. It was Dorothy Parker, and she wondered if I could fly up to San Francisco that afternoon to a Conference of Western Writers. Yale fumbled and lost the ball, and I said I would.

On the plane were fellow writers, Joel Sayre, Humphrey Cobb, Dorothy and her husband Alan Campbell. The conference was distinctly Left Wing, being run by sort of a Western branch of the League of American Writers, an organization set up in New York the year before "to get writers out of their ivory towers and into the active struggle against Nazism and Fascism." I didn't know anybody in the hall where the meeting was being held, or any of the speakers, but I was particularly impressed by the speech of a man who spoke with a sort of Cockney accent and whose name was Harry Bridges. He had been introduced amid tremendous enthusiasm as a Labor Leader, and I thrilled at the thought of such a man speaking to writers. This was getting closer to the real thing.

Then, with equal enthusiasm, there was introduced "the

courageous untiring fighter against Nazism whom we all know, the widow of the great Lincoln Steffens, our beloved Ella Winter." I dimly remembered from my youth Steffens' muckraking articles in father's bound volumes of *McClure's* magazine, and I awaited gray hair and a few sad but brave wrinkles. To my astonishment, there came to the front of the platform a handsome middle-aged brunette who had the most extraordinary black eyes, alternately luminous and flashing as she spoke in a charming British voice. Her words were charming, too; she "welcomed especially the humorists who had come from Hollywood, because what the Movement needs is humor, humor and more humor," and added "Dorothy Parker and Donald Ogden Stewart in one sentence can help us more than a thousand jargon-filled pamphlets." By this time I was ready to help "our beloved Ella" do anything.

After the meeting we all met in a bar where she introduced me to Bridges, who instantly won my heart with his dry humor, his good sense, and his ability to drink large quantities of bourbon. Then Ella (she was "Ella" by then) took Harry and Dotty and the rest of our good old Hollywood delegation to the apartment of Paul Smith, a friendly young newspaper editor whose walls featured admiringly autographed photos of Lincoln Steffens and Herbert Hoover.

Next day came more thrills for the romantic convert when at Humphrey Cobbs' request we were taken over to San Quentin prison to interview Tom Mooney. The afternoon was featured by another meeting of the Western writers at which I pledged Hollywood's undying help, was promptly attacked as "just a giver of lavish publicity-seeking dances" by a furious all-out left wing writer and defended most ably by an even more furious flashing-eyed beauty named Ella Winter.

In Lincoln Steffens' *Autobiography* (which I promptly read) Ella is described as a "dancing girl," and I decided to see if he was as wise in that department of life as he was about politics. A month later Ella made a flying visit to Hollywood to raise money for a weekly magazine she was editing and after a try-out or two at the Trocadero I was able to give the *Autobiography* – and her – my unreserved admiration. This seemed to compensate somewhat for reports from Broadway that my play *The New House* was proving even more difficult to sell than *Insurance*. No reasons were give by Leland Hayward, other than "They just don't seem to care for the theme."

Two days from Christmas I got a frantic telephone call from Bea.

Ames had caught a bad cold, it had developed into pneumonia, and the crisis was expected hourly. Bernie Hyman's eyes filled with tears as I told him, and he released me from my contract. I got to the farm Christmas eve. Bea and I were fearfully together all night in the face of our first tragic reality; the next morning the local doctor saved Ames' life by performing an emergency operation on one lung.

Our spirits rebounded, and we celebrated Christmas in a somewhat symbolic mixture of champagne and leftover fumes from the doctor's ether. Bea had had all she wanted of rural life and the new house; as soon as Ames was well enough to travel she took him, "Duck" and a nurse to Florida "for an indefinite period." I was broke again, and accepted an offer from David Selznick to return immediately to the Coast to work for his new company which was being financed principally by the Whitneys. In view of my determined efforts in the past year to escape from Hollywood illusion into Political Reality, the title of my next job – *The Prisoner of Zenda* – had a certain ironic ring.

The prisoner, however, escaped after four months, for which welcome relief his gratitude is largely due to David Selznick himself. Irving Thalberg had had his faults, but he had never made the mistake of thinking of himself as a gifted writer. Nor had he ever made the mistake of allowing the employer-employee relationship to come into the open in all its dictatorial onesidedness. The day that David shouted at me, "Don't try to tell *me* how characters make love!" was the end of the honeymoon, and the three-picture contract which I had luckily had the instinct never to sign, was terminated "by mutual consent."

The visit to Zenda did, however, have its positive advantages. It was on this script that I became acquainted with the bewildering processes of Hollywood censorship, which had been self-imposed under the name of the "Will Hays Office" after the Fatty Arbuckle scandal and was guided rigidly by the moral code of the Catholic Church. In the *Prisoner* story, Ronald Coleman played the dual role of an Englishman on a visit to the kingdom of Zenda, and of the King. Our script, following the novel, explained this striking resemblance of the two men by the fact that some three centuries before there had been a very gay Englishwoman who was Ronald's great-great-etc. grandmother. On a trip of Zenda, around, say, 1620, this carefree minx had caught the eye of the equally gay, light-moraled King, and so forth. At the very beginning of our story, therefore, Ronald explains this to a friend (and the audience) on a walk through the family manorial hall where hang the portraits of his ancestors – not what you might call an inspired bit of scriptwriting, but mercifully short and effective. However, when this came back from the Hays office, which was then being run by a genial Irish Catholic named Joe Breen, we were informed that since this great-great-great etc. grandmother had committed a sin, she must, according to God's laws, atone for her act. But how? "Well," the Office suggested "how would it be if she died in childbirth?" That was no problem for an an experienced screenwriter, and on the 4th of March, 1621 the poor lady came to her end (off the screen, fortunately) with the required amount of atoning pain. After I became more experienced in the workings of the Hays office "code," I used always to write three or four scenes which I knew would be thrown out, in order that we could bargain with Joe Breen for the retention of other really important episodes or speeches.

There were other more rewarding educational benefits during my Anti-Nazi League days. I made the acquaintance, as chairman for their speeches, of André Malraux and the English Ralph Bates, two devoted (at that time) anti-Fascist warriors who had fought in Spain and who joined my pin-up gallery of Left Wing Heroes. The Spanish Civil War had given Hollywood another opportunity for education in political realities, and an Anti-Franco League (of which I was president) organized several highly successful meetings in the huge Shrine auditorium. Ernest Hemingway had come out to the Coast after inspecting at first hand the Spanish situation and, at a private dinner at Robert Montgomery's house, had raised a thousand dollars from each of the ten guests in the interest of ambulances for the Loyalist side. As I had by now become pretty widely tagged as a Red, I was not invited to meet my old friend, but I was tremendously pleased that he and I were once more on the same side.

From the distance of Hollywood the issues in Spain seemed very clear and I did not want to get my enthusiastic fight against Fascism confused (as by now had Dos Passos, Edmund Wilson, Doc Walker and most of my old friends) with the bitter disputes over Trotskyist and other types of "true" Communism. My main reason for closing my eyes to those ideological struggles was, however, a profound distrust of myself. I knew that if I wanted to, I could too easily find excuses like "Trotskyism" for avoiding the consequence of taking my stand as a Russophile. I was too new a convert not to be almost pathologically distrustful of any "out" for myself. It was, in a way, a good joke on me that I had come so late into the Movement that most of the friends whom I had expected to welcome me joyfully had already taken up anti-Russian positions which made me an even bitterer enemy than I was during my Capitalistic joy-ride.

But I didn't yet realize the extent of the bitterness of the anti-Stalin movement, and I went blissfully on my anti-Fascist way. One mistake which I did make at this time was my idealization of Russia as the first Socialist republic. I discredited too readily the reports of the terror in Stalinist Russia during and after the trials of the mid-30's, and accepted too eagerly the myth of the universal humanity of my Socialist dream-country. But in the fight into which I had so recently plunged it did not seem the time to examine very closely some of the possible realities of my ideal. In a certain sense I had "got religion," and I didn't want to examine the realities of my heaven until I was sure I would not use any possible disillusionment as an excuse for deserting to the "individualism" of those who were "above the battle."

By the time I returned to New York, therefore, the gulf between me and my former life had become much wider than I had previously been willing to realize. I had never hesitated to discuss my revolutionary ideas with my friends; I remember one such discussion of the previous summer on Jock Whitney's yacht when Jock had laughingly declared that he would be enthusiastically for Socialism if it meant that he didn't have to play polo any more. But the jokes were getting a little strained, and I felt myself becoming more and more separated from people of whom I was still very fond. It was with a sad sense of this that I played my last game of golf on the Whitney links. I hadn't meant it to be the last, but when I came to the final tee I realized that the Long Island play days were ending and I rather despairingly took a deep breath and hit the best drive I had ever made. My partner, Stuart Symington, was amazed and demanded, "What's happened to you?" I couldn't tell him – and I never played golf again.

This chasm was further widened by a speech I made shortly after at Carnegie Hall. My political activities had previously been confined to Hollywood, but now I had the opportunity of making my *auto da fe* in the East. The League of American Writers had organized an anti-Fascist meeting, of which Archie MacLeish was to be chairman, and various writers, including Ernest Hemingway, were to speak. It gave me tremendous pleasure to be on the program with these two, and I eagerly looked forward to our reunion "on the same side."

It didn't work out that way. As we gathered at Carnegie Hall, Archie was so disturbed by the appearance of the Communist Secretary Earl Browder on the platform that he paid little attention to my presence – and Ernie hadn't shown up at all. MacLeish abandoned the chair and went in search of Hemingway, and after one or two other speeches I launched into mine. It was, like the Hollywood anti-Nazi speech, one of the thrilling high points in my life. Bea was in the audience, with Phil and Ellen Barry, and Adele Lovett. So, on the other side of the hall, was Ella Winter. After my speech Archie returned to the platform with Ernest, and the enthusiasm reached its height during his very moving attack on the Fascists in Spain. It was a most successful meeting, even though my hoped-for reunion with my two oldest literary friends was a dismal disappointment.

The next two days were occupied with conferences and papers by members on the various tactics by which writers could fight Hitler, Mussolini and France; there was also an unsuccessful attempt by the Trotskyists, of which I was only vaguely aware, to remove control of the League from the Communists who had been responsible for its origin. At the final meeting I was elected president for two years, to replace Waldo Frank who no longer wished to be associated with us Reds.

A few weeks after this I heard from Leland Hayward that Sam Goldwyn was very anxious to have me come out to Hollywood to work for him. On the farm I hadn't been able to get ahead on a new play, and as I respected Sam for his desire to make a picture which aimed at something more than mere entertainment, I made him the offer (to Leland's horror) to work for him for free. It was to be on an original idea of mine about the "ghost" towns in the West, and if he liked my final script, he was to recompense me for my work; otherwise, it would cost him nothing but the office space and a secretary. Sam quickly accepted, and I as quickly began to find that an "original" was not something that one could knock off in a few weeks. My own rather shaky financial situation and my renunciation of salary led me to live, for the first time since the Hotel Mark Twain days, in a small cheap room in the Ojai apartment house, a couple of blocks above Hollywood Boulevard. I ate most of my meals alone in cafeterias and with the exception of occasional dinners at the

Goldwyns' my "social" life consisted almost exclusively of anti-Nazi and Screenwriter's Guild Executive Board meetings.

For a while I rather romanticized this return to the simple life of my early years, and it certainly gave me plenty of time to catch up on my reading and thinking. One of the joys of my study of Marx and Engels was that the old boys opened up exciting fields of research in subjects of which I was profoundly ignorant, such as philosophy, history, and anthropology. It was like returning to college, with the important difference that I now had a reason for studying other than the passing of examinations. Dialectical materialism, with its theory of life as a continuous process of change, an ever-expanding growth rather than a closed repetitive circle, gave me the key to a changing world full of hope and beauty. It was on this that I concentrated rather than on the economic theories (which I didn't really understand very well). Most exciting was my newfound belief in the techniques of Science as the means by which Man might gradually come to know his world and, after testing his knowledge scientifically, be prepared to change it and control his own destiny. The blind alley, from which crazy humor had been one despairing means of escape, thus became the open road. And in celebration of this joyous fact I got gloriously drunk late one night, stepped unscientifically into an open road, and was promptly knocked for an ever-expanding loop by a speeding automobile.

When I recovered consciousness I was in a hospital, with less than fifty-fifty change of recovery from a basal skull fracture. That I hadn't died already was due largely to a screen director and Anti-Nazi League colleague named Herbert Biberman. When I had been hit, the police had no clue to my identification except a copy of the League weekly on which I had written Herbert's telephone number. He rushed into action, took over the process of getting me to the Cedars of Lebanon hospital and under the care of two of the best brain surgeons on the Coast; shortly after daybreak they were able to give him some slight hope.

Kay Francis had also heard of the accident and had as a token of friendship spent the early morning hours in the hospital room next to mine. She telephoned Bea, who flew out from New York with Joan Payson. The next day I began to get out of danger. According to my doctors, my first conscious words were the worried query of every drunk who can't remember passing out: "Did I do anything awful?" They reassured me, and when I sighed with relief as I relapsed into unconsciousness they took it as a hopeful sign that I wanted to live.

I certainly did. I even smiled over the somewhat illogical premise that God had spared me so that I could continue to fight against Him – or at least his churches. Another curious reaction was my realization of how very easily death could come. I just wouldn't have known anything about it. But I certainly knew about the terrible headaches of the first few days of my return to life. After that came three quite happy weeks with both my worlds gathered around my bedside, including my sister Anne who had come out from Columbus to visit her daughter and granddaughter. Bea and Joan had returned to New York by Christmas, but Clark Gable and Carole Lombard brought me a wonderful tree loaded with crazy presents in gleeful appreciation of the Hollywood rumor that because of the accident I had lost my mind. On New Year's Day I left the hospital and stayed for a week at Clark and Carole's home, then returned to New York.

To my surprise and in spite of – or perhaps because of – the rumors about my brain, I was back in Hollywood within a fortnight. Columbia Pictures needed an immediate script for *Holiday* and it was too good an offer to miss, especially as the hospital and doctors' bills had to be faced. It was a thoroughly enjoyable return to a payroll. Katharine Hepburn and Cary Grant were starred. George Cukor directed, and my fellow-writer was Sidney Buchman, whose wife Beatrice was one of the hardest-working supporters of the Anti-Nazi League.

It must be mentioned in this connection that I contributed very little to the running of the League besides my name and an occasional speech. All the daily grind of collecting dues, planning meetings and radio programs, and getting out the newspaper was done by four or five devoted members who were, I had been told, members of the Communist Party. In this, as in other organizations of which I belonged, it was largely the Communists who did the work.

Inasmuch as various Congressional committees in their wisdom later decided that all of these "premature anti-Fascists" must have been Communists, and that all Communists are to be sent to jail if they refuse to reveal the names of other Communists. I regret that I cannot give specific credit to these courageous men and women with whom I am so proud to have been associated. It was also with deep sorrow that I later had to watch so many of my fellow fighters give in to the demands of the Congressional committees and abjectly crave pardon for being "duped." I have no call to be self-righteous in my condemnation of the many whose jobs and livelihood for themselves and their families depended on their submission to the anti-Red hysteria. I was never subpoenaed, and if I had been I was fortunately in a financial position to risk defying them. For those who did defy them, even to the point of going to prison, I have the most profound admiration. And for the others, I am certainly not the one to throw the first stone. I only regret that such an unjustified smear has been allowed to obscure the real Americanism of those who participated with me in what I regard as one of Hollywood's finest hours.

When I got back from *Holiday* my wife had news for me. She came to the farm on Mothers' Day to tell me that she wanted a divorce in order to marry Count Ilya Tolstoy, a grandson of the writer and a "defectee" from the Soviet Union whose government had sent him a year or two previously to an Iowa Agricultural College in order to perfect himself in the art of raising horses for the Russian farmers.

I had had no suspicion of anything. My enthusiasm for my own "rebirth," which I had hoped would make her love me all the more, had blinded me to the fact that we had been drifting apart for some time. In the meantime I had fallen in love with Ella and she with me. But I also loved Bea, and would not have left her. She was my wife and the habit of marriage to her was strong. Everything in the house was a reminder of her. I was momentarily angry at her "desertion," especially at a time when I was becoming increasingly isolated because of my beliefs. My pride was also hurt. But she convinced me that in Tolstoy she had found her real love, and I agreed to her request.

Thus, in its eleventh year, came to an end a marriage which had been a gay one, often a happy one, but very rarely a real one. The name of my play should have been *The Doll's House,* not *The New House.* The luncheon which followed Bea's tidings to me was symbolic. She had brought to the farm from New York her sister Jerry, and a very good screen-writer friend of mine named Phil Dunne, both of whom knew the purpose of the journey. So we sat around the luncheon table gaily pretending that nothing had happened, just as Bea and I had pretended for ten years that our happy life could continue indefinitely if we just didn't look too closely at it. After luncheon we even walked through the looking glass into Ames' life and tried to persuade the ten-year-old that mummie and daddie were going to be just the same after the divorce. But Ames wasn't buying that. His frightened tears brought a little reality, and made us feel that it wasn't going to be quite so easy for those who couldn't pretend. Bea and Jerry and Phil then took the afternoon train to the city and I was left with my kids in the wreckage of the "new" house which was now a year and a half old. I was in a strange state of shock. That evening I telephoned Ella who was in New York and told her in German (out of deference to the local telephone operators) what had happened.

22

While I didn't feel very joyful about my divorce, there was a certain welcome sense of relief from pretense. My playboy era had now definitely ended. I resigned from the Racquet and the River clubs. When a request came from Hunt Stromberg at M-G-M to come out for a job on Clare Boothe Luce's *The Women,* I was glad to get away from the memory-filled farm.

The only worrisome thing about *The Women* was that I was expected to work on it with Scott Fitzgerald. Our paths had separated widely in the eighteen years since our St. Paul friendship at the dawn of our careers. Scott's literary skyrocket had apparently burned itself out; his *Tender Is The Night* had been badly received by the Depression-era critics. Worst of all, Zelda had gone insane. I hadn't seen him since the 20's when Bea and I had walked out of one of his famous Great Neck weekends, unable to enjoy the stupid drunkenness. As I entered the gates of the new Irving Thalberg Memorial Building I didn't quite know what to expect, especially as I had greatly disliked his confessional *The Crack Up.* The book was probably a little too close to home. My own crack-up as a writer had been in many respects quite as reprehensible and as disappointing to those early 1920 hopes as had Scott's. But now, I felt, I was back on my feet, still capable of fulfilling my promise.

Esquire / 1936

To my great surprise and delight, so was Scott. He wasn't drinking and he was, in fact, much more understanding than before and infinitely more human. In our month together our old friendship came back, and it was like those eager starry-eyed days in St. Paul when he was reading Masefield to me in front of the fire in his living room.

"Be with me, beauty, for the fire is dying." But the fire still wasn't dying in either of us. He told me of *The Last Tycoon,* and I tried to explain my "conversion." Scott had apparently come close to Marxism when living in Baltimore, but the "artist" in him couldn't go over the fence. He sympathized with me about Bea, and we had fatherly discussions about his daughter at Vassar. He made helpful suggestions about a speech I was writing in reply to the coast-to-coast radio attack by Congressman Martin Dies on the "Communistic Un-American Hollywood Anti-Nazi League." He seemed to enjoy with a sort of kind grandfatherly benevolence the spectacle of me as one of the eager socially-conscious beavers.

After Scott and I finished our version of *The Women* (which wasn't shot), I got an offer of another job, this time with Leo McCarey on a picture for Charles Boyer and Irene Dunne called *Love Affair.* Leo, although a violent anti-Red, was a delight to work with, as was also my fellow-writer Delmar Davies. Political discussions were carefully smothered in laughter, and I was sorry when the script was completed.

Bea meanwhile had successfully obtained a Florida divorce and I was free to marry Ella. There was, however, one small hitch: She wasn't in any particular hurry to get married. Her hesitancy arose partly out of concern over presenting without careful preparation her eleven-year-old son, Pete Steffens, with a stepfather. The relationship between Pete and Lincoln Steffens had been extremely tender and close. So when I started on *Love Affair,* Ella brought Pete out and we took up trial residence in a small Westwood village house. Ames and Duck were entered at a boarding school in the Ojai Valley. Beatrice had become the Countess Tolstoy. The only remaining problem of the changeover was the outcome of my efforts to convert the son of Lincoln Steffens to the Stewart brand of paternity.

The problem was solved in a rather unexpected way. One evening in early March, 1939, Ella was helping Pete with his lessons when he suddenly looked up at her and asked: "Say, Mom, how long is it going to be before I can call this guy 'dad'?" That did it, and we were married the next day at the court house in the nearby town of Ventura. That afternoon I made a speech before a Negro Youth Club and in the evening Joan Payson gave us a party at the Beachcombers, a new restaurant featuring a rum drink called a "Zombie."

The next morning "dad" instructed son Pete on the dangers of excessive rum drinking and a very happy family life began, to which

Pete contributed considerably by his immediate and warm acceptance of two younger brothers. Ella likewise was a godsend in the difficult role of stepmother to two rather spoiled and unintelligently brought-up children.

Joan wasn't the only one of Bea's and my old friends who was kind enough to welcome the new wife. Frances Goldwyn invited us to one of her parties, and we had a hilarious evening with Clark and Carol at their home, which ended with Clark patting Ella encouragingly as he kissed her goodbye in a slight alcoholic haze and murmured tenderly, "Don't worry, little girl – we'll protect you from Hitler."

This came shortly after I had acted as master of ceremonies at a huge gathering in the Los Angeles stadium to welcome Tom Mooney after he had been released from San Quentin by the newly-elected Governor Olsen. It was another of those moments on which I look back with pride, even though poor Tom quickly became a much less significant figure than he had been when in jail. The Mooney celebration was the largest meeting I ever chaired, but there were many others that year, including a talk by Harold Laski who had been Ella's professor in her days at the London School of Economics. Professor Laski was staying with Charlie Chaplin, and we had a memorable "question period" in our living room after the speech, in which the President of the University of California at Los Angeles briefly participated.

The Red scare was beginning to penetrate the colleges, but it was the publicity the Congressional committees got from the film stars which was directing the chief spotlight on Hollywood. Nevertheless, the growing menace of Hitler kept our anti-Nazi League alive and kicking, and there were other causes, such as the struggles of the migratory workers in the California fields and orchards, which gave Ella and me abundant outlet for our "un-American" activities.

In June we went on to New York for the biennial meeting of the League of American Writers. Once more a crowded Carnegie Hall cheered our anti-Fascist speakers, who this time included Thomas Mann from Germany, Eduard Benes from Czechoslovakia, Louis Aragon from France, and Sylvia Townsend Warner from England. The best speech of the evening was made by Vincent Sheean, a moving appeal, simply written and quietly delivered, urging all writers to remember that

Writers of the past were themselves a small and special class, writing, until the mid-nineteenth century, for a still smaller special class. We are many and we write for many . . . . Our responsibility is to that brotherhood whose progress we wish to accelerate, to our brothers who work in other materials, in the mines, on the railroads, in the cotton fields, and not only in one country. Our effort, thus understood, will be integrated into the general effort of the American workers, industrial and agricultural, white and black. It will be integrated into the general effort of the mass of mankind against social and economic reaction everywhere. We have no guarantee against the transplantation of the Fascist techniques into this country. We have, indeed, the contemporary certainty of native reactionary forces which are similar to Fascism in every respect except that of technical development. What we have to oppose them is the collective will and instinct of a whole people which must not, if we can prevent it, ever be chloroformed or paralyzed. We cannot exercise our particular function as writers without engaging to some extent in a struggle which is already going on everywhere; that struggle is one of the prime conditions of our lives; we know that it will be long and that its course will be studded with failures . . . . But the adult contemporary writers of this country have found their place and will not abandon it.

Those were the ideals of our League in that June of 1939. Our enemy was not American Capitalism unless it used its power for the destruction of human rights. For two days after the Carnegie Hall meeting we discussed the ways in which we might, as writers, enlist in the struggle to defend the principles of Vincent Sheean's speech. Papers were read by Dorothy Parker, Norman Corwin, Dashiell Hammett, Alan Lomax, Langston Hughes, Joseph Freeman, Max Wylie, H. V. Kaltenborn, and many others. We were attacked as Reds by the Hearst and other papers. We laughed at that. Roosevelt was also being attacked, and great things were happening in our democracy under Roosevelt. The Federal Theater Project, for one example, was reaching masses of people who had never before been to the theater. The C.I.O., firmly on its feet under the new Labor acts, was giving hope to the hitherto unorganized millions. Father Coughlin and other followers of the Nazi techniques were not really getting anywhere. Our meetings at the New School for Social Research radiated enthusiasm and hope.

After the final get-together, at which I was reelected president for another two years, I collected all the papers and speeches and signed a contract to edit their publication. Before leaving for California Ella and I visited the Worlds Fair – "The World of the Future" – and in front of the Soviet pavilion felt proud that we were helping Stalin and Roosevelt make that future world a truly better one for all the people who were still being kicked around.

The Stalin-Hitler pact was signed in August. I was president of two anti-Hitler organizations, and my first angry reaction was along the lines of "How can that guy Stalin *do* this to us?" It was the first test of my new philosophy, and it took a little while for the picture to clear. I won't say "for my mind to clear" because I was only an amateur Marxist, and I didn't have many of the real facts about the Soviet Union or, for that matter, about international politics, any more than anyone else had who was not on the very inside. So I didn't think myself into an acceptance of the pact as much as I felt that there must be a reason for it.

This feeling was deeply based on the emotions which, only four years previously, had caused me to change sides from the successful few to the many who needed help. Those Many were for me not only the Jews in Germany, although they were undoubtedly the reason for the large majority of our anti-Nazi League memberships. Hitler was for me only one of the cancers in the world, and I trusted the Marxism of the Soviet Union to have the right answer for the advance of the international Many towards the fulfillment of all their capacities. To that extent I was an "internationalist," no longer a "patriotic" American in the "my country right or wrong" sense.

But my internationalism was American in that I wanted to fight for Socialism in America as the next step toward Abraham Lincoln's speech about the "revolutionary right of any people to overthrow their government" in their march toward liberty and justice, and I accepted with it the Marxist doctrine of the need for a "final conflict" in view of the fact that those in possession of the means of production were not going to surrender them without a hell of a fight. The philosophy of Marxism had come to me, as do all philosophies to all men, in response to a need, and, in my case, to a cry for help from a man who was drowning in a world which didn't make sense. I took from Marxism what I needed for myself. I was American, and my Marxism was American. But Russia was the only country of Marxism, and I didn't think I could abandon Stalin without surrendering my life raft. I was completely unaware of the extent to which Stalin had already betrayed Marx. So I didn't decide, in this first crucial test, to "cultivate my garden" as had Voltaire's sadly disillusioned idealist, and as did so many of my companions in the Movement. The best of all possible worlds was still on my agenda – with, of course, the wisdom which I had acquired from Marxism that "best" is only another illusory absolute in a world which must be forever changing. "Better" was the correct adjective; in spite of Stalin's incredible pact there was still much to be done in the struggle for a better world. I didn't resign from anything. Neither, however, did I accept the suggestion from a prominent Communist functionary that, inasmuch as Vincent Sheean had now attacked Stalin in the *New Republic,* I omit his speech at the Writers' Congress from the forthcoming publication which I was editing.

This was my first rejection of the American Communist Party's interpretation of Marxism, although here again my action did not come from any well-thought-out analysis of the situation as much as from my feeling that I just couldn't do unjust things like this. I didn't agree with Sheean's analogy of "Stalin equals Napoleon," but it seemed to me that Sheean's words at Carnegie Hall expressed beautifully the American writers' purpose in their struggle against Fascism; the defence of Soviet Russia "right or wrong" was not the reason that writers joined the League. But from the same not-very-well-thought-out system of ethics, arrived at via Exeter and Yale, I just couldn't be unfaithful to my friends or my side. So I didn't denounce any Communist-controlled organizations of which I was president or to which my name was helpful. My growing doubts about the American Communist Party's interpretation of Marxism didn't affect my belief in the superior wisdom of the remote Soviet Union which, being so distant, in no way challenged my personal ethics as had the decision about the Vincent Sheean speech. I was still at heart a bourgeois and if I had been living in Stalinist Russia, I wouldn't have been living for very long – provided, of course, that I would have had the courage not to conform.

My doubts and confusions were greatly increased by the war, which broke out while I was in Carmel editing the Writers' Congress book.

Ella and I had gone there after the Congress, and were staying with the kids at the pleasant oceanside frame dwelling in which Lincoln Steffens and she and Pete had lived after their return from Europe.

The decision of the American Communist Party to mobilize the country for peace, on the grounds that the war against Hitler was a "phoney" one, was a rather questionable pill to swallow, and our refusal to support this "line" gradually widened the breach between us and some of our Communist friends. But because I trusted the Soviet Union to have the correct Marxist understanding of the situation, I refrained from publicly criticizing the pact and the party's theory about the war. This is where I reached the lowest depths of a sense of final severance from my few remaining past friends, including, worst of all, Bob Benchley.

I had gone down to Hollywood in connection with a possible job on the script of *Kitty Foyle*. Bob and John McClain and I were finishing what had been a gay dinner when unexpectedly Bobby began lecturing me about my hypocrisy as an anti-Nazi in not attacking Stalin's pact with Hitler. As his anger mounted, my fear grew that a dangerous can of tomatoes was at last being opened. There was good reason for my fears. All along, since my "conversion," I had been deeply sure Bobby respected me for my political activities, even though he wasn't at all interested in them, with the exception of rights for Negroes, about which he felt very strongly, and for which he had once or twice let me use his name on a committee. But now, as he kept pressing me with increasing scorn about the Stalin pact, I felt a horrible gulf opening between us; worse than that, I realized that my confident assumption that he had understood my "new life" and had sympathized with it had been an illusion. I couldn't answer his questions, other than to plead that Stalin must have had good reasons. "What reasons?" shouted Bobby, and his contempt for me was so violent that I couldn't answer. If McClain hadn't been there I might have tried to explain, as I have for the first time here in these pages. But John, John McClain who was so comparatively recently one of Bobby's friends, was tauntingly on his side.

I felt sick and betrayed, and when, after dinner, the joint attack on me continued in Bobby's Garden of Allah rooms, I left them without saying goodbye. But it *was* goodbye; I was completely sunk and I found myself repeating, "Well, that's the end of Bobby" as a taxi took me to my hotel. The driver noticed my despair and remarked, as I paid him, "If you ask me, Mac, I think that guy Stalin ought to be hung." I didn't ask him. The next morning Bob telephoned, and my heart leaped with joy. I thought he had called to say he was sorry. But he had merely phoned to ask if I would speak to a director about considering him for an acting job. I said I would, and hung up.

The fact that Bobby apparently hadn't been aware of what the evening had meant to me made it, somehow, all the worse. Something very precious, almost the most valued possession in my life, had gone.

After I had finished the unexpectedly long and arduous job of editing my Writers' Congress book, I decided to call it *Fighting Words* because of a remark by the publicist Edward Bernays that "in the next war, words will be as important as bullets." By the time it was published, however, the climate both inside and outside the League had so changed that my high hopes for the book had to be written off as another casualty of the Stalin-Hitler pact.

Those last months of the '30s were not by any means an unbroken series of discouraging happenings. In Carmel I met and spent exciting evenings with all of Ella's and Lincoln Steffens' close friends, among whom were Robinson Jeffers, Langston Hughes, John Steinbeck and Martin Flavin. This picture of Ella's life was an extraordinary contrast with that which I had been leading on Long Island and Hollywood during that same period. Ella and I made rewarding trips to San Francisco where she introduced me to others of her old riends. I had doubts as to how these serious intellectuals along the Coast would regard Ella's new screenwriter-playboy acquisition, but whatever criticism they may have had did not prevent them from making me feel most welcome. Ella also was most anxious to show me that she had not lived a life entirely surrounded by high-minded eggheads, so she proudly engaged a table at what she called the really gayest spot in San Francisco, where, she said, she and Steffens always dined when in town. I was duly impressed, but also extremely surprised when the head waiter and the hat check boy both greeted me by name and warmly inquired about Beatrice. Ella was not exactly pleased, even after I explained that they had known me in my Trocadero Sunset Strip days.

On another memorable occasion in San Francisco we delightedly watched Harry Bridges, on one of the many investigations into his Communism, give Dean Landis of the Harvard Law School a few of the facts of life about the realities of the Pacific Coast labor movement. Another of my heroes of those days, Irwin Shaw, came up to Carmel while working on a new play, and we spent many good evenings, aided somewhat by the *vin du pays*.

To Carmel on a visit also came the most precious of my new acquaintances, a brilliant young Exeter and Harvard graduate named Robert Lamb, who was a member of the staff of the La Follette Congressional Committee investigating the violations of civil liberties on the Coast. Bob Lamb became for both Ella and me a never-failing source of enlightenment in politics and economics; his intelligence, his integrity, and his extraordinary power of insight made his death from cancer a few years later one of the irreplaceable losses in our circle of friends.

Another loss, one which happened while we were still in Carmel, was that of Ella's beloved brother Rudi, who was living near us with his wife Thea and little daughter Sylvia. It was one of those deaths about which one could only despairingly demand "Why?" He was one of the most lovable and unselfish men I have ever known, and in two days, after a streptococcus infection, he was gone. So, for a while at least, was the charm of Carmel, and we drove with Pete rather disconsolately down to Beverly Hills where we found a house on South El Camino drive. Pete and Duck started at the local schools, Ames was again with Mrs. Lynn at the Ojai Valley school, and I continued to work on *Kitty Foyle*.

Pete Steffens, DOS, Donald Ogden Stewart Jr.

DOS's house in London – 103 Frognal.

ST. MARTIN'S THEATRE

West Street, Cambridge Circus, W.C.2 Tel.: Tem. Bar 1443

Licensee: J. M. Cook   Lessees: Bright Enterprises Ltd.
Managing Directors: J. M. Cook and A. M. Cook

By arrangement with Bright Enterprises Ltd.
CAMPBELL WILLIAMS for
The London Arts Theatre Committee Ltd.

presents

FAITH BROOK
LYNDON BROOK
DERMOT WALSH

in

THE KIDDERS
by DONALD OGDEN STEWART

with

GORDON TANNER
PETER JAMES

BETTY McDOWALL   RICHARD CALDICOT

Directed by PHIL BROWN

Setting by STANLEY MOORE

EVERY EVENING at 8 p.m.
Matinees: Tuesday 2.30, Saturday 5.0

C.L.J. (1958)

*Playcard of **The Kidders**.*

*DOS with the cast of **The Kidders**.*

DOS with W.E.B. Dubois in the backyard of DOS's house in London.

A gathering for Paul Robeson (center) in the backyard at 103 Frognal.

Prime Minister Harold Wilson with Sir Charles Chaplin, DOS, and Ella Winter, on the day Sir Charles was knighted, March 1975.

Salka Viertel and DOS.

Donald Ogden Stewart, 1955.

Photo: W. Suschitzky

Donald Ogden Stewart and Ella Winter.

23

The 20's had ended with the Wall Street Crash, the 30's with the outbreak of World War II, and the 1940's didn't look any too promising for my "world of the future" either. Hitler was triumphantly sweeping through France and blitzing England. Stalin, now apparently an active partner of the Nazis, had occupied the Eastern half of Poland, annexed the Baltic states, and conquered Finland. But because of my faith in Marxist historical analysis, I still stubbornly refused to join in the mounting chorus of anti-Soviet rage. Robert Sherwood's *There Shall Be No Night,* attacking the Russian war on "brave little Finland," echoed American middle-class sentiments as he had done so successfully in all his plays. I had stepped out of that class – at least in my thinking – and I viewed with contempt the panicky retreat of former "progressive" writers to the safe harbor of "Communism is the same as Fascism."

But neither could I go along with the American Peace Mobilization campaign of the Communist Party, and I found myself reviled by the Right and suspected by the Left. The Hollywood Anti-Nazi League, of which I had been so proudly the president since its beginning, slowly but inevitably fell to pieces when the new Communist "peace line" was insisted upon, and I informed the League of American Writers, when they tried to force upon their membership the same policy, that I did not wish to be considered for president at the next Congress.

It was a year of defeated hopes and cooling enthusiasms, but it was also a valuable year of self-testing. And also, strangely enough, I remained on the "preferred" list of the film studios. After R.K.O.'s

Kitty Foyle, for which I was to share credit with Dalton Trumbo, I was asked by M-G-M to write the screenplay for Philip Barry's *Philadelphia Story,* an opportunity at which I leaped with joy. Katie Hepburn was to star, as she had so successfully on Broadway, old friend George Cukor was to direct, and the cast included Cary Grant and a young Princeton graduate named James Stewart.

My only doubts concerned the producer, Joseph Mankiewicz, the brother of Herman Mankiewicz. Herman had been one of my close friends in the early Algonquin and Hollywood days but had recently become one of the most vicious of detractors not only of Dorothy Parker and myself but of all attempts to bring "social consciousness" to Hollywood or to establish an effective Writers' Guild. Herman was one of the "enemies" whom I have, all my life, never hesitated to devastate with a barrage of brilliant wit, leaving them aghast at the overpowering revelation of their faults. This verbal lashing, of course, never occurs in their presence; usually I am lying alone in bed and the hour is 4 a.m. Anyway, I didn't particularly look forward to working for Herman's brother. But Joe and I cooperated quite happily by carefully avoiding political subjects, with the single exception of Finnish War Relief, of which he was the M-G-M chairman and to which I politely declined to contribute. *The Philadelphia Story* was the least-deserving-of-praise bit of script writing I have ever done, since Philip Barry had written it so beautifully that my task was mainly an editing one. My chief contribution otherwise consisted in a few added scenes for Jimmy Stewart, and the Oscar which I received for the screenplay was probably one of the easiest ever obtained.

After my M-G-M job Ernst Lubitsch asked me to help him with an original of his called *That Uncertain Feeling.* It was a fluffy bit, designed for Merle Oberon and Melvyn Douglas, but I had always wanted to work with Ernst and we had a lot of fun putting it together. Once more, politics were politely relegated to occasional bits of kidding. Lubitsch, a Berliner of the 20's, knew his political onions, and craftily mocked my starry-eyed innocence. Anyway, I was pleased that as a writer I had made good with the maestro.

All this was happening in a whirlwind of increasing rage at the presence of any Reds, particularly the successful ones, in Hollywood. Organizations were formed "for the preservation of American ideals." Costly full-page advertisements were taken in the trade papers; one of them, denouncing me for my Writers' Congress speech, was contributed by old friend John Lee Mahin. The

American Legion joined in the attack. More subpoenas came from Congressman Martin Dies, and more lawyers made tidy sums clearing stars of "un-American" charges. California legislators discovered the publicity value of attacks on Hollywood, and hastened to get into the act. A Tenney Un-American committee in Sacramento published a voluminous list of us rats. I was cited seventy-four times (next highest to Paul Robeson) for having joined something or signed something. Ella was only cited thirty-two times, but my superiority was explained by the fact that I had always been a pushover for joining organizations, even as far back as prep-school days in Exeter.

But in spite of all this opprobrium, M-G-M courageously trusted me not to put Communistic propaganda into a Joan Crawford vehicle called *A Woman's Face*. I was to work on it with Eliot Paul, a bearded oracle whose knowledge of where to find decent French cooking in Los Angeles was a delight. The job itself was also extremely intriguing since all we had to start with for a story was a Swedish film starring an unknown actress named Ingrid Bergman. A genial Englishman, Victor Saville, was our producer; George Cukor was to direct, and supporting Joan were Melvyn Douglas and two famous Germans, Conrad Veidt and the aged Albert Basserman.

Both were refugees from Hitler; the latter, undoubtedly the greatest of German actors, had refused all Nazi inducements, including the safety of his Jewish wife. And it was he who now contributed to one of my educational experiences as a screenwriter. I had spent quite a bit of time and effort on his rather short but important part, constructing each sentence of his dialogue meticulously for its cadence and for the exact correctness of each word. After the shooting of the picture had started, I decided to go over to the stage to see how the great Basserman was making out with my precious words. He wasn't on the set, but I finally discovered him in a dark corner, conversing with another German. When I got closer, I discovered to my horror that this friend was reading his dialogue to him and the old actor, without understanding the meaning of a single word, was learning the sentences by heart and repeating them in what sounded like the mechanical sing-song of a Chinese mandarin. My heartbroken protests to the producer were unheeded, and perhaps it was just as well, for when the picture was released Basserman almost stole it from Joan with what the critics called "a performance of supreme sympathetic understanding of the part."

This work carried me over into March of 1941 when two events of great importance to me occurred on the same evening. The first was a speech I made as one of three or four representatives of Hollywood on the coast-to-coast broadcast of the "Town Meeting of the Air," a radio series which had high popular rating in those days. Walter Wanger, in charge of this particular production, had been extremely courageous in letting me, the Red, be one of the "voices of Hollywood," and although I can't remember anything about my speech, I was very proud to be on such a top-drawer program. The only thing I do recall is the moderator's nervous fear that I might say something "untoward" or "un-American" during the question period (my speech had been carefully screened) and sure enough, just before the end, someone in the balcony yelled down at me a question about Communists in the studios. As I took a deep breath and stepped to the mike, delighted with this chance to make character by defending the industry, the moderator clanged his bell, the town meeting was adjourned, and my unseen audience was saved from the danger of possible subversive thoughts.

Then Ella and I walked across the street to the Biltmore for the Academy Award banquet. Since *The Philadelphia Story* was up for selection as the best screenplay, we sat in evening dress at the Louis B. Mayer table. Another screenplay nominee was *Kitty Foyle.* Bob Hope was in marvelous form as toastmaster, but I got a little fed up when the winners began getting modest and coy about "not really deserving this great honor." And when Ginger Rogers tearfully announced that she owed her Oscar exclusively to her dear mother, I rushed out to throw up or get a drink or both. When I returned, Hope was just announcing that I had won the "Best Screenplay" award, and I strode happily to the mike to tell the world that the success of *The Philadelphia Story* was due to me and nobody else. Luckily I got a big laugh. It was a marvelous evening, and an Oscar is a wonderful thing to carry home to one's family. Next morning Pete and Duck rushed up to my bed with the morning paper, on the front page of which was a huge headline "Stewart Wins Award." Both were a bit let down when I explained that James Stewart had also won an Oscar for his work in *The Philadelphia Story.*

In June, Duck and Ames went to Florida to be with their mother at Marineland where Count Tolstoy had been put in charge of an aquarium financed by Sonny Whitney. Pete wanted to spend the summer in Carmel and Ella and I went to the farm. On the way we stopped for the fourth – and last – League of American Writers

Congress.

It turned out to be a rather sad affair. Four years ago I had proudly stood up in Carnegie Hall and nailed my flag to the left-wing mast. Now Carnegie Hall was no longer available to us, and I sat on the platform of some strange hall, feeling like an outcast, surrounded by strange men and women who had submerged the anti-Hitler struggle into the "mobilization for peace." I was made more uncomfortable by the glaring spot-lights from camera crews of fellow Skull and Bones man Henry Luce's *Time* magazine as they filmed the proceedings for some future "Time Marches On" program, presumably on the subject of the unpatriotic traitors in our midst. I was asked to make no speech and my last act as retiring president was to read a telegram from Theodore Dreiser announcing that he was joining the Communist Party. Cheers – and exit President Stewart.

I was grateful to the Communist Party for giving me the job; I had enjoyed it, and I went through with this final public ceremony because of that gratitude and because I thought I ought to share the unpopularity of the people who had been largely responsible for electing me. And I had no intention of resigning from the Movement although the bright path of my first joyous steps did not now seem so straight and well-marked. Before going up to the farm I happily agreed to write a humorous weekly piece for a new publication called *The Week*. This was my first go at this kind of writing since the *Chicago Tribune* and the *New Yorker* and I welcomed the chance to see if the old Stewart humor mill was still working after ten years of Broadway and Hollywood.

Meanwhile, Leland Hayward had dug up an intriguing new proposition for me. I had told him that I was once more – and this time definitely cross-my-heart-and-point-to-God – finished with Hollywood, at least until I had written another play. "I couldn't agree with you more," said the agreeable Leland. "Now – how would you like to write a musical for Rodgers and Hart based on the Ludwig Bemelmans *Hotel Splendide,* a best-seller about his experiences as a waiter at the Ritz?" Since I didn't have any definite story or idea for a play of my own, this sounded tempting and rather easy. Ella and I lunched with Bemelmans at the Ritz and liked him so much that we immediately suggested that he come with us to the farm where he and I could work uninterruptedly. Ludwig agreed, provided that he might be visited occasionally by his wife and daughter. It looked like it was going to be a wonderful summer.

And it was. Not because of Bemelmans. He *was* wonderful, and the collaboration was a happy one. But what made the summer memorable for Ella and me occurred towards the end of June. I was driving alone on my way to Rockwell Kent's farm where Ludwig had dined with Rockwell and his English wife Sally who had replaced Frances two or three years previously. It was a beautifully clear, calm, star-filled night, and I was listening to some dance music on my radio. It was a Cole Porter tune which Ella and I happened to call "ours" because we had danced to it at the Trocadero when we were just falling in love. "I've got you under my skin – I've got you deep in the heart of me." Suddenly the music stopped. After a moment, "We interrupt this program to tell you that this afternoon the German armies invaded the Soviet Union and a state of war now exists –" I listened, and I unexpectedly began to cry. Not with pity for the Russian people: I wept with joy and relief. I was once more on the "right" side, the side of all my old friends. Now we were all fighting Fascism, or, at least, fighting it in Germany and Italy. When I got to Rockwell's we held a celebration. Ludwig, although he hated politics, loved celebrations of any sort, and when we brought the news to Ella there was more rejoicing. It was one of the happiest nights of my life. I could continue believing in my remote dream, the country where the true equality of man was becoming a reality under the philosophy of Marxism and Leininism and the leadership of the great Stalin.

Then, after Churchill's enthusiastic welcome of his new ally, began the wonderfully satirical picture of the great American switcheroo. We must now all love the Russians. The fashionable chairmen of Bundles for Britain and Finnish War Relief tried to melt as imperceptibly as possible into supporters of American-Russian Friendship. In Robert Sherwood's *There Shall Be No Night* brave little Finland was transformed overnight into "brave little Greece," and the uniforms of the beasts changed, as if by magic, from Russian gray to Nazi green. Ella and I were invited by various local organizations to make the collection of contributions palatable to the socially elite, headed by the leading upholders of free enterprise. My dinner jacket emerged from its moth balls and my Hawes and Curtiss dress shirts were shiningly happy in their return to social consciousness. It was indeed a wonderful summer – at least for Ella and me. The clouds had lifted and we were fighting beside Roosevelt,

Churchill and Stalin for our "world of the future."

And at the same time, there was the fun of working with Bemelmans. Ludwig was similar in some ways to Rockwell Kent; both were artists, but Rockwell's Bohemianism had been of the American twenties and had matured into an active sense of responsibility for humanity. Rockwell was a force, a driving force – and God pity those who got in his way. Ludwig was European and he was a child – lovable, sometimes undependable and self-centered like a child – but always charming, with a child's beautiful and fantastic imagination, and an insatiable readiness to play. It was, for me, a delightful temporary return to my own playboy world – a world which existed to be enjoyed. Money meant nothing to Ludwig. If he had it, he shared with all. If he was broke, he borrowed. Apparently he had none of my fears of unpaid bills, or my childhood training in thrift. I remember on one trip we made to New York, as I was paying for my lunch I dropped a nickel behind my chair and got down on my knees in an attempt to find it. To my amazement, Ludwig roared with laughter at the spectacle of anyone stopping to pick up a nickel. My bewilderment was at the idea of *not* doing so. I feel guilty at the fact that sometimes (not often) I throw away a tube of toothpaste without having squeezed out the last possible drop.

Ludwig brought up with him a pocket-size Mexican hairless dog named Tintoretto who was the most disagreeable animal I have ever had to spend a summer with. To make it worse, when we had left the Coast Ella had found herself unable to part company with three doubtful cats which she had picked up in different alleys (a habit of hers) and shipped to the farm. What she hadn't known was that every cat was happily pregnant, so that by the time Tintoretto arrived there were some seventeen or eighteen felines on the place. Such fun – for Tintoretto – and Ludwig was very sensitive to any criticism of his pet.

To add to the rural *joie de vivre,* there arrived unexpectedly one night a handsome young Italian named Tony who had just been released from the Matteawan State Institution for the Insane, having been sent there nine years previously to be "rehabilitated" after been saved from the electric chair by a remarkable New York psychiatrist, a close friend of ours. The psychiatrist, Dr. Frederic Wertham, had come into Tony's life the morning after the sixteen year old boy had killed his mother with a kitchen knife; after an heroic court battle Dr. Wertham had convinced the jury that the lad should be cured rather than killed. The cure, nine years long, had been successful, and it was then the psychiatrist's advice that Tony should have three or four weeks in a quiet friendly atmosphere before plunging into the realities of New York life. So – there was Tony on our doorstep, and we and Ludwig welcomed him with great interest and pleasure, without, of course, telling Bella our cook or John her father any of the story.

It is not, however, as easy as might be imagined to have a "cured" murderer as your guest. Ella and I suddenly found that the most harmless everyday expressions, such as "I could have killed him" or "The critics knifed her" were constantly on our lips. And then, during breakfast one day, Bella came into the dining room and asked Ella if she had any idea where the largest kitchen knife had gone. The search which followed was suspenseful and intense, and it was finally discovered that Tony had borrowed the implement for some upholstery work he was doing for us (he had learned that trade at Matteawan). The relief was immense, even if not quite complete for a few more days.

Other slightly less dramatic visitors that summer were Ludwig's beautiful wife Mimi, and daughter Barbarita. Of the latter I shall say only that at the age of six she was very pretty and slightly less irritating than Tintoretto. Most of Bella's best culinary efforts were greeted with "I don't eat that," and her fond father would thereupon take her on midnight picnics where in the best Ritz hunter-and-trapper fashion he would build a fire beside our trout stream, warm a can of spaghetti with tomato sauce, and follow it with chocolate eclairs. I have heard that dear little Barbarita has since grown into a stunningly attractive woman, which reaffirms my belief that God moves in a mysterious way.

Before Bemelmans left, we were also visited by Harry Bridges, on his honeymoon with his new bride Nancy. Harry, as he does to so many, intrigued Ludwig with his intelligence, his integrity, and his "true story" insights into the darker side of the labor movement on the Pacific Coast. Ludwig later wrote a sympathetic profile of Harry for the *New Yorker,* which Harold Ross published while the labor leader was once more on the front pages as being on trial for deportation as a Communist. Truth, in our free press, also moves in a mysterious way.

24

Then, in December, came Pearl Harbor. Ella and I were able occasionally to contribute our patriotic bit by writing for radio programs or composing speeches for various War Administration big shots. I was even invited by Earl Robinson to contribute one of the programs in an extremely important radio series called "This is War." I chose as my subject an actual happening in a small Ohio town where, in a truly joint effort, each person contributed labor according to his or her ability. For the first few weeks, the war effort became democratic in the sense in which I hoped all of America might some day become, that is, of people working together in equality and for each other instead of competing in a rat race for financial security and status. I wanted to call my script "This is the Real America." When I had finished it was apparently accepted with enthusiasm by the Office of War Information which was at that time headed by Archie MacLeish. I remember thinking proudly to myself, while flying over the farmhouses and towns of Kansas, "You down there are going to be listening to this program in a couple of weeks." I eagerly awaited the day of the broadcast. A program from Washington was announced in the papers – but it was not my sketch. I called Earl Robinson there from Hollywood; he seemed a bit embarrassed, but assured me that it had probably been postponed. I waited for three more weeks, then flew to New York at my own expense to see what I could find out. I could find out nothing, except that my contribution would definitely not be broadcast. My last desperate call was to old friend Archie MacLeish in Washington. His irritated response to my appeal for information was "Don, there's a war on!'' and he hung up.

I spent the Christmas holidays in a nightmare household situation for which I was entirely to blame. Ever since my divorce I had been nourishing the happy illusion that first wives and second wives could and should be friends, especially in the interests of the children. So I hung mistletoe on all chandeliers at the farm and blithely invited Bea to join Ella, Pete, Ames, Duck and me in a jolly old get-together, just one big family around the tree, with a hey-nonny-no, sing wassail. Ella wasn't quite so optimistic about my expectations; she was right. The last Christmas Bea had spent on the farm as my wife had been amid the ether fumes of Ames's operation, and by the final day of her return visit I was longing to ask Dr. Culver to bring up some more of the same and put us all out of our misery. But having no ether I began to resort to wassail, with the result that shortly after dinner I passed completely out, leaving Ella the task of driving our Yuletide guest some twenty miles to the nearest railroad station. I recovered consciousness at about two in the morning. Ella had not returned, and the most terrific of sheet and hail storms was raging. The telephone was out of order. Desperate with anxiety, hangover and guilt I started to drive to Elizabethtown, where I thought perhaps Ella would have stopped at Louis Untermeyer's house. The roads were hub deep in ice and slush and I crept crazily and fearfully along through the sleet, expecting every minute to come upon our overturned car. On the outskirts of Elizabethtown my brake refused to hold on an ice hill and I slid back into a ditch. The last mile on foot was as awful a walk as I have ever made. But Ella was there and, better still, Bea wasn't. Louis had driven her to the train and my little Christmas fantasy of Wife-Past and Wife-Present was ended, with Wife-Present delivering a few final well-chosen words as the curtain came down.

In the midst of this domestic infelicity had come an invitation for the most tempting Hollywood job I had ever had. Not only was it for Katharine Hepburn and Spencer Tracy, with Victor Saville producing and George Cukor directing, but the story itself, a novel by I. A. R. Wylie called *Keeper of the Flame,* was perfectly made for my desire to contribute to an understanding of democracy's war by exposing the danger of un-Americanism within our own gates. The story begins with the five-star funeral in a small town of one of America's favorite sons, someone like, say, General MacArthur. Spencer Tracy is a New York reporter who has been sent to cover the event, and attempts in vain to obtain an interview with the widow (played by Hepburn). Accidentally they meet, and he becomes increasingly suspicious that the lady is not telling the true story about her husband's death. The further he probes, the more the mystery deepens. Finally he becomes convinced that in some way she was responsible. There had been a mysterious telephone call on the stormy night of the death. The Great Man had driven hurriedly away alone, after a violent scene with his wife. A bridge had been washed away by the storm, and his speeding car had plunged him to his death. Tracy collects evidence that the wife knew about the bridge before her husband left, and confronts Hepburn with the accusation: "You didn't warn him, did you!" Katharine breaks down, confesses, and then tells her reason. Her husband, the great national hero, had become the spearhead of a plot to overthrow the Roosevelt-like government and substitute a Mussolini-type dictatorship in the name of "greater democracy." The backers of this *coup* were a group of the country's most powerful industrialists and financiers who saw in the extension of the power of the people a dangerous challenge to their own type of Free World. The plot had in those days strikingly believable parallels, including Hitler's successful takeover of his country with the backing of Krupp, Thiessen and other powerful Germans under the name of "national workers' socialism." The plotters in our film had used the popularity of the Great Man's name and Air Force officers were in on the *coup;* on the night of his death our National Hero had received the signal and was on his way to head the "march on Washington" which would have brought "greater democracy" to America. So Katharine, by letting him drive to his destruction, was both a murderess and the savior of her country from Fascist dictatorship. It made a wonderful film, the one I am most proud to have been connected with. Here was my compensation for the sabotage of my radio attempt to do my bit; here were my "war aims" which coincided, I believed, with those of Roosevelt and all good Americans, and I thrilled with pride as I sat beside Ella amid the huge audience at the Radio City Music Hall which was excitedly and with applause watching this exposé of the real un-Americans. I heard afterwards that in that same audience was Louis B. Mayer, great friend and supporter of ex-President Hoover, and that "L.B." had walked out in a fury from the show when he discovered, apparently for the first time, what the picture was really about. Certainly such a picture could never have been produced later, after the

Congressional committees had begun to instruct Hollywood in the "true" brand of Americanism, and the producers had abjectly gone down on their knees to the McCarthy definition of patriotism. But in those days Roosevelt was still the hero, the Anti-Nazi League and the League of American Writers had helped educate the movie colony in the need for an artist to be a politically aware person, and it is to the glory of Hollywood's war effort that such a fine "politically conscious" picture was allowed to be released. It was still a Hollywood where, when Ginger Rogers' mother came out with the cry that "share and share alike" in a film star's dialogue was Communist propaganda, she was met with derisive laughter. Russia was still an ally in need of help, fighting in Stalingrad with its back to the wall. Sam Goldwyn came through with a magnificent Lillian Hellman pro-Russian picture, directed by Lewis Milestone. Jack Lawson was writing an heroic epic of the American convoys in the North Atlantic which were carrying supplies to Murmansk. Warner Bros. did a version of *Mission to Moscow.* And M-G-M got into the act with its *Song of Russia,* engaging as technical adviser none other than Anna Louise Strong, throughout her long life one of the most ardent friends of Communism and the Soviet Union. I almost fell over when I saw her name on the elevator directory in the front office of the Irving Thalberg Memorial writers' building, especially as her office was situated in the close vicinity of two of the leading red-baiters, John Lee Mahin and Howard Emmett Rogers, neither of whom was speaking to me. The script writers were in daily hot water about Soviet political realities which did not jibe with M-G-M standards. Louis B. Mayer refused to allow the dangerous words "commune" or "collective" to be used in connection with a huge Soviet farm until his attention was called to the 100% American usage of "Community Chest." L.B.'s fears were not entirely ridiculous; after the war he and other producers were grilled mercilessly for their pro-Russian folly by Congressmen who had already erased Stalingrad from their political geographies, and seven million dead from the credit sheet of Russia's own contribution.

With *Keeper of the Flame* I entered, at forty-eight, upon what might be termed the crucial period of my productive life as a writer, and the fourth and final movement of the symphony of my life as a whole. I entered it *con brio.* I was on firm ground, both in my actual condition of living and in my philosophy. Thanks to Ella, I had stopped spending money as fast as – or faster – than I earned it. At the time of my divorce I was broke, with the exception of the farm and my life insurance, on which I had borrowed to the limit. I now had, with luck, beaten Capitalism at its own game, and I gleefully set about my job of waging war on it with my own gift of humor and my training as a dramatist and screen writer. My quarrel, you will note, was with the system of Capitalism, never with the individuals. I treasured – and still treasure – my friendship with the wealthy people with whom I had fun in my playboy days. But that didn't prevent me from using every club in my bag to fight against what I believed was an outdated system which would use every club in *its* arsenal in order to postpone the advance of what was called in those days the "Century of the Common Man." The odds were fairly even – at least they seemed so to the eager confident crusader as he reached for his typewriter.

I decided that the climax of my new play – as in *Keeper of the Flame* – was to be the revelation to my hero or heroine of the forces in America working, even in war time, against the victory of democracy. I had heard from Bob Lamb and other reliable sources stories about goings-on in the huge motor industries in Detroit, of the efforts of Henry Ford among others to disrupt the unionization of the autoworkers. I had collected quite a lot of data on the strong-arm practices of Ford's right-hand man, Harry Bennett, who, according to these tales, had not been averse to the use of gangsters and various Ku-Klux-Klan-like "shirt" organizations in his attempts to terrify and divide the workers, particularly the large numbers of Polish and Negro employees on the Ford payroll. There was also Father Coughlin and his Fundamentalist-White-Protestant equivalent, said to be subsidized heavily by the motor industry, who used the radio stations for the spread of anti-Semitism and other hate-the-foreigner ideas. In other words, I had reason to suspect that it was possible that at Ford the war was being fought on two levels. In support of the America vs. Germany, Italy and Japan war, Ford was turning out large quantities of war material. Not entirely without profit of course, but with sufficient conformation to the War Board's requirements to justify praising old Mr. Ford as a great patriot and an outstanding contributor to our democratic war effort. But, at the same time, his continuing use of anti-Semitic white-supremacy gangster tactics in dealing with employees could almost make one imagine that he saw quite a lot to be said in favor of the Hitler idea. Perhaps he even thought America was fighting the wrong war; he wouldn't have been alone among the Upper-Bracket Power Elite with that idea. At any rate, as I pondered the spectacle, a play began to form in my head. "How would it be," I asked myself "if old Harry had a young grandson who was fighting on the American side – an only grandson, who really believed in the American ideas of equality and democracy, and who, in his desire to be equal – and not just Henry Ford's grandson – had enlisted as a private?"

That seemed like a possible springboard into serious drama. The basic conflict would be between the Henry Ford-Harry Bennett "free enterprise" struggle for power among the Few, and this new world of the increasing sense of brotherhood among the Many, of which the idealistic grandson was getting his first taste as a private in the Roosevelt army of democracy. Let's say that young Ford has been wounded and is home on leave. Then there would be his father and mother. The Brady family. The young grandson was Sam, his mother Emily, his father George. And there would be old Mr. Brady and his hatchet-man Jeff Martin.

How would it be if Emily Brady was an intelligent woman, courageous, eager to help in the war. Which war? Old Man Brady's or her idealistic son's? She had given Sam his ideals of democracy which she had got from her father, who was, say, a professor, not rich but wise. Does he know about the two wars? Or, more important, does *she* know? Why wouldn't she? Because old Mr. Brady and his Jeff Martin don't want her to. But she begins to be curious. Why? Because she's worried. Why? Because George has begun to act strangely – perhaps to drink too much. Something's driving him nuts. Is it about the business? The War? She knows she can't go to Old Mr. Brady about this; he doesn't like women who ask questions. What about asking Jeff Martin, who, everybody says, knows everything. She had learned early in her married life not to show any curiosity about the goings-on at Brady Motors. "Woman's place is in the home" was Old Mr. Brady's admonition – and no one, including son George, ever dared oppose anything the old man said. But Emily, in her desperation, ventured down to Jeff Martin's office. That is where I began my first act. With great excitement I discovered that what I had stumbled upon was a possible thriller – a Bluebeard story. By the time I brought the curtain down on Act Two, Emily had made a series of increasingly horrifying discoveries as she courageously ventured further and further into the skeleton closet of one branch of "the American Way of Life." To Jeff Martin, as he tried to block her way, she was "one of the Pearl Harbor crop of 'new women' – crazy about democracy and the four freedoms, especially the freedom of women to stick their noses into places where it don't belong." Emily explains her "new woman-ness" to her father in this way: "Here I have been for years dutifully presiding at Garden Clubs and Hospital Drives, trying to pretend that I was a valuable member of the community when I knew that all they wanted was the great name of Mrs. George Brady. And then the war comes along and for the first time I began to feel that I'm really a member of the community and not just someone sitting way up there in a private box. I talk to other women – women who are being air raid wardens and women working for the first time in factories and they feel the way I do – sort of a release. I feel alive – that's all: And I don't want anybody to tell me to go back up to my private box and stop asking questions!"

Act Three takes place in a downstairs room in Emily's home at ten in the evening. She is alone on the stage. In the dining room (offstage) George is giving a dinner in Sam's honor to which have been invited a cross-section of the more important loyal subjects of the Brady empire – the most powerful newspaper publisher in the Mid-West, the owner of the most important radio chain, congressmen, senators, state supreme court judges, generals, bankers, the president of the state university, and Jeff Martin. Emily hears from the radio in the room the voice of President Roosevelt in one of his Fireside chats: "There are a few in this country – only a few but their power is great – whose voices are becoming shrill and arrogant as victory seems to be coming nearer to us and our allies. These voices from the powerful few would have us stop talking about the Four Freedoms, especially freedom from want and freedom from fear. The many have fought the battles of this war – the few would now step forward and grasp the fruits."

The education of Emily Brady is gradually completed. Her son has been wounded in a war against Fascism; her father-in-law is fighting a secret Fascist war against Democracy; and her husband, caught between the two, has retreated into a schizophrenic alcoholic world of "know-nothing-ness." When she demands that they send for Sam, they refuse. "You're afraid of him!" cries Emily. "The starry-eyed boy with his wound stripe!" Jeff calmly suggests "Sam will learn the facts of life in time – the same as his father did." "Yes" agrees Emily "He'll learn – but from me. From his mother, who dared to open the wrong door." "For God's sake," cries the distraught George, "Not now!" And the curtain falls as the triumphant Emily announces, "I can wait."

Well, that was that. It had taken me over a year after I had started at the farm in the summer of 1942. We had moved down to an apartment in New York in the fall. There had been several drafts, but I now was sure that I had written a good play – and that I had said what must be said. But I was soon to discover that there was apparently no market on Broadway for my broadside. "But Don," would be the exclamation, "What are you *saying*?" At first I would spell it out for them. "I am saying that the struggle for power in competitive Big Business inevitably incorporates anti-human practices, including gangsterism and murder. It involves defiance of democracy, especially of the Bill of Rights. It demands that human beings be regarded as commodities, to be manipulated for profit, without regard to their worth as individuals or their natural need for self-fulfillment. I am saying that Jeff Martin is not a villain; he is a necessity. There must always be a Jeff Martin to do the Old Man's dirty work. And there always will be decent chaps like George who are caught between their fundamental need for brotherhood and the requirements for success in competitive Big Business. These Georges can only save themselves from schizophrenic madness by creating the illusion that they don't know what the Jeff Martins are doing. A part of Big Business is – and has always been – more or less successfully concealed inhumanity. But in spite of saying this, my play is a play of hope, of great hope, Emily's curtain line implies that in time the acceptance of man's inhumanity to man will lessen, that the buddies in the war against Hitler will have learned the value of working together and will, like Emily, begin to ask questions."

I took the play first to Herman Shumlin, a producer-director whom I greatly respected for his close connection with the plays of Lillian Hellman. Herman was interested and made helpful suggestions for rewriting, but seemed a bit doubtful about production. As I rewrote, his doubts increased. Then, after Shumlin, came an increasingly dismal succession of interviews with "possibles." Leland Hayward soon stopped pretending that the play was produceable. Elliot Nugent said that he just didn't believe that such things were possible in America. I began running round to odd little hotels or to odd people in big hotels. "There's a very rich woman at the Plaza who's crazy about the theater" – and I would put on my Brooks Bros. suit and discover that she was also crazy about hashish.

Or, "why not try my aunt Estelle? She loved your *Perfect Behavior*" – and there would be the job of explaining to Aunt Estelle that *Emily Brady* wasn't quite as funny as *Perfect Behavior*. I got a lot of friendly lunches out of it, and could probably have sold a lot of automobiles or life insurance, but always, at a certain point, the prospect would insist on reading the play – or have somebody also read it – and then would come the discovery, in spite of my nice table manners and my clever dropping of impressive names, of what my play was really about. It was a horribly discouraging winter and I felt angry and humiliated at the spectacle of myself, hat in hand, humbly having to peddle it around.

The discouragement and gloom would have been considerably deeper if it hadn't been for Ella's fighting spirit and her faith in me. And the picture wasn't one of unrelieved gloom by any means. We were living in the Village, in the upstairs half of a duplex at 25 West 11th Street. Below us was our landlord, the distinguished Liberal lawyer Osmond Fraenkel. Duck was with us, attending school at the nearby Little Red School House and then the Town and Country. The other boys came down for Christmas: Pete from Harvard, Ames from South Kent School in Connecticut. My name had got onto the New York list of "available toastmasters" and I was always ready to slide down the pole into my dinner jacket and gallop off to the nearest plate of left-wing chicken, mashed potatoes and peas. Sometimes it would be in honor of the Veterans of the Abraham Lincoln Brigade or Paul Robeson's "Council for African Affairs"; on other occasions I would preside over Carol King's favorite organization, "The Committee for the Protection of the Foreign Born." My one interlude from left-wing after-dinner speaking in this period came when I was invited to speak at the annual banquet given at the Biltmore by the New York alumni of my old school Exeter. It had been thirty years since my graduation, and I was terribly pleased at the honor, especially as others at the speakers' table included Judge Learned Hand and the Morgan partner Thomas Lamont, Senior. It seemed good to be back among these friendly respectable citizens and I felt happily relieved that my own contribution to the evening was to be purely humorous, with no obligation to collect money for sharecroppers or Jewish refugees. The only possible fly in my happy old-school ointment was the presence at the speakers' table of Westbrook Pegler, who was not an old Exoman and certainly not my favorite Red-baiter. But I had been assured by the committee that he was there to talk only about sport, and I relaxed further into my memories of old familiar faces. My reverie was rudely interrupted by the word "labor." It was Pegler speaking, and he was telling the spellbound audience of the menace to the American war effort of labor unions which, according to him, were a much worse threat to our freedom than Germany or Japan. He finished amid tremendous applause, and I heard the toastmaster introducing me as "probably, along with Robert Benchley, one of the funniest Exeter graduates ever produced." I had wanted to be funny but consciously so; the spectacle of me in a dinner jacket defending "labor" had much of the humorous quality of the old Exeter Golden Branch debating society solemnly arguing "Resolved; that labor unions are a good thing." But I didn't argue. I merely said that I disagreed with Mr. Pegler. I was quite unprepared for the boo's and cries of "sit down!" with which this remark was greeted by my fellow alumni. I had never been booed before, and my humor is not the kind which thrives on opposition. I retired as gracefully and quickly as possible from any claims to being one of the funniest of Exeter graduates.

Characteristically, I didn't get angry at the time. I still believed that hatred aroused by my beliefs could not possibly be directed personally at me. In Hollywood I had come to accept the snubs and the sneers of the "enemy." But here in New York, living as it were on the edge of my old successful playboy life, I was still, to myself, both a "Red" and also the "old Don" who wanted to be well liked by everyone. What I hadn't realized was that as a "Red", I had enabled people to put me on their list of those to whom they were superior – just as I had once felt superior to Jews. "At least I'm not a –" is a very human failing in a competitive world. Occasionally I would be tempted to drop in at Tony's or 21 "just to see who was there." One New Year's Eve, when Ella had gone to bed early with a cold, I found myself walking up Fifth Ave, playing with the idea of having just a New Year's quick one at the 21 bar. I knew that I would get a friendly welcome from Jack and Charlie, and also from Mac whom I had first known when Jack had taken me to his young brother's Brooklyn high. I couldn't now ever really "go back" to any part of my past, no matter how brightly it sometimes glowed in the ashes of memory. It was about this time that Ella, after dining with Thomas Wolfe and listening to his fevered evocation of certain aspects of his past, commented: "What you're saying is that you can't go home again." There is always that bright happy place in one's memory, often the unconscious memory, where one was happy and safe. Perhaps the last step to maturity is the final acceptance of the illusory nature of that "safe warm place," and with maturity comes the recognition of the reality of the world and an understanding of one's responsibility to change it for the better, which, to my mind, constitutes the beginning of an individual's freedom. It had taken me a long time to grow up.

25

The New Year, 1944, didn't seem to be in a hurry to listen to me. *Emily Brady* at first attracted no additional interest, although the kindly John Golden offered encouragement and hope with, however, one unfortunate proviso: that I rewrite the play to turn its exposure of undemocratic and inhuman practices in Big Business into a paean of praise for the American way of life, and an indictment only of a "villain," Jeff Martin, who was betraying his "good" employers. Anxious though I was for a production, I couldn't agree to this. The villain in my play was the dark side of a competitive acquisitive society which could not be "cured" by the reform of individuals a la moral rearmament. But John Golden wouldn't buy this.

Nor apparently, would anyone else – until, one bright spring day, I discovered that Jane Cowl was looking for a play in which she might star. The part of Emily intrigued her, and she showed it to Billy Rose, who sent it out to Orson Welles in Hollywood. Then followed a week of incredible suspense for Ella and me. She had been offered the extremely desirable job of foreign correspondent in war-time Moscow for the New York *Evening Post,* but had hesitated as it meant leaving me alone in the depths of my despair over *Emily Brady.* M-G-M had asked me to come out to work on the script of Philip Barry's play *Without Love,* but I had been unwilling to abandon *Emily* without one more struggle.

And then, one evening, the telephone rang. "Mr. Orson Welles calling from Hollywood." Ella and Duck rushed to the extension upstairs, and I tried to seem nonchalant as I listened. I didn't stay nonchalant. Orson loved the play, was "more excited than by anything for a long time. Could I come out and talk about it?" I could. Then he continued, "There's only one thing . . ." My heart sank. I knew about that "one thing." It had been asked by John Golden and God knew how many others. I swallowed and asked, "What one thing, Orson?" "I don't think Jane Cowl is right." "Is-is that all?" I gasped. "That's all," he replied. I'm afraid it wasn't very fair to Miss Cowl, but I didn't argue the point. Neither did Billy Rose. The next day I had a contract, and he had the production rights for a year. Emily had been saved by throwing Jane overboard. A pity – but that was show business.

Another thing about show business is the way one little bit of financial enthusiasm about a play can revive a writer's enthusiasm about himself. No matter how sure I was that *Emily Brady* was a new and important contribution to the American theater, I needed the reassurance of a production. A play between the covers of a book, no matter how "important," is still in the womb; the baby must be exposed to the world. The fact that the Broadway world was a very special and limited cross-section of humanity didn't bother me at the time. I had conquered them with *Rebound,* and Emily was a vastly superior creation – at least to my mind. And now, after two years of discouragement and despair, I had a top producer, an excited and exciting director, and an almost certain fall production.

So – Ella signed with the *Post* to sail for Moscow, and I agreed to go out to Hollywood for *Without Love.* It was not a very appropriate title for my mood. I loved everybody and everything, including Billy Rose, Orson Welles, and the fact that the picture was for Katharine Hepburn and Spencer Tracy, with an old friend Larry Weingarten producing. Before "Fidget" took off (I had recently invented that nickname for her) we had lots of farewell parties for lots of friends. Bob and Helen Lamb came down from Boston where he was teaching Economics at M.I.T. Barrows Dunham, a Professor of Philosophy at Temple University, drove over from Philadelphia with his wife Alice. Another Philadelphia visitor was Sam Darey, whom Ella and Lincoln Steffens had first known when he was the secretary of the Communist Party, from which he had recently been expelled in the dispute over the new "Browder link."

Ella sailed secretly in May on a cargo ship loaded with dynamite – a fact which I fortunately did not know at the time. Her destination – if the Nazi U-boats would permit it – was Egypt and thence, via

Teheran, to Moscow. With luck she was to be back for the opening of *Emily Brady* and certainly by the end of the year. I didn't realize, until a half hour after she had gone, how much I was going to miss her, especially as there wasn't any chance of getting a letter from her for several weeks.

Meanwhile, *Without Love* beckoned and I reported for duty at dear old M-G-M where, by now, I was almost the oldest living graduate. Larry Weingarten was fun to work for. He laughed at my jokes, and his own weren't bad, either. And he had just married a remarkable woman named Jessie Marmorston who was not only the first good-looking woman doctor I had ever known but the first good-looking woman I had met who was making experiments with cancer in mice and also liked to dance. Not at the same time, of course, and I didn't discover about the dancing until we had had several serious talks about medical subjects including my own health. I wasn't particularly worried about it, but I was fifty years old and I wanted to write several more plays before my fires began to die down.

So Dr. Marmoston arranged to give me a checkup at her office, including something called a basal metabolism which involved strapping several tubes onto me at various places and then switching on a pump. All went well until she turned the electric switch, at which all the fuses in the building blew out. When we had stopped laughing it seemed as though the next step was to ask if she thought Larry would mind if we continued the checkup at the Mocambo. Larry didn't mind, and as he didn't enjoy dancing and she did, Jessie and I had a lot of fun that summer. She was a great-hearted generous person, as well as being a first-rate doctor. Her office was always crowded with poor patients from whom she never expected a fee, and Larry never knew when she was going to bring home some forlorn refugee to live with them "just because he (or she) is very discouraged and needs a good meal and a little friendship."

But *Emily Brady* began to look as though she needed more than a basal metabolism – or perhaps it was Orson Welles who needed one. When I had first arrived he had greeted me with the decision that the only actress who could play "Emily" was Agnes Moorehead. I had never seen Miss Moorehead act, but I was willing to trust his judgment. I also trusted his professed enthusiasm for the play – and that was where I was to become gradually aware that I was dealing with a "genius." Such characters are often extremely charming and lovable in fiction and on the stage, but the charm began to wear a bit thin when I found that he apparently had not the slightest intention of doing anything about *Emily Brady*. His chief occupation, as far as I could gather from his newspaper publicity, seemed to be a series of performances of magic in which he featured sawing Rita Hayworth in half. I wired him that sawing a playwright in half was perhaps not quite so neat a bit of trickery. I received a telephone call reassuring me of his continued enthusiasm for the play. That was the last I ever heard from him, nor was I ever able to see him or contact him in any way. Billy Rose in New York became equally inaccessible, and Emily slowly died. There have never been any post mortems, and to this day I do not know what happened. My nearest guess would be that somewhere along the line someone had decided that an exposition of possible Fascism in the United States was inadvisable – or out of date. The opening of the Second Front had driven the Nazis back into Germany, the Russians after Stalingrad were pressing westward, and the victorious end of the war was in sight. Presumably, Fascism had been defeated for ever and ever – and the only clouds in the sky were those rolling up behind the Red Army as they raced the Allies towards Berlin. The Cold War and the Red Scare were just around the corner, and Emily Brady was perhaps one of the first victims.

Of course, the changeover didn't happen as quickly or as complete-ly as all that. Out in Los Angeles we had crowded the Shrine auditorium after Stalingrad to cheer a superb speech by Charlie Chaplin beginning: "Comrades – and I mean comrades!", after which we had followed the lead of Walter Huston in singing our tribute to "the victorious banners of the glorious Soviet Army." A dinner at the Beverly Wilshire in praise of that same victorious army was pack-jammed with top Hollywood star names. We worked enthusiastically for the election of F.D.R. and Harry Truman. It was, for a brief moment, like the return of the good old days when we had put on white ties and tails in order to persuade the producers that something must be done about Hitler. And now that something *had* been done – and in alliance with Soviet Socialist Russia – I indulged for a moment in the hope that the alliances of the war might con-tinue as a guarantee of further victories. Emily Brady was dead, but her spirit might go marching on.

Personally, there were low moments, too – partly because of Emily and partly because of loneliness for Fidget. In one of those moments I called up Bob Benchley and found myself once more, after a long separation, in his bungalow at the Garden of Allah, with a happy highball in my hand. There was a knock – and unexpectedly in came John McClain, in naval officer's uniform, on leave from service in the Pacific. This led to what might be described as "a heightened mood," and when Bob handed me my third or fourth highball I felt called upon to make a reassuring affirmation. "Would you like to know something interesting?" I announced. "I've got alcohol just where I want it. Completely under control."

That is an extremely dangerous statement to make, and an hour later I found myself in the Beverly Hills jail on a drunk driving charge. It was the second time I had been there. Some five years previously, after acting as toastmaster at a Yale-Harvard-Princeton banquet, I had felt a bit "sleepy" on the way home, drawn my car up to the curb and been arrested an hour or so later for what is called "drunk in auto." I am not complaining that I did not have it coming to me. But I had never before been placed alone in a room where the door knob turned round and round without opening the door, where I could not get to a telephone, where all my personal possessions were examined and commented on before being dropped into an envelope. And in the morning, in a cell, in addition to the nausea of hangover, was the additional shame of having betrayed my political "cause." Ever since I had grown out of my playboy life I had considered it part of my obligation to the movement not to get drunk – and I had kept fairly well to my self-imposed sobriety. I dreaded the publicity, especially when I thought of it reaching Ella in Moscow, Ames and Duck at school in Connecticut, and Pete at Harvard. I had been lucky the first time, but this would surely mean a jail sentence. I had finished *Without Love* and made all preparations to return East. And now, just because on a foggy night, going very slowly, I had rammed the fender of a car parked at the curb! But when my trial came up, my luck held out. Perhaps partly because I lied about having to hurry to New York "to put on my play," but chiefly because I had a very good lawyer named Charles Katz, I got off with a stiff fine. And no publicity. It was one of the most sickeningly depressing experiences I had ever had – and my depression did not lift that evening when I went to say goodbye to Katharine Hepburn, where I found old friend Tallulah Bankhead in one of her less attractive Dixie belle moments in which she practically spit in my eye for being a traitor and a Communist.

On the way East I picked up my sister Anne in Columbus and took her to New York with me. Her husband Charles Outhwaite had recently died, and we both needed cheering up. We did our best, but it was a dreary December in which there crept over me a strange Dead Sea feeling. I was fifty, I had been in the movement for ten years, and while I had not lost my belief in Socialism, the personal nature of my contribution somehow seemed to have got sidetracked, especially with the sinking of *Emily Brady*. The exciting days of anti-Hitler and pro-China had been taken over by the Roosevelt administration, as had also the ferment of the struggle for labor organization and all anti-Fascist activities. Our side had won the war. My belief in Stalin had not wavered. Socialism was certainly closer – or seemed closer. But without Ella my life lacked a center, and at that particular moment Beatrice came back into the periphery.

I had gone up to the Christmas vacation exercises at the South Kent School where Ames and Duck were enrolled. And there was Beatrice who, after two marriages following ours, was living alone in a small two-roomer in New York. She was, as far as I could observe, the same old Bea. After a couple of drinks at her friend's home near the school where she was staying, I became the same old Don. There were a lot of laughs. Ten years seemed to have rolled way and caused a return to the days when nothing mattered but fun and present laughter. Bea knew better than anyone how to apply alcohol to my "Life of the Party" complex. It wasn't that she wanted me back as a husband, but she hated Ella, and I was fool enough not to see the picture. I was so sure of my love for Ella that I didn't see any harm in a momentary return to former companionship, especially as I had never been able to retain my anger against Bea.

So when I took the boys back to the Madison Square hotel where they lived with Anne and me, the old Stewart family had several get-togethers. Bea and I went shopping for Christmas presents, one of which was a tuxedo for Ames, aged sixteen. That gift was, in a way, symbolic of the two-world fantasy which I didn't seem able to shake off. I was, in my philosophy, a revolutionary Socialist, and yet I was willing to have my children exposed to the same world against which I had revolted – the world of exclusive schools and tuxedos and Racquet Clubs. It cannot be said that my revolt was a phony one or that I didn't sincerely believe in the class war. It was rather that I didn't ever cease being a bourgeois. I never really hated my former friends in the upper class and, America being what it was, I didn't feel that I had the right to bring my children up under the handicap of being "different." In my plays and speeches I could hate Big Business, Fascism and the National Association of Manufacturers. But in New York that Christmas I could also readily accept Bea's suggestion that we pay a visit to Joan and Charlie Payson who, after all, were still the godparents of our youngest son. It was a delightful visit, I felt unembarrassingly welcome, and afterwards I walked down Park Avenue with Charlie who, in white tie and tails, was on his way to the Waldorf for the annual banquet of The National Association of Manufacturers. We parted at the door with a laugh as I declined his invitation to attend the banquet. I felt no betrayal of Ella or of my beliefs. I didn't know that the word was spreading around 21 and Hollywood that Bea and I were together again and that I was divorcing Ella. Bea and I bought a Christmas tree and prepared for the "family" celebration. It wasn't the family. Ella had taken over the boys when they were four and eight; she had gone through the hard years of training and educating two badly spoiled children, whom Bea and I had turned over to nurses and governesses. The boys loved Ella, whom they called "Muffet," and wanted her there for Christmas. So did Pete. And so, most of all, did I.

On December 22nd came a cable from Florida. "Arrived. See you tomorrow." It was signed "Fidget." So the boys had two Christmases – and I had the happiest in my lifetime. Ella hadn't known about Bea but she had, strangely enough, become worried about Jessie Marmorston whom I had praised in my letters from Hollywood. God, as I have said, moves in a mysterious way.

A few weeks later Ella and I moved up to Cambridge partly because of Pete who, as a cadet in the Harvard Naval Officers Training Corps, was soon to graduate into active service. Ella also wanted to be near our old friend Angus Cameron who, as one of the heads of the Boston publishers Little Brown and Co., had offered to help in the preparation of her book on her recent experiences in wartime Russia. My own job was to write a new play. I didn't have a clue, except that I felt impelled, after the discouraging fate of *Emily Brady*, to return to my gift for humor. Twenty years ago, after *Aunt Polly* had flopped, I had dived happily into the crazy humor of *The Haddocks*. So – let's have some of the old Stewart comedy. But of course with a serious theme embodying my criticism of certain American fallacies about "the free world." Sort of a mixture of *New Masses* and *New Yorker.*

Living in Cambridge, in the shadow of Harvard University, was quite a change from Hollywood. I discovered to my horror that when one was invited to tea, tea was what one got. It didn't seem to me that that was what we had fought and won the Revolution for. But we soon found other – and younger – companions. Chief among these was Professor F.O. Matthieson of the English Department and through him we met another English professor, Theodore Spencer. Matty was short, stocky, fierce, and radical; Ted was tall, graceful, good-tempered, conservative. We grew to love them both. Another good friend was the wife of Professor Howard Mumford Jones, and as head of the Soviet-American Friendship Society, we saw something of Henry Wadsworth Longfellow Dana who was living in his famous great-grandfather's house. In a nearby suburb lived my old Yale room-mate Phelps Putnam. Put, like Matty and myself, was one of the few Bones men who had "swung to the Left" in the depression period of the 30's. Unfortunately his fierce unrelenting asthma had finally triumphed; he spent most of his days in bed, still trying desperately to fulfill his great early promise as a poet. His mother and father were taking loving care of him, as was his sister Frances who had married the Unitarian clergyman Stephen Fritchman. It was wonderful to find in Put at least one of my old friends who shared my enthusiasm for what were becoming increasingly publicized as "un-American activities."

But before the full fury of the Cold War could be unleashed, the Hot War had to be finished. Our great hero F.D.R. died in April. Ella had been invited to the White House shortly after her return from Russia, and her report on the President's physical appearance at that time had been rather alarming. But his death came as a terrible shock – and no one on the Left knew what to expect from Harry Truman. On April 25th came the beginning of the formation of the United Nations in San Francisco and in May the unconditional surrender of Italy and Germany. There were newspaper photographs of the fraternizing of Russian and American troops. No one knew what deals had been made at Yalta, but there was alarm at the Red Army occupation of Poland, Hungary, Bulgaria and Romania. I saw it as the spread of Socialism and was delighted. I still believed in Stalin's Marxism, and was not at all aware of the contradictions involved in the imposition of Socialism "from the Top."

Meanwhile I had been having trouble with my new play. I was

attempting a sort of parallel to Goethe's *Faust,* with Faust himself a modern American Liberal, and Mephistopheles his "Mind" – or, more correctly, that section of his mind which supplies him with the logical excuses for remaining a "Liberal" instead of moving into the dangerous territory of progressive politics. I was trying to give a humorous depiction of the struggle within myself to resist the temptation to play safe and not "shoot the works" in active participation in a political fight for Socialism which I saw as the next step toward real democracy. But although I knew in general what I wanted to say, I had not been able to devise any interesting characters or dramatic situations. I had a theme but no play, so when in June Jack Warner telephoned from New York that Clarence Day's widow wanted me to adapt *Life With Father* to the screen, I leapt happily at the chance. Howard Lindsay and Russell ~~Krause~~ had written such a successful *Crouse* play that there wasn't much need – or indeed much allowance – for any screen writing, and after a couple of understanding consultations with Mrs. Day I was able to finish the job by the end of July.

All this had taken place in a large rather tomb-like Cambridge house we rented from a Greek professor, full of classic busts (rather ominous words for a playwright) and heavy woodwork, one sample of which lingers in my memory because of a horror connected with it. In a coy Victorian attempt to conceal a water closet there was a section of heavy black oak book case which (if you knew the secret) swung outward into the room, and quickly closed after you as you entered the sacred precincts. One Sunday our pet kitten tried to follow me in, and I had the sickening problem of what to do with a hopelessly crushed body. No veterinaries were available. I tried to drown it in a large tub of water and finally had to knock it unconscious. To this day I cannot get out of my mind the look in that animal's eyes as I killed it.

The atom bomb was dropped on Hiroshima three days later, and in the mushroom cloud dissolved the last hopes for the Roosevelt-Wilkie "One World." Ironically, it was the A-bomb which gave me the "go-ahead" for my play. My *Faust* became a professor of astronomy in a Southern university worried, among other things, about the ghastly possibilities of an atomic Third World War. He had lost his only son in the final offensive against Germany. He was my "liberal" on the verge of asking the question which Henry Wallace, then Secretary of Commerce, was later to ask Truman – and lose his job: "Is there not some justification that Russia has begun to believe that we regard another war as inevitable, or at least that some military men in the U.S.A. are in favor of a preventive war?" He quoted "the size of our defense budget, the testing of more and more A-bombs in the Pacific, the efforts to obtain air bases abroad." My astronomer, however, had already begun to ask other political questions to which his Mind had given him what seemed like doubtful answers. The relationship between the professor and his worried protective Mind (invisible, of course, to all other characters) was supposed to be the source of a good deal of comedy, as though the parts could have been played by Jack Benny and Rochester, or any of a long line of such comic acts dating back to Weber and Fields. The character of the astronomer, to whom I gave the name of Lem, was really the same as that of Emily Brady. Lem was the man of science suddenly realizing his obligation as a world citizen and his need to probe the true reality of democracy and the free world. To his Mind's dismay, he was inquiring about such un-astronomical subjects as labor unions and racial equality and the increasing control by the Army and Navy of various universities' (including his own) scientific departments. Although he didn't know it, he was heading for trouble as a possible "Red." His wife knew it, though; so did his daughter and his best friend, the president of his university. They were trying to aid his Mind by heading him toward safety.

And then, just as they seem to be succeeding, when Lem is alone in his study, there appears to him, almost as in a dream, a beautiful woman, rather poorly dressed, with a knapsack over her shoulders. This is Lisa. Who she is, where she comes from, is a fascinating mystery to Lem, especially as she seems to know a great deal about astronomy and is particularly concerned about a series of celestial photographs he is taking in search for a possible new planet. Lem is intrigued – but not so his Mind. "Get her out of here!" is the almost frantic warning. "And quick!" The Mind, of course, recognizes the danger. Lisa is Lem's Conscience – more specifically, his conscience about humanity – and the fight between her and the Mind increases in intensity, and often in humor, as they struggle for the soul of this tormented professor.

Finally, in the last act, the question of "un-American activities" among the faculty comes to the attention of the university. Lem is out on a limb, and when confronted with the possibility of the loss of his job because of his political activities, including speaking out for the rights of Negroes, he is persuaded by his Mind that he cannot do this to his wife and daughter. Lisa appears, and the final showdown begins. "You're asking me to shoot the works," groans Lem. Lisa quietly remarks that "other men have," and adds a quotation from the Talmud: "If not I, who? If now now, when?" "I'm a professor of astronomy," cries Lem, "That's my job – not politics. I have a wife I love, a daughter I love." At that moment Lem's assistant comes rushing in, waving some photographic plates. "Professor Stevenson!" he cries. "Your planet!" Lem grabs the plates. "Where?" "There!" points the assistant. Lem looks sharply, then exclaims "But it's a star!" "That's right" exults the assistant. "You've discovered a new star. It's just as important. Stevenson's star!" Lem excitedly sends the assistant off to cable the announcement to other astronomers. His Mind rushes in to congratulate him. And then they notice Lisa. She is gazing into the heavens, tears running down her cheeks. "Gone" she cries "Gone. My world. My planet where we had started an atomic war – where no one had the courage to cry out, 'You fools! Would you blindly destroy everything rather than let all men share our blessings!' Gone! Cities, fφrms, people, children – and in one evil flash of senseless hatred they become death, flame, ashes, smoke – a pinpoint of light on an astronomer's photographic plate. A new star. Stevenson's star." And Lisa exits. The Mephistopheles Mind looks at Lem ready to shoot the works. The discovery of a new star has possibly saved him his job. But Liza has saved something much more important – the courage of a man to search for truth rather than yield to the subtle importunings of his reason in the direction of the safety of collaboration with one's employers.

The play was, of course, about myself – except for the heroic resolution of Lem's struggle. There have, however, been heroic Lems in the course of history, and to me my obligation as a playwright compelled me to end on the hope that there will be many more. To that extent I was a playwright with a message – and as my message was political, it was even more reprehensible: it was propaganda. If Lem had been a Russian astronomer named Lemski, my hopeful conclusion that he would continue his courageous search for truth would presumably have put me on the side of the angels. But I knew nothing about conditions in Russia, nor about what went on in the minds of Russian scientists. I am an American, I knew about myself and I wrote critically yet hopefully about what I considered the deepest problem of our time. But, as with *Emily Brady*, I was unfortunate in my timing. My play, begun in 1945, was not finished until 1947. In the interval Winston Churchill had delivered his speech warning America of the danger to the "free world" from the evil ambitions of Russia for world conquest; the Truman doctrine had been proclaimed with the dispatch of American troops to Greece and Turkey; and as the Cold War grew in intensity Lem's individual search for truth was beginning to be viewed as treason, or at least as a fear of standing up to the Godless Soviet desire for world domination.

We stayed in Cambridge until the end of 1946, having moved from the Greek professor's mausoleum to a small apartment on Linnaean Street where we joyfully found James Aldridge and his beautiful Egyptian wife Dina. Ella had met them in 1944 in Moscow where Jim like Ella was a war correspondent; he had come to Cambridge, also like Ella, to take advantage of Angus Cameron's editorial help in the preparation of his next book. These were serious days of work for all of us, interrupted only for me by a telephone call in November of 1945 from Philip Barry to tell me Bob Benchley was dying. I hurried to New York but was unable to see him. There was no funeral, which was perhaps just as well: No church, no stadium could have been large enough to hold the friends who wished to honor this most lovable of men. How many times since then have I longed to talk to him, to go to him, to hear his laughter. My loneliness for him has grown. I dream of him and always wake up comforted.

By mid-1946 Ella's book was published under the title *I Saw the Russian People*. It was an honest, moving account of the heroism of the common people during the war; it was equally honest about her discovery of certain disquieting developments since her original visit in the early thirties, which she had told about in her *Red Virtue*. Her new book, like my play, was unfortunately completed in the face of the growing fears and apprehensions of the Cold War. The heroism of Russian resistance to Hitler and the "One World" hopes of the wartime alliance were beginning to be overwhelmed by the post-war actions and reactions of East and West.

Early in 1947 we moved back to New York to a brownstone front at 8 East 10th Street. We lived in the lower floors and basement and rented the top section to Ring Lardner Jr.'s divorced wife Sylvia. I had decided not to submit my play to the Broadway agony which I had gone through with *Emily Brady* until I could find a director or a star whose enthusiasm would help me over the bumps. I had recently signed a contract with M-G-M for five pictures in five years, and when they called me out to do Sinclair Lewis' *Cass Timberlaine* I had hopes of finding out there a "progressive" director who would not be frightened by the "message" in my play. I made the laughable mistake of going first to Elia Kazan, whose answer was that "he just wouldn't know how to direct such a play." But then, shortly after this came a miraculous telephone call from Garson Kanin. He and his wife, Ruth Gordon, loved the play and would like to produce it in the fall! Ella and I leaped into the air and in our enthusiasm brought a house. It seemed the least we could do, especially as it was on Maybery Road in Santa Monica, overlooking the Pacific, with our beloved Salka Viertel only five doors away. Among our guests at the house-warming were Charlie and Oona Chaplin, and Charlie tells the story (which might just possibly be true) that I took him on a tour of the new house. "And this," Charlie swears I announced, "is the main bedroom"; at which I blithely proceeded to undress and retire for the night, leaving Charlie alone to find his way back to the other guests.

Life was once again full of wonder and hope, and I began once more to wrestle with the problem of whether I should accept the Pulitzer prize or perhaps the Nobel Peace prize.

26

From our new house the M-G-M studio was a forty-five minute drive each morning and *Cass Timberlaine*, with the amiable Arthur Hornblow Jr. as my producer, was providing me with one of the most interesting and difficult scripts of my Hollywood career. The novel interested me because the locale could have been the Columbus of my early youth and most of the characters were the Minnesota equivalent of the country club Society group in which I had grown up. The leading character, to be played by Spencer Tracy, was a judge, as had been my father. The difficulty lay in the fact that while Sinclair Lewis had written a powerful and fairly comprehensive study of middle-and upper-class life in an American city, he had not written a play or a film. Every time a successful novel is transcribed to the screen, there are countless wails and angry howls from lovers of the book that "Hollywood has ruined another work of art!" Inasmuch as this was the next to last film job I was ever to be allowed to complete in my native land, and since I am quite proud of what I did to ruin Sinclair Lewis's novel, I would like to devote a few moments of memory to the processes of film production in the case of this particular picture. The working conditions for a writer were fairly ideal. One had an air-conditioned office on the first or second floor of the large Irving Thalberg Memorial Building, the third floor of which was occupied by Louis B. Mayer, other top executives, and a producers' dining room. Every writer had assigned to him a first-class woman secretary. I always made sure to select one who thought my jokes were funny.

The working hours were from around nine until half past five;

lunch was usually eaten at an excellent commissary on the lot. Writers ate at "Left Wing" or "Right Wing" tables, depending on their political views, since the Red scars had not yet closed down on all tongues and minds. Surrounding the writers were tables for actors, directors, camera men, and all the hundreds of employees concerned in the various productions. A large long center table was reserved for top stars and directors, although most of the biggest stars ate in their private bungalows. Beer could be obtained with lunch; two or three cocktail bars were in the neighborhood, but film making by now had become a serious and extremely competitive business. A writer's life was real and very earnest and the grave was just around the corner – after one or two unsuccessful pictures. Self-protection was one of the first lessons a writer had to learn, since almost from the start of every picture the jockeying began about whom to blame if the production was a flop – and usually it was the writer, especially if he (or she) had had the courage to depart from the original "property." Another lesson, mentioned much earlier, involved the formation of the protective shield against being hurt too much by caring too deeply about one's own individual creative contribution. Both of these lessons were painful and destructive: They showed finally that a writer, no matter how much he was paid, was damaging, perhaps irreparably, his one great treasure, his creative originality. Film making *is* a cooperative venture, to be sure, and no one person can ever really take the bows for a success. But to a writer the "cooperation" of a producer, director, and star can be at times a bitterly discouraging experience.

Cass Timberlaine, however, was not on the whole such an experience. My salary was impressive enough to give me a certain amount of authority – at least, a good table whenever I went to Romanoff's. The chief problem about "Cass" involved the fact that Spencer Tracy as the forty-five-year-old judge didn't really have a very good part. He falls in love with Jinny, a lively and much younger girl from "the wrong side of the tracks" and marries her against the opposition of his upper-class neighbors on the exclusive Heights. O.K. so far, but not particularly original. And for the rest of the novel Cass sits around with what in show business we call "egg on his face" while Jinny takes over. She wants "life" – at least a better life than is offered by the rulers of the Heights. Cass waits for her to settle down. Jinny acts in the local drama club. Cass sits in the audience. Jinny flirts. Cass suffers. Jinny wants to go to New York.

Cass tags along. Jinny gets diabetes, also gets pregnant and loses the baby. Cass suffers some more. Finally Jinny falls in love with Cass's best friend and goes off to New York to live with him. Cass waits for her to come back and takes long walks.

This brought the book to within fifteen pages of the end, and I began to feel the need of a long walk myself. A despairing writer at Metro has a choice of several walks. One is around his air-conditioned office. This leads to a certain amount of nervousness on the part of the secretary. Another walk goes up and down the long corridor outside the offices and leads the writer to think he is on one of the lower decks of the *Titanic,* which in turn suggests how wonderful it be if one were in a lifeboat and the patient kindly Minnesota judge were at the bottom of the Atlantic. One then walks out of the Irving Thalberg Memorial Building, across the beautiful flower-bordered lawn to the Main Gate of the studio, outside of which are clustered the daily gang of youthful autograph collectors who greet the writer with hopeful inquiries such as "Hey, mister – are you anybody?" This followed by shouts of derisive laughter if you are idiot enough to say "I'm a writer." The first stop for the creative artist inside the Main Lot is at Jim the barber's shop from where, since all the chairs are occupied by executives, one moves to the commissary for a cup of coffee. Perhaps one sits there alone, thinking of other pictures which had seemed just as hopeless as *Cass.* This gets one rapidly nowhere, so one wanders further through the Lot, past the huge concrete warehouse-like sound stages where other productions are being shot. Beyond Stage 12 begin the outdoor sets – the "New York Street," the "corner of old Paris" (which last week was the corner of old Las Vegas). One thinks of the impermanence of these sets – like the impermanence of everything in Hollywood. During the preparation and shooting of a picture people work together in the closest and most intense intimacy. The characters in the story become momentarily real. Occasionally electricians and hairdressers weep. Then – the final scenes are shot, there is a farewell party on the set, everyone gets a little drunk, the stars give expensive presents to the head cameraman and the director, less expensive ones to lesser lights. The party is over; the company departs. The Night Crew arrives for work and begins to dismantle the set. The stage is needed for another picture, starting tomorrow.

But that "next picture" was also Hollywood – and always there were new hopes, new possibilities. *Cass Timberlaine* with Spencer

Tracy could really say something important about something other than the marriage of an older man to a young girl. As I left the "corner of old Paris" and wandered back to my office and my patient secretary, I began to get an idea. Cass was a judge, born into and surrounded by the upper class of his home town. Supposing *that* problem were to enter the picture? Supposing a judge had to fight for his judicial integrity and his self-respect against a danger of which he was only dimly aware – his affection for and belief in his "best friends." That would involve Cass in a struggle as important as his husband-wife drama, and much more interesting to me in my belief that success and status are much more powerful in America than is ever supposed to be admitted in a democracy. Fortunately for me, with my reputation as a Red, Sinclair Lewis had painted a graphic picture of the upper and lower middle classes in the town and his description of the true natures of Cass's "best friends" made it easier for me to convince the studio that I was not introducing propaganda.

What I was introducing, however, was significant in the progress of my life as a writer. I had originally gone out to Hollywood some twenty years before on the pretense that the screen offered me a vastly increased audience to whom I could "say something." It was not entirely pretense, but the dreams were certainly more predominant than I would have acknowledged to myself at the time. The "somethings" which I myself had contributed to the screen in these twenty years had come largely under the head of "entertainment," which was what my employers were paying me for. But in *Keeper of the Flame* and now in *Cass Timberlaine* I felt that I was beginning to fulfill my original purpose in becoming a screenwriter. In adding to a novel about marriage what a judge is forced to learn about classes in a democracy, I was using the screen for what seemed to me one of its neglected purposes – the telling of truths to millions of people instead of merely entertaining them.

M-G-M had not bought the book for its "truth"; they had purchased a vehicle for an extremely valuable property, Spencer Tracy. My first job, therefore, was to sell my idea to him. Spence was one of the few really good actors in Hollywood; he was also one of the most insecure of human beings, especially about scripts. Fortunately he had recognized the weakness in the part of Cass. So had Arthur Hornblow, the producer, and I was given the go-ahead.

I went ahead quickly and happily. Ella and I were enjoying the Santa Monica house, with the beach and bathing at our doorstep.

Ames came out to prepare for entering UCLA. There was little "political activity" and we rarely went out in the evenings, usually to Salka Viertel's where we met a fascinating German refugee couple named Berthold Brecht and Helene Weigel. Sometimes we dined with the Chaplins, sometimes with Jessie and Larry Weingarten. Sunday evenings were usually spent quietly at Katharine Hepburn's. Garson Kanin and Ruth Gordon came out, and we did some final polishing of my play which we decided to call *How I Wonder*. Rehearsals were to start in August or September, as soon as a cast could be got together. Life was beautiful.

In June Ella accepted a suggestion from her publisher that she consider a new book based on the state of Europe two years after the war. She promised to be back in time for the opening of *How I Wonder*, and from New York, just before she flew to Berlin, she telephoned that she had just seen the first tryouts for the part of Lisa in the play and that a girl named Meg Mundy was marvelous. Ames and I celebrated by having dinner at the Brown Derby. A couple of tables away from ours was an heir of one of the famous Southern tobacco companies who surprised us by delivering a noisy tirade against the Jews. I couldn't believe it at first, and even though he was drunk I thought somebody ought to tell him to shut up. To my surprise, I found myself doing the job, and to my greater surprise he called me a son of a bitch, jumped up and started towards me. I jumped up too, and to my delight I wasn't at all frightened. It was the first time since the bull ring at Pamplona that I had needed my physical courage. Ames was standing up, too, and I think we could have handled the situation, but luckily the waiters rushed up, grabbed him and got him out of the front door. Ames and I sat down feeling pretty good and then Jack Warner leaned over from the table next to where the Southern gentleman had been and said, approvingly, "Nice work, Don. We were all behind you." A little later good old Jack, when asked by the Un-American Activities Committee (investigating the injection of communist ideas into films) if I was a Communist, replied: "If he isn't, I don't know who is."

Meanwhile, the "Communism" which I was injecting into *Cass Timberlaine* came to a head in a scene in which the judge turns down Jinny's plea that he became a New York corporation lawyer, tells her that his duty is to return to Minnesota even though that means rendering a decision against his friends on the Heights, and walks out on her instead of vice versa as in the novel. Love and his marriage are not as important as his judicial obligation to justice to all classes of people. Whether or not readers of the novel thought it had been ruined, I never knew. Arthur Hornblow liked the script. So did Spence. Lana Turner was given the part of Jinny, and with George Stevens as director shooting started. And that left before me the joyful prospect of my triumphant return to Broadway.

When I reached New York in the middle of August "Gar" Kanin had exciting news for me. Raymond Massey was crazy about the play and very very anxious to play the part of Lem, the professor of astronomy. When we met at his house, Massey told me that he had the same feeling about *How I Wonder* that he had when Robert Sherwood sent him *Abe Lincoln in Illinois*. I floated home on a happy cloud of euphoria and bourbon. The euphoria increased during the process of casting the other parts. Everett Sloane gave up a big TV contract in order to play Lem's Mind. Meg Mundy had already been chosen for Lem's Conscience. Carol Goodner came back into my life from the Bob Benchley-Music Box review days and was selected as Lem's wife. The past rose up again when we selected Bethel Leslie for Lem's daughter; her father Warren had always been one of the Payson boat race party, and he had last been seen by me while acting as Bea's divorce lawyer. His wife Jane had divorced him, and she and Bethel took me to the Stork Club, the first time I had been there since "the old days." It was wonderful to be "back" with a play which uncompromisingly expressed all the reasons why I had "gone away." I went to 21 for a drink and Ernest Hemingway pulled me affectionately down to his table. It was wonderful to tell Hem that I had a play going into rehearsal; he pounded my back enthusiastically and I loved him again. In fact, I had never stopped loving him, but we had certainly drifted far apart. And now, in a few weeks, when my play opened, I was to regain his respect as a writer or so I hoped. I very much wanted his respect – and that of all my companions of the 20's and 30's, who thought I had "sold out" to Hollywood or Stalin.

Ella returned from Europe just before rehearsals were to start. I was at the airport, on the roof. "The plane from Paris has now landed." The passengers came down the ladder. No Ella. And then, after a wait, a little distant figure, hurriedly carrying a typewriter, two overweight bags hidden under some coats. A bag fell open, and everything spilled out. That was my Fidget. It was a joyful reunion. She had had a fascinating trip. Berlin (still in ruins), Prague, then cross country by jeep in Yugoslavia with a *Time* correspondent, and at the end a long interview with Tito in Zagreb.

Rehearsals opened at par and my temperature steadily mounted during the next three weeks. It was so good to be back in the theater. It was so good to have in Garson a brilliant director who respected the writer and would not change a line – or let the actors change a line – without consulting me. I wrote a piece about that for the Sunday *Times*, kidding myself for having complained that in Hollywood my best lines were always changed, whereas now, when *How I Wonder* opened, every line, God help me, would be mine – and I was terrified that I had no one to blame if the play failed. But I really had no thought of it failing. The actors were getting better and better, especially Ev Sloane, who was developing the Mind into the truly comic Mephistopheles I had imagined. The only cloud on the horizon – and it was a small cloud at first – was that someone had gone to Ray Massey to warn him that the play was Communist propaganda. I reminded him of his initial enthusiastic comparison with Sherwood's *Abe Lincoln*. He acknowledged that but his doubt persisted. Finally I had a showdown with him at his club, the Century. It was tough going. The clouds of the Cold War crept in at every window. Ray was a Canadian. His brother was Governor General of Canada. "But Ray," I protested, "this play is not about Russia. It's about America – and the destruction of the world in an atomic war. Russia hasn't got the atomic bomb. What is Communistic about the play? Isn't it true that the Army and Navy are subsidizing the scientific department of universities? Isn't it true that large corporations control the boards of trustees of many colleges? And that professors are already losing their jobs because of the mere suspicion of un-American activities? And that a scientist might have "dangerous thoughts" which he would have to suppress – or else? Is it un-American for a scientist to think?"

"No," replied Ray "but –"

"But what?" I asked.

"In the first act," he said, "in that scene with the president of my university, I say that there are men in America who *want* to declare war on Russia – right now."

"Don't you believe that?" I asked.

"It sounds pro-Russian for me to say," he replied.

"O.K." I said. "Let's change it. Let's say that perhaps possibly there *might* be men who want to drop the bomb on Russia. That's what you're trying to find out. That's your 'dangerous thought.'

O.K.?"

"Well –" hesitated Ray.

"Look, Ray" I said "That's not what the play is about. It's only your suspicion – a first-act springboard into action. You're looking for a criminal. But the whole rest of the play is about something else. What's your lines in your final scene with your wife – the ones beginning 'I was looking for a criminal –'."

Ray hesitated, then gave me the line. "I was looking for a criminal," he said, in that wonderfully expressive voice, "up here, alone, underneath the stars –"

"Skip to 'I've found the criminal'," I urged. "Your wife asks 'Who?'"

" 'Me' " continued Ray. " 'I turned my telescope on to this earth and discovered that the criminal was – myself. A little man, afraid for his job.' "

"That's what the play's about" I cried. "The very last line – the curtain line – your message from God. What's that?"

" 'Special from God to all mankind'," said Ray. " 'Your job is to make the earth a fit place for Me to dwell in. If I need any more stars, I'll make them myself'."

"Curtain," I said. "Is that a communist play?"

At the end of the evening Ray and I shook hands and I felt that I had satisfied his doubts, perhaps almost restored his original enthusiasm. My own enthusiasm reached a high at the dress rehearsal. Gar and Ruth had provided an absolutely overwhelming scene, in which Lam's rooftop "office" was set under the stars of a huge cyclorama sky. Fidget and I sat hand in hand, close to tears. It was my dream, beautifully realized.

That was the high point. The audience of the New Haven opening did not like the play, did not enter into the rooftop dream world. What I had hoped was a bit of *A Midsummer's Night's Dream* became frosted with a touch of *The Winter's Tale*. After the final curtain there was little enthusiasm. Gar and Ruth disappeared with Thornton Wilder, who presumably briefed them on what was wrong. Max Gordon and George Cukor added further discouragement when Gar returned and we called off the after-opening conference. My old Bones-mates Larry Tighe (now Treasurer of Yale) and Doc Walker (who was in the Industrial Relations department) disliked the play for different reasons, as did their wives. The cast was discouraged, especially as the reviews were not good the next morning.

Boston was a little more encouraging. The performances were improving, Ev Sloane was beginning to get his laughs, the reviews were more understanding. Phil Barry was enthusiastic, as were Put, and Professors Matthieson and Ted Spencer. Professor Harlow Shapley of the astronomical department at Harvard, whom I had consulted for my scientific facts while writing the play, brought a party of his students and reported appreciative pleasure. But the audiences on the whole remained doubtful. On some nights, particularly both Saturdays, they responded with encouraging laughter and what I believed was understanding. I still hoped, as I had when I started the play, that my comedy would charm the audience away from opposition to my serious "message." I still hoped that when we got to Broadway both the comedy and the message would find the right critics and the right audiences who would appreciate the novelty of my having restored the soliloquy to the stage by means of a humorous struggle between Mind and Conscience for the soul of a man – and the salvation of the world from nuclear destruction. So I was not discouraged by New Haven and Boston, and after what seemed like a particularly successful Saturday-night closing Ella and I had a gay train return to New York with the company – with the exception of Ray Massey who was driving down, and Gar and Ruth who chose for some reason to sit in a different coach. What I didn't know was that Ray was becoming convinced that he had been duped into a Communist play, and that Gar and Ruth were debating whether or not to close the show without any New York opening at all.

But it did open, at the Hudson Theater. Ella and I didn't go. She was busy preparing a party for the cast, and I was too jittery. I lingered outside the theater during the first act, had a manhattan at the next-door bar, and peeked continually into the lobby during the intermission. The only person I recognized was Eliot Nugent in white tie and tails, and what he was saying sent me scurrying gloomily back to Fidget and fireside. Then, for some reason (and it was not alcoholic) a strange calm settled over me. It was as though some gland had been functioning – the disaster gland. When the cast arrived (but not Ray Massey, Gar or Ruth), with confirmation of the non-recognition of my masterpiece by the audience, I devoted myself to cheering up the actors. The old Life-of-the-Party spirit sprang once more into the breech and when the last guest had departed I sank into bed not so much depressed about *How I Wonder* as terribly pleased that we had given such a good party.

Next morning Professor Barrows Dunham who, with his wife Alice, was staying with us, got up early and went out to the news stand so that if there were any good reviews he could show those to me first. It was a thoughtful but fruitless gesture. There were no good reviews. My comedy, it seems, was no comedy and my "message" had apparently been written by Stalin. One critic even brought Ella into his attack by heading his reviews "The Winter of Don's Discontent." Another referred contemptuously to the fact that Stalin's representative Vishinski had already delivered my message to the United Nations the preceding Thursday. The afternoon reviews were worse than the morning ones, and there was no relief when the weekly magazines appeared. I went backstage the second night to try to cheer up the poor actors. They were brave and loyal, except Ray Massey who wanted me to close the show. I didn't want to. I believed in it, and when I watched the performance that night I was still very proud. I told Gar and Ruth that, and they very decently decided not to close it; there had been a large enough advance sale from charities and various organizations to keep it going two or three months. I wanted to keep it going. So did most of the company. There was always the chance that it might pick up (every writer always believes that). What I underestimated was the power of the critics, and the extent of the Cold War fears and hatreds which I was thinking could be appeased with laughter and overcome with truth. Even before my play opened the Un-American Activities Committee had opened their own show in Washington; this one featured Hollywood, with writers, actors, producers, directors hurrying to affirm their hatred of Russia and Godless Communism – and to give names of suspected "un-Americans." Some bravely defied the Committee, and were later to pay for it with jail sentences.

One morning the New York office of M-G-M asked me to drop in and I thought, "Oh, oh. Here we go!" I had already been named in Washington by three or four of the patriotic "friendly witnesses" eager to hold on to their jobs. But what Metro wanted was that I go to London to look at another possible vehicle for Spencer Tracy, since everyone was apparently quite happy about *Cass Timberlaine*. This one was a hit play called *Edward My Son* and I was to sail the following Saturday. I was delighted. The gloom around the Hudson Theater had taken the joy out of New York. Bad reviews diminish one's desire to be seen at Sardi's – or anywhere else. On the night before sailing, however, we went again to see the play, at a benefit performance which had been subscribed to by a progressive political organization called the National Society of the Arts, Sciences and Professions. It was the kind of audience which could understand the play. They loved it and I loved them. What seemed horrifying to me then (in 1947) was the almost universal ignorance of Marxism and the steadily rising fear and hatred of Communism which was making it impossible for anyone to study Marx with an un-prejudiced mind. No one was able to realize that there was at the bottom of it a basic love of humanity, and that there was in dialectical materialism a philosophy of hope for all mankind. The one big mistake of which I was guilty was that I linked my philosophy too rigidly and too naively with the Soviet Union and particularly with Stalin. The bait was that the "first Socialist country" could not be doing anything other than following the humanism of Marx, which was like believing that the Inquisition could do no wrong because the Catholic Church had been founded on the rock of Jesus Christ. But of such was my "Communism" made, and besides, there was nothing in *How I Wonder* or *Emily Brady* or in any of the films I ever wrote that could not have been written by the most patriotic believer in democracy and a free world – which, indeed, I was and still am.

27

And now kind reader (sorry to wake you up) I think that this would be as good a point as any to have a brief "post logue" and lower the final curtain. At the end of 1947 I was 53 years old. I wrote two more plays, neither of which reached Broadway – although one of them which I consider my best ever was quite a bit of a hit in London – and I also was commissioned by M-G-M to do two more screenplays (*Edward My Son* and *Huckleberry Finn*) before they lowered their own curtain and demanded that I clear myself of the suspicion of Communism by humbly confessing that I was "duped" into assuming a left-wing position in my political and personal philosophy. It had also been suggested to other dupees that they could cooperate by naming a few of their associates in the Communist party, and I am sorry to say that quite a few Hollywood friends whom I had hitherto respected for one reason or another actually did "clear" themselves in this manner.

Anyway, by 1950 I was officially on the Black List which The Producers themselves, without any acknowledged pressure from the House Un-American Activities Committee, had created. Ten courageous Hollywood writers and directors had served a term in the country's penitentiaries because of their refusal to submit to the Un-American Committees questioning. In this period I had written two more plays – one called *Joy Boy,* during a joyful 1947 Christmas festival with Ira Wolfert and his wife at our farm. The play concerned a "Joy Boy" who happened to be the mayor of New York and if this causes you to think of Jimmy Walker, you are not far from the target. Ira, in addition to being a first-rate novelist, is also a superb writer of comedy and a very well-informed observer of the American political scene. I have never understood why our play was not acceptable for Broadway production – but that has happened to a great many even better comedies.

The other play, which I called *The Kidders,* was based in part on a book by Karen Horney called *The Neurotic Personality of Our Time.* From this book I developed the idea of showing that underlying the psychology of the people of the United States, the Greatest, Most Powerful Country in the World, were certain neurotic fears which led to the development of "kidding" as a protection against facing the truth of these fears. The characters were living in an American midwestern city (like my own Columbus) and were employed in the District Office (as I had been just after college) of a huge corporation with its controlling offices in a 68-story skyscraper in New York (my American Telephone and Telegraph Co.). The play opened with the arrival from the 68th floor of Agnes, the older sister of Jenny. Jenny is married to Dan who works in the District Office. This unexpected visit from the distant Top Floor which controls their jobs sets off the fear that the District Office is to be closed which would mean the loss of jobs and livelihood. Gradually, as the fear grows, the personalities become more neurotic and we have the spectacle of a cross-section of American urban civilization as it might react to various disasters, such as bank failure and unemployment, originating in causes (on the 68th Floor) of which they have no knowledge and over which they feel they have no control. As the fears increase the American "kidding" becomes more and more bitter as a defense mechanism to protect them from gazing down into the fearful chasm over which they have lived their lives.

The producer Robert Whitehead chose Harold Clurman to direct an excellent cast and we tried out in the summer of 1950 in an off-Harvard theater in Cambridge. Whitehead wasn't quite satisfied and the Broadway opening was postponed.

As I have said, it is still in a state of postponement. Writers, especially those who have spent some time in Hollywood, are at times apt to succumb to strange prophetic visions. For example: Occasionally, as I lie in bed at night, there enters into my imagination a beautiful dream of Broadway theater; the year is A.D. 2072, and the audience is cheering as they throw corsages of orchids onto the stage. And the name of the author of the play?

The author occasionally (although those happy occasions are getting a little less frequent since I went on the Wagon) has the same lovely visions about some of his early books – especially about *Mr. and Mrs. Haddock Abroad.* Incidentally – a word about that wagon. On November 30, 1969 the author achieved the age of Seventy-Five. He decided that he would postpone any more drinking of spirits until he had reached the age of One Hundred. Five days after this noble resolution he found himself discussing (with himself, of course) the nature of the first drink he would have on the morning of November 30th, 1994. He finally decided on champagne, and that, of course, led to the remembrance of the many happy champagne birthdays I had helped various friends to celebrate. It then began to seem somewhat heartless to abandon completely these friends, so I began compiling a list of celebratable birthdays – a list which gradually lengthened to include such relative strangers as Buddha, Martha Washington and the wives of various other former presidents of the United States. I have very faithfully celebrated those patriotic occasions.

Anyway, when I was finally tapped for the Hollywood Un-American Activities Black List, Ella and I decided that we might have a go at corrupting some other country than the United States, so we piled our subversive thoughts and our evening clothes into the car and started to explore un-American countries such as France and Italy and England. Late one night in 1951, deep in Regents Park, London, our car ran out of what the English call petrol. I faced a long walk in a dark unknown country in an even more unknown park when, to our surprise, the very first car that passed us stopped – a tall gentleman got out, came over to us and asked, "Can I help you?" And he did – by driving to the nearest garage and returning with some petrol.

Well, in our many years in New York and Hollywood this had never happened to happen, so we decided right then and there that England might be as good a country to corrupt as any of the others on our list.

A Last Word

It has been several years since I started to write this book, and since then I've realized the some of the events of our years in London deserve at least passing mention. When I left America the most active part of my career ended but I did not, after all, go into hibernation. Bear with me then, for a few more moments before we part company.

When Ella and I decided to stay in London we set about finding a new base for our subversive activities. We lived temporarily in a number of houses and flats, none of which satisfied us. One of the houses was painted entirely in brown, with black dripping from the ceiling. Ella repainted the whole thing white but when the owner of the house, who had been away for a year, saw what Ella had done she demanded that we paint it brown again.

Our agents kept searching, and one of them mentioned a funny old house on a hill in Hampstead which had belonged to Ramsay Macdonald. It had been unoccupied for many years and had become dilapidated. There was dry rot and rising damp, the curtains were moth-eaten, the roof leaked and the garden was an overgrown jungle. The paint was chipped and there was no furniture to speak of. It was in such poor condition that the Macdonald family didn't want to rent it, fearing what they would have to pay to fix it up. We stayed there for a long time without either renting it or buying it. Ella loved the house but the work that had to be done scared us both.

It was Katie Hepburn who came and saved us from our indecision. She is very interested in old houses and when she saw this one she said that it was a beautiful place and why don't we rent it for a year.

She came every day for about six weeks with a packed lunch from the Connaught Hotel and helped Ella fix the place up. She took a scythe and hacked away at the grass in the back yard, which was over six feet high. She and Ella would sit on crates in what is now the kitchen and Katie would dab at the chips in the wall with paint from a little can she had brought. Somehow they managed to make the place liveable (while I sat carefully observing them) and we decided to rent it.

Meanwhile Katie continued to come and work on the house. One day she said to Ella, "Are you going to buy this house or aren't you?" Ella was still indecisive and said that she didn't know. "Well," announced Katie, "if you don't buy it I will pour creosote over it." That made Ella's mind up. We eventually bought the house and have never regretted doing so. Katie comes every year to inspect the place and always re-affirms how delighted she is that we bought it.

In addition to serving as a home for us, our pictures, and a constantly changing menagerie of cats, dogs, a monkey and assorted other creatures, our house has been a gathering place for many friends from many countries. Ingrid Bergman always comes to see us when she's in London, as do the Chaplins and Ring Lardner, Jr. Jim and Helen Thurber were here several times before Jim's death, and so were Edmund Wilson and Ella's old friend Robinson Jeffers. We had parties for the Berliner Ensemble and for the Moscow Arts Theater. Dr W. E. B. Dubois came with his wife Shirley Graham. Many American friends came to see us after they had escaped the net of the blacklist. One of these was Paul Robeson, who had just had his passport returned by the State Department and was able for the first time in several years to travel out of the U.S.

Paul got his passport back as an indirect result of my having gotten mine. One of the first punishments dealt to us un-Americans who hadn't answered questions in the early fifties was taking away one's passport. They took mine while I was here in England. When I went to have it renewed (it was 1954, I think) they stamped CANCELED all over it and clipped off one corner. Ella got the same treatment, though she was able eventually to get a British passport. For four years I couldn't leave England. When *The Kidders* was performed in Aachen, Germany, I couldn't even go to see that. I had been unable to go to Venice to finish work on *Summertime,* a movie I wrote for David Lean, and someone else finished the job.

In 1958 I tried again (I had tried several times before) to get the damned thing back. No one who had refused to answer questions had been able to do this. Our lawyer Leonard Boudin went to the State Department and told them all the reasons that I should get my passport back. It was pretty clear by that time that I wasn't going to answer any questions and the political atmosphere was not quite so bad as it had been earlier. Still, my case didn't get very far at first. The State Department finally asked me whether I had been in either the American Embassy or the Passport Office in recent years. Apparently they wanted to know what contacts I had had with Americans in London.

It just happened that I had, through an accident of sorts, been at the American Embassy. I told the State Department this through an affadivit submitted by our lawyer and they asked (again by affadavit) why I had been there. I told them, truthfully, that I had been invited to a party given by the Ambassador for Martha Graham (an old friend). When the people at the State Department heard this they wanted me to prove that that was the real purpose of my visit. I replied: "It's very easy to prove because (a) I wore my blue pin-stripe suit and (b) I had two double martinis." I don't think that was what convinced them to give me back my passport, but I did get it back, and that statement is still in the State Department files.

After I got my passport back we made a number of trips throughout Europe, staying with the Chaplins at their home in Switzerland. We didn't have any long-term adventures, however, until 1964, when I got a letter from President Nkrumah asking me to come and teach Ghanaian students how to write for television. He had just bought several million dollars worth of television equipment and realized that no one in Ghana knew how to make programs for it. W. E. B. Dubois' widow had been visiting Ghana and recommended me as a likely teacher, and down we went.

This was very exciting for me: I had always wanted to teach, and here was my opportunity. There were about twenty-five students in my class, all around twenty or twenty-five years old, and I came to feel a great fatherly affection for them. What I had to do was to take the lessons I learned in Hollywood and apply them in underdeveloped Ghana. I did this by trying to get the students to write interestingly about their own lives. They would give me samples of their work and the next day in class I would read a few of the samples and say what was wrong with them. Translating M-G-M practice into Ghanaian terms wasn't easy, and my students were not very good at the beginning. But little by little something began to happen, and the scripts started to get better. This was very encouraging and made me very proud. I felt that I had taken fifteen of my children and taught them to look into their own lives with greater understanding, to produce something that was interesting as drama.

Whether my efforts were successful may never be known. The minute I left the government made a contract with an American company to get American and English television programs on Ghana's stations. The woman who was in charge said that she did not want anything about Ghana. So they got *Dr. Kildare* and I got very upset.

My quarrel, incidentally, wasn't with Nkrumah. He was a wonderful guy to us, and we parted great friends. I only had one thing against him. Every morning at around five the telephone would ring and it would be Nkrumah, wanting to talk to Ella about gardening. I don't quite understand what they talked about but I do understand my desperation as I tried to go back to sleep. Other great friends we made in Ghana were Conor Cruise O'Brien and his wife. O'Brien, who was vice-chancellor of the university, did have a serious split with Nkrumah over the stocking of the university bookstore. O'Brien had the bookstore carry some non-Socialist books. Nkrumah wanted them removed, O'Brien insisted, and Nkrumah fired him. When we went to see the O'Briens the night he was fired their house was dark and deserted. They sat alone in the dark, feeling very low. Clearly, Nkrumah could be cruel and far from understanding when he wanted to.

We came back to England after that and have more or less stayed put. I got very interested in cricket, going to every match I could and feeling confident enough to shout "well bowled!" or tell fellow spectators who were talking to shut up. I even understood the game, which I believe is something of a rarity among Americans. I've also spent time talking to those unfortunate Ph.D. students who have come to me with questions about Hemingway and Fitzgerald and Benchley and Thurber and so on. Aspiring playwrights and screenwriters sent me their scripts for a while, though they've stopped doing that for some reason. I don't know whether it has anything to do with the fact that many of the scripts are still sitting in my attic.

People sometimes ask me whether I feel upset at having had to leave my successful career in the United States. Of course, those years at Culver City were marvelous. With the money I was making I could even be rude to waiters. But in another way it was a great relief to get out of the Hollywood syndrome. I didn't have to earn that impossible salary anymore, didn't have to be a Success. I don't regret that at all. My life has been for me a successful one, and in many ways a happy one. Can one ask more?

HARRY DAS ? - 698

HOLIDAY - 240
P. STORY - 253

Smilin' Through - Red Dust - no credits? - 199

Dinner - 204

FORRESTAL - 214

propaganda plays - 219

Emily Brady - 246 ft